Praise

FRENCH KIDS EAT

"It takes a brave couple to move two picky-eater kids into a French small town and convert them to foodie omnivores. We have much to learn from European food traditions, and the contrast between French and North American school lunches is a striking example. A must-read for teachers and parents."

— Marion Nestle, professor of Nutrition, Food Studies,
and Public Health at New York University
and author of *What to Eat*

"A fascinating and valuable read." — Lynne Rossetto Kasper

"Karen Le Billon has written a book that every parent of young children will want to read. After she moves to France with her two young daughters, both with North American eating habits, their family palates are slowly educated to the French way of eating. She and her children learn that it's okay to feel hungry between meals, turn to mindful eating, and learn the importance of enjoying one's food. Humorous as well as instructive, this culinary adventure will change the lives of parents and children alike."

— Patricia Wells, author of *The Provence Cookbook*

"This book is not only about how to teach children (and yourself) to eat well and happily for life, it's a book about how to help build and maintain the foundations of any civilized society. I loved it. Essential reading, whether you have children or not."

— Laura Calder, author of *Dinner Chez Moi*
and host of *French Food at Home*

"Le Billon . . . strategically identified questions she faced while living abroad: Why were French kids tidier eaters? Why did they sit quietly at restaurants? Why did her daughter's teacher suggest she see a therapist when she wanted to pack her school lunch?"

—BonAppetit.com

"A wonderful—and important—book. One family's topsy-turvy culinary transformation becomes an in-depth exploration of the habits that have kept French kids loving food (and eating spinach) for centuries." —Elizabeth Bard, author of *Lunch in Paris*

"A breezy but practical volume for hurried parents looking to keep their kids well-fed. . . . [The] tone is straightforward, generous, and gentle. That Le Billon concludes with a small collection of kid-friendly recipes makes this foodie manifesto all the more accessible."

—*Publishers Weekly*

"[Read] with a pencil or highlighter in hand. . . . The ten 'rules' she comes up with are really commonsense ideas you probably, however vaguely, already know. But if you're like me, you may find them excellent, if not also habit-changing, reminders of how things should be. Or can be." —Forbes.com

"If you're looking for a dietary overhaul for your family, this book will get you well on your way to better eating." —SeriousEats.com

FRENCH KIDS
EAT
EVERYTHING

Also by Karen Bakker Le Billon

Privatizing Water (Cornell University Press, 2010)
Eau Canada (UBC Press, 2007)
An Uncooperative Commodity (Oxford University Press, 2004)

Illustrations by Sarah Jane Wright

FRENCH KIDS

EAT

EVERYTHING

How our family moved to France,

cured picky eating, banned snacking,

and discovered 10 simple rules

for raising happy, healthy eaters

. . . .

KAREN LE BILLON

WILLIAM MORROW

An Imprint of HarperCollinsPublishers

Illustrations © Sarah Jane Wright.

HarperCollins books may be purchased for educational, business, or sales promotional use. For information, please e-mail the Special Markets Department at SPsales@harpercollins.com.

A hardcover edition of this book was published in 2012 by William Morrow, an imprint of HarperCollins Publishers.

FIRST WILLIAM MORROW PAPERBACK EDITION PUBLISHED 2014.

Designed by Diahann Sturge

Library of Congress Cataloging-in-Publication Data has been applied for.

ISBN 978-0-06-210330-7

20 21 OV/LSC 10 9

To Philippe

Contents

FRENCH KIDS
EAT
EVERYTHING

Prologue

This book is a very personal story about our family. But it also addresses issues that affect all of our children. Because of poor eating habits, the current generation of North American children will suffer far more health problems—and perhaps have a shorter life expectancy—than their parents. We may be training our kids to eat themselves into an early grave.

It's hard to change the way our families eat. Although we know what we *should* be eating—more fruits and vegetables and as little processed food as possible—we don't do it. Or, even if we prepare healthy food, our children often won't eat it. Food insecurity (unaffordability, lack of access) is a serious issue, but even families with adequate resources don't always eat as healthily as they should. So we need to figure out better strategies for *how* as well as *what* to feed our kids. This is where the French approach to food education offers valuable lessons. Living in France taught our family that children *can* eat well and enjoy it too. The healthy eating habits, smart routines, and tasty recipes used by French families and schools were the basis of our family's reinvention of our approach to eating. They inspired us, and my hope is that our story will inspire you too.

But this is not solely a question of parental responsibility or personal behavior. In France, schools, governments, and communities have worked together to create food and education systems that support parents in feeding their children well. In North America, it often seems as if the opposite is true. So we urgently need to have a collective conversation about how to reinvent kids' food culture—in homes and schools, on farms and in stores via market and governmental reform. My hope is that this story (which is not about haute cuisine, but rather about how ordinary French families are empowered to feed their children well) will inspire you to join in that conversation.

1

French Kids Eat Everything
(and Yours Can Too)

Le plaisir de la table est de tous les âges, de toutes les conditions,
de tous les pays et de tous les jours.

The pleasures of the table belong to all ages, all conditions, all countries,
and to each and every day.

—Jean Anthelme Brillat-Savarin, *The Physiology of Taste* (1826)

𝒜sk my children what their favorite foods are, and the answer might surprise you. Seven-year-old Sophie loves beets and broccoli, leeks and lettuce, mussels and mackerel—in addition to the usual suspects, like hot dogs, pizza, and ice cream. Claire, her three-year-old sister, loves olives and red peppers, although her all-time favorite is creamed spinach. Living as we do in Vancouver, where the world's largest salmon-spawning river flows through one of the continent's most Asian cities, our daughters also happen to love seaweed, smoked salmon, and avocado sushi.

Our daughters' enthusiastic eating habits are no surprise to my French husband, Philippe. But they still surprise me, because food fights used to be frequent at our house. Before our family moved to France and embarked on our (unintended) experiment with French food education, dinnertime was parenting purgatory. Fries were my daughters' favorite "vegetable." Anything green was met with clenched teeth. Whining stopped only when dessert appeared. Our daughters subsisted on the carbohydrate and dairy-rich diet that is the mainstay of North American families. Our standbys were Cheerios, pasta, and buttered toast. We considered goldfish crackers to be a separate food group.

Sophie was a picky eater right from the start. By the time she was three, she had developed a fear of new foods that reminded me a lot of myself as a child. Anything objectionable on her plate would trigger her little "crazy food dance" (as we called it): arms waving, eyes rolling, Sophie would whine, sometimes yell, and even jump up from the table to avoid being confronted with the fearsome food in question. Her somewhat quirky tastes didn't make it easy to avoid setting off this behavior. For example, Sophie didn't like vegetables, or anything white or creamy: cheese, yogurt, any sauce of any description, or even ice cream. And she refused to eat things that most other children like, including macaroni and cheese, and sandwiches of any kind.

In contrast, Claire—her younger sister—was our little Buddha baby, calm and contented. *You've won the lottery,* our midwife told us on the day she was born. While Sophie specialized in twenty-minute naps (but only while being walked in the stroller or snuggled in the baby carrier), Claire would enjoy lazy two-hour siestas and still sleep for a blissful ten hours at night. And she ate almost anything. That is, she *would* eat almost anything until she started behaving like her older sister. This gave me a serious case of parental performance anxiety, combined with a good measure of guilt.

You see, my husband's friends, parents, aunts, uncles, cousins, and other sundry and assorted relatives all expected our daughters to eat like French children. And French kids eat *everything,* from fruit salad to foie gras, spinach to stinky blue cheese. They eat things most North American kids (and some of their parents) would never dream of eating, like cardoons. (Don't worry, I'd never heard of them either.) They also regularly consume things that most of us wish our kids *would* eat, like salad. I have seen my French nieces and nephews greeting radishes with as much delight as popcorn. I have witnessed three-year-olds devouring seafood of all sorts and toothless babies sipping everything from béchamel sauce to vegetable bouillon. Some have even more exotic preferences: Didier, who would cheerfully savor *la langue de boeuf* (beef tongue), or little Fabrice, whose favorite food was *museau à la vinaigrette* (pickled pig snout), or baby Claire, who gummed her daily ration of Roquefort cheese with obvious delight.

Now, French kids don't eat this way because of some genetic predisposition for liking exotic foods. Just like kids anywhere, their favorites include things like pasta, potato chips, chicken, and chocolate. But that's not what they usually eat. As amazing as it may sound, French children love all kinds of food, and most of what they eat is healthy. True, you might find the rare French child who has an aversion to specific foods (cauliflower, in my husband's case). But, for the most part, French kids consume anything put in front of them. They eat in a straightforward, joyous, and all-embracing way that seems baffling to the ordinary North American. And everyone assumes this is normal—including the kids.

This is, in fact, a junior version of the famous "French Paradox," which has had scientists scratching their heads for years. In a nutshell:

French adults spend twice as much time as Americans eating, and they consume foods like butter, pork, and cheese in apparently uninhibited quantities, yet are less overweight (and very rarely obese) and have lower rates of heart disease than Americans. Yes, this is one of those unfair facts of life: the French, it seems, can truly have their cake and eat it too.

The way French kids eat is equally paradoxical. French parents gently compel their children to eat healthy food. They expect their kids to eat everything they are served, uncomplainingly. They ask them to spend long hours at the table (where they are expected to be extremely well behaved) rather than watching TV or playing video games. Despite this, French kids think eating is fun. And that's not all: France's rate of child obesity is one of the lowest in the developed world. And while rates of overweight and obese children are at an all-time high and are rapidly increasing in most wealthy countries (with the United States leading the pack), they are stable and even declining in France. This is not because they're all on a weight-loss program; diets for French children are relatively rare because few of them need it.

Before we moved to France, I was stumped about how French parents achieved this. I knew (and worried) about the negative effects of poor diet on my children's health, teeth (cavities!), sleeping patterns, school performance, and even their IQ. But I felt powerless to do anything to change the way they ate. I wanted to change, but I didn't know how.

The "strategies" used by parents we knew in Vancouver didn't seem very satisfactory. Force and pressure tactics didn't appeal to me (although I admit to trying them). And I didn't like bribing kids to finish (or even start) their meals. Vitamin pills seemed like a cop-out, particularly after I read that they don't supply nutrients the same way fresh food does. So I bought the cookbooks that suggested sneaking healthy foods into kids' meals, and I tried concocting specialized menus that required the skill of a chemist and the savoir faire of a chef. As I wasn't a particularly enthusiastic or efficient cook, I found this approach to be incredibly time consuming. And it didn't really work; in fact, it backfired. Sophie's sensitive "yucky food" detectors would be put on alert by the faintest whiff of anything odd, and she became even more suspicious of what was on her plate. And even if the "sneaky" method had worked, it made me wonder: Would my kids keep putting cauliflower puree in their brownies after they had left home? I didn't think so.

Admittedly, my failed attempt to sneak healthy foods into my kids' meals was, in part, a reflection on my limited cooking skills. Soon after we married, Philippe christened me *La Reine des Casseroles Brûlées* (the Queen of Burned Pots), given my unfortunate habit of going on the computer, or diving into a really good book, in the middle of making a meal. My cooking repertoire was limited to four or five dishes (at most) that would cycle over and over again, with potatoes featuring heavily throughout. This is the way I was raised. My mother came from a farming family; *her* mother had eight children to feed and little time for fancy extras. Every night, she would prepare one dish and serve it without ceremony. "We ate," remembers my uncle John, "because we were hungry. And no one ever encouraged us to eat. If we didn't eat our share, so much the better: there'd be more for everyone else." My grandmother's favorite was *stamppot*, a dish produced by boiling potatoes together with kale and then mashing everything up (yes, this results in green mashed potatoes). Dollops of butter and dashes of salt and pepper were the only flavorings used (my relatives considered garlic to be an exotic spice). That *stamppot* is still one of my favorite dishes tells you a lot about my culinary credentials.

So it was unsurprising that my first forays into French cuisine—as a consumer—were unsuccessful. The first time Philippe brought me to see his parents was perhaps the worst. On the spur of the moment one rainy April morning, just after we started dating, he invited me to visit his parents' house in Brittany. From Oxford (where we were both studying), it was only a short drive to Portsmouth, where we caught an overnight ferry. We left under gray clouds and drizzle, slept on the boat, and awoke to a magical sunrise, with breaking waves surging on the rocky shore surrounding the stone citadel of Saint-Malo. We drove in Philippe's battered Renault 5 car through one tiny, charming village after another, and then along the coast, alternating between rocky cliffs and enormous white sand beaches gleaming in the sun. It was the first time I had set foot in France, and I was utterly seduced.

We arrived at his parents' house—a picture-perfect stone cottage covered in vines—in time for lunch. The meal, for me, was unforgettable. Bathing in sunlight on the *terrasse*, Philippe and his parents treated themselves to a plate full of local seafood, most of which was suspicious-looking shellfish the likes of which I had never even seen, much less tasted. When I was a kid, the closest I got to fish (and the closest I wanted to get) was the canned tuna casserole that my sister and I loathed, and that my mother topped with potato chips in an attempt to bribe us to eat. (My sister usually caved in, but I never did.)

I gave the shellfish a pass, only to find myself confronted with a large sole purchased that same morning, Philippe's mother proudly announced, fresh off the fisherman's boat at the local wharf. Confronted with a whole fish on a plate, I felt totally helpless; never having eaten anything like this, I had no idea where to start. So I sat, cheeks burning, while Philippe cut up my sole in front of his bemused parents. It was years before I felt at ease eating fish, and I confess to feeling ambivalent (to say the least) about serving it to my children. So you could say (and I certainly felt) that my daughters came by their limited eating repertoires somewhat honestly.

Philippe, however, was frustrated by our family's eating saga. On most matters, the relaxed attitudes of North Americans suited him just fine (in fact, he preferred them to the more rigid, formal French manners). But he was perplexed by the way our daughters ate, particularly in comparison with their French cousins, all enthusiastic eaters. And his extended family back in France was more than perplexed. They were quietly (and sometimes not so quietly) outraged.

Looking back, I now realize they were expecting me to educate my children about food. According to the French, this should start when children are very young, well before their first birthday. After all, eating is one of the first acts that an infant performs consciously, and then independently, even before walking and talking. This provides a wonderful basis for discipline: firm but gentle guidance about life's rules. I use the word "rules" hesitantly, because although the French approach to food education is highly structured, these are not rigid regulations. Rather, they're more like commonsense routines, or social habits: unwritten, and often unspoken, but collectively accepted. Like most cultural codes, these rules are often mysterious to the outsider, but not particularly complicated once they've been explained; in fact, they are often deceptively simple. This was the case with the first "food rule" that I figured out:

French Food Rule #1:

Parents: You are in charge of your children's food education.

The belief that parents should actively educate their children about food in a gently authoritative way is at the heart of the French approach to kids' food. Deep down, I knew that this approach—which was much more authoritative than my approach—might benefit my children. But for a long time, I resisted it. Fostering independent eating was an important step in building autonomy, right? The kids should be in charge of their own eating, right?

Absolument pas! Absolutely not! That is a recipe for disaster! warned my mother-in-law, my sister-in-law, the cousins, aunts and uncles, and Philippe's friends. Given how their children ate, I had to admit they seemed to have a point. During our first visit back to France after Sophie was born, when she was just eight months old, I watched in amazement as other babies her age devoured everything their parents gave them and contentedly napped for hours after every meal. Sophie, meanwhile, was fussy at mealtimes. She played with her food, spat it out, and clearly viewed eating as an annoying interruption in her daily schedule. Most of her meals—the sweetest apple puree, the smoothest mashed banana, the creamiest yogurt—would end up dribbled on her bib, her hands, and my lap (where she preferred to sit, regarding the highchair as some kind of torture device). It's not that she wasn't hungry. But when she woke up during the night, or after her achingly short naps, she wanted milk. And *only* milk. She had, to say the least, an ambivalent relationship with solid food, which didn't improve as she got older.

At the time, I assumed that Sophie took after me rather than after the French side of the family. One of my sister's favorite photos—and the first one she showed to Philippe when I took him home to meet the family—is of me in a highchair: pursed lips, cheeks red from crying, carrot puree smeared on my psychedelic 1970s-era overalls. The wallpaper behind me has a retro orange texture (a closer look reveals methodical splatters worthy of *Extreme Makeover*). The way my family tells it, I won every food fight we ever got into.

"Sophie is just like me," I would sigh. "I hated vegetables when I was young."

"*Mais non!*" I was told, "she just hasn't tried them enough times yet. When she's really hungry, serve them again. Then she'll eat anything and everything." At this point, I started to wonder. *Maybe, just maybe, the French know something I don't.* And I was right. They did know some things I didn't. French parents are provided with very different information about food, and about children's eating habits, than American parents. This is because French doctors, teachers, nutritionists, and scientists view the relationship between children, food, and parenting very differently than do North Americans. They assume, for example, that all children will learn to like vegetables. And they have carefully studied strategies for getting them to do so. French psychologists and nutritionists have systematically assessed the average number of times children have to taste new foods before they willingly agree to eat them: the average is seven, but most parenting books recommend between ten and fifteen. So whereas I often assumed that my children didn't like a particular type of food, my French friends would simply assume their children hadn't tried it enough times. And their children usually proved them right. French children cheerfully taste new things with an air of calm curiosity that I've rarely seen displayed by American adults, much less children.

How exactly do the French manage this, you're thinking? What strategies do French parents use? What do they cook? And what do they say (and, just as important, *not* say)?

I couldn't answer these questions until we moved to France. When we were visitors, the French politely ignored my (to them) odd eating habits, and an allowance was made for my status as a foreigner. But once we had chosen to settle there—in the village where Philippe grew up—everything changed. The French are not known for their tolerance: there is normally one right way to do things (which, unsurprisingly, is almost always the French way). They are never shy about letting their views be known, and they have little tolerance for culinary faux pas. So our family, friends, and neighbors took on the task of teaching my children—and me—how to eat properly (in other words, like the French). In restaurants and grocery stores, at school and at day care, on the playground and in people's homes, my beliefs about food, kids, and parenting were challenged.

Slowly, I began to understand how the French think about children and eating. The first thing I had to do was redefine how I understood the word "education." I kept being told that I had to "educate" my child, and so I would hasten to assure people that I had, in fact, already started saving for university. But that's not what they were talking about. The word *"éducation"* covers a lot of ground in French: it includes the knowledge acquired through formal schooling, but also the manners and behaviors, habits and tastes developed through discipline in the home. The goal is to produce a child who is *bien éduqué* (or *élevé*): who is well spoken, well mannered, and well behaved. In other words, a major goal of French parenting is to produce a child who knows and follows the unwritten rules of French society—which are much more strict than those in North America. French parents are very respectful of these social rules: training children to be *bien éduqué* is just as important as giving them self-esteem (in fact, they believe that the latter depends, in part, on the former).

Now, healthy eating is one of the most important skills that parents help their children develop. Underlying this focus on food education for young children is a simple principle:

Chances are, my children are not going to grow up to go to Harvard, or to be major league sports stars, concert musicians, or NASA astronauts. But no matter who they grow up to be, how and what my children eat will be of great importance to their health, happiness, success, and longevity.

Don't get me wrong: it's great to encourage kids to be the very best they can be. But from the French perspective North American parents often cram schedules so full that little time is spent teaching kids some of the most basic, important things they need to know, like the proper way to prepare, cook, and eat healthy food. In order to explain to myself how important this really was, I finally settled on a simple comparison. French parents think about healthy eating habits the way North American parents think about toilet training, or reading. If your children consistently refused to read, or even learn the alphabet, would you give up trying to teach them? Would you be content to wait for your children to toilet train by themselves, assuming that they'd eventually "grow out of it" or "figure it out"? Probably not. You'd probably figure out strategies to help them develop this essential life skill. Philippe tried to sum this up by explaining a famous French dictum to me: *tell me what you eat, and I'll tell you who you are.* In North America, many parents will simply shrug if their child refuses to eat well. The French, meanwhile, are thinking: *show me how your kids eat, and I'll know what kind of parent you are.*

The idea that French parents place high value on their children eating well is obvious. What is less obvious is *how* French parents get their children to eat well. Before we moved to France, I had my suspicions. Maybe tyrannical French parents *force* their kids to eat everything, I thought. Maybe this is just another version of the Asian "tiger mother" syndrome: the fierce French parent who insists that her children *mangent absolument de tout* (*must* eat some of everything). In fact, what we saw in France was just the opposite; fights over food were rare, and I never saw a parent force any child to eat anything.

So maybe it was the recipes? The meals that I saw ordinary French families eating were simple and quick to prepare—while still being healthy and tasty. But when I dutifully copied down a few promising recipes and tried them at home, they certainly didn't have a similar effect on my children.

What did French parents know that I didn't? More important, what did they *do* and *say* that I didn't? How, exactly, did they get their kids to eat everything *and* enjoy it? As I learned during our year in France, the secret lies not only in *what,* but also *how, when,* and (most important) *why* French kids eat.

Learning this secret was not the reason we moved to France. I am not a foodie, and Philippe is one of the rare French men I've met who has relatively little interest in food (which helps explain why he could entertain the thought of marrying a foreigner). I had little desire to improve my cooking skills; if anything, the thought of having to cook French food filled me with a vague sense of dread.

But living in France awakened my interest in how French parents cook for, eat with, and educate their children about food. I began to ask questions, and also to voice my objections. *My kids won't eat that way! It's too expensive! I don't have the time!* Luckily, the French love talking about food. In many French households, the most common topic of conversation around the breakfast table is what will be eaten for lunch. And at lunchtime, almost without fail, someone will bring up the topic of what should be eaten for dinner. Discussing food— *how* as well as *what* we eat—is the national hobby of the French. So when I asked questions, people were only too willing to talk.

From my many conversations with parents and teachers, doctors and scientists (and from the research I did to back up what I was hearing) I learned that feeding children well doesn't need to be conflict-ridden or complicated. I learned simple tricks for teaching children to enjoy eating a wide variety of foods, and I also learned that nutrition and healthy eating habits, while important, don't need to be the main focus. Rather, enjoying your food is the focus, and healthy eating habits are a happy by-product.

This view (food is fun!) helped inspire our family to reinvent the way we eat. Over the course of our year in France, we discovered ten Kids' Food Rules. Applying these rules challenged some of my most deeply held beliefs about children, food, and parenting. This was sometimes uncomfortable, but our quest to reinvent our family's food culture was also an experience that brought us closer together. I was inspired by seeing the French families all around us who fostered a healthy love of food—and a love of healthy food—in their children. I hope that our story will inspire you to do the same.

Alors, on y va!

2

Baby Steps and Beet Puree

We Move to France and
Encounter Unidentified Edible Objects

Au nom du père
(In the name of the Father)
Parent touches the child's forehead

Et de la mère
(And the Mother)
. . . the nose . . .

Et de l'enfant
(And the Child)
. . . the left eyebrow . . .

Tout ce qui est bon
(Everything tasty)
. . . the right eyebrow . . .

S'fourr là-dedans!
(Gets stuffed inside!)
. . . and pops the food in the child's mouth.

—French nursery rhyme

Living in France is not like visiting France, my husband warned me before we moved. I couldn't understand what he meant. We'd spent enough time there, I thought, that I truly felt at home. It was true that we had never *lived* in France. But when we were studying in England, we spent every spare moment we could there. Most of our friends were other international students who soon left England and scattered around the world. We did the same; a year after we were married, we moved to Vancouver, a city that neither of us knew. Despite the birth of our two daughters, we never really settled in, and I daydreamed about moving to France someday to be closer to Philippe's family. We'd find work somehow, I told myself. Our daughters would learn French and spend more time with their grandparents and cousins. I wanted out of the rat race, and rural France seemed like the perfect place to retreat.

As our children grew, so did my nostalgia for all things French. A brown donkey named Gribouille was partly to blame. At about the same time we returned to North America, our English friend Andy left New York to travel across the French countryside with Gribouille for a companion, and wrote a contemplative book about his journey. Later, I realized that his book wasn't really about living in France, as he didn't stop long enough to settle in. But at the time, his account of "finding tranquility in a chaotic world," as Andy put it, seemed compelling. Where better to find tranquility than in the French countryside?

Finally, when Sophie had just turned four and Claire was a toddler, we decided—or rather *I* decided—that we'd make the move to France, to the small village where Philippe grew up: Pléneuf Val-André (population: 3,900), on the northwest coast of Brittany. Philippe didn't share my enthusiasm; he preferred living in a big city, with the mountains and ocean at our doorstep. As much as he missed his family and loved his large circle of intensely loyal French friends, he didn't want to move back home. Even his parents were ambivalent.

"What will you do here?" asked Jo, my father-in-law. "The village is so small."

I tried to tell them that this was exactly what I was looking for. A big-city girl, I craved a cozy village life for my kids. I found it hard to understand why Philippe had left. In the end, we compromised: we'd try it for a year. Both of our employers (universities that often granted temporary leaves of absence) agreed that we could telecommute for one year. I was ecstatic.

We arrived in mid-July, at the height of Brittany's short summer season. Our new home was an old stone house overlooking the bay, only a few minutes' walk from where we had been married in a small chapel dedicated to local fishermen (we took our vows under a handmade replica of a schooner, proudly suspended from the plaster ceiling).

Although it had only five rooms (three of which were bedrooms), the house felt delightfully clutter-free and uncomplicated. We had traveled to France with only two suitcases; everything else was in storage back in Vancouver. Arriving with so little suited Philippe, who still had mixed feelings. But I couldn't share his ambivalence. Clichés sprang to life: fresh baguettes tucked under arms, cobblestone streets, church bells, café courtyards in the sun, ivy trailing up stone walls of our house. It was the height of the local farm festival season (complete with pig roasts and cornfield mazes for the kids); between farm visits and family visits, we spent our days wandering the local countryside. Our local village radio station—"Radio Bonheur" (Radio Happiness)—fit the mood perfectly, with its non-stop French country music (think: accordions, and more accordions).

Just below the house was the beach: a glorious expanse of smooth white sand running a mile wide and half a mile deep at low tide, ringed by rocky cliffs and turquoise water. I knew that so much sand could only be produced by storm-driven waves, and I was well aware of Brittany's reputation as an incessantly rainy place, but as July turned into August, the weather was mostly balmy. The girls played for hours in the sand while we read books, lounged, and dozed (me) or sailed, windsurfed, and kayaked (Philippe).

Le paradis!

Gradually, we began meeting our neighbors. Early one rainy

morning, I glanced out the window to see a man suspiciously clad in a large garbage bag, which he had fashioned like a cape by poking a hole through the end. He was standing amidst the bushes that separated our house from his, searching carefully through the leaves, popping things too small for me to see into another large garbage bag he was holding in his hands.

"What's he doing?" I whispered to Philippe.

"Collecting snails," he replied, after a quick look out the window.

"To eat?" was my astonished response.

"If you're really nice, maybe he'll share!" teased my husband.

The neighbor did invite us over the next day to sample some of his harvest, which I politely declined (although Philippe happily went to eat a plateful of baked snails with garlic and came back two hours later looking highly satisfied).

Thankfully, Mr. Snail (as I took to calling him) was not our only visitor. In fact, a stream of family and friends came by to welcome us. Philippe was one of the first members of his family to leave the region, and many of his relatives hadn't strayed far from home. His mother and her two sisters—talkative, stylish, domineering matriarchs—now lived less than five miles from where they had grown up in a small farming hamlet. They typically visited in a pack—aunts, uncles, and cousins in tow—and would take over the kitchen for hours, cooking family meals, endlessly telling stories, filling the house to the brim.

Although I would often half-heartedly offer to help out with cooking, I was usually shooed away. My reputation as a cooking novice had been established soon after meeting Philippe's family, with a memorable culinary disaster. My sister-in-law, Véronique, had just met her future husband, Benoît, and they had traveled down from Paris to introduce him to the family. This being Benoît's first visit, Philippe and I had made the trip over on the ferry from England. When we arrived, my mother-in-law, Janine, was fussing over the arrangements for the meal. Boldly asserting that I could make a great apple pie, complete with a homemade crust, I proudly rolled up my sleeves and did indeed produce a lovely looking *tarte aux pommes*— with pastry so hard that it was impossible to cut. When enough force was applied, the crust shattered into tiny pieces. I had apparently come up with a great recipe for flour-based cement. After that, I was pretty much banned from cooking, which suited me just fine. I would do the dishes, or just sit and enjoy the endless bantering, yet affectionate, conversations.

Listening to Philippe's family talking to my daughters, I began to learn the endearments that the French reserve for small children. Many of them revolve around food. Janine's favorite was *ma cocotte* (*mon coco* for boys), literally, "my little chick." Much to his discomfort, she still occasionally called my husband *mon petit chou* (my little cabbage). I soon learned some of my own endearments and would tease Philippe by calling him *mon trognon de pomme* (my apple core). Jo, Philippe's normally reserved father, would call his grandchildren *mon lapin* (my rabbit), which is, of course, an edible animal for the French.

Food was even a theme of the children's songs that our daughters learned from their cousins: "Savez-vous planter les choux" (Do you know how to plant cabbages?), "Dame tartine" (Bread-and-butter lady), "Les temps des cerises" (Cherry season), and my personal favorite, "Oh l'escargot" (an ode to snails that sounds wonderful in two-part harmony). Food, it was clear, was an important part of how French families interacted with their children. But before we moved to France I didn't really understand the central role that food plays in formal French education.

That all changed when Claire started day care in mid-August. The plan was that she would be settled before Sophie started school in September. But she wasn't settling in well at all. And eating, in particular, wasn't going well. Claire was expected (like all French children) to eat the freshly prepared three-course lunch prepared on site by one of the staff. But Claire's diet at the time was like that of many North American toddlers: made up largely of cereals (in her case, buttered toast and crackers), complemented by largely symbolic attempts at feeding her the standard vegetables (carrots, peas), most of which she simply refused to chew. This was normal, I thought. But, as I soon found out, that's not what the day-care staff thought.

It all started with beet puree, in an episode that was the first of my many culinary faux pas. In the last week of August, we were invited to a meeting at the day care: an information session, or so I thought, remembering the equivalent back home, where we had discussed hand-washing hygiene with a public nurse and toured the facilities. My expectations were wrong. When we dutifully arrived at 4:30 in the afternoon, no nurse or antiseptic hand wipes were to be seen. The smiling staff welcomed us with elegant *amuse-bouches* (a term for cocktail nibbles that literally means "entertain the mouth"). On the first tray, intriguingly colored dips were perched on top of delicate puff pastries: bright pink, light green, creamy off-white. *How imaginative,* I thought. *How French.*

Fleeting images of potato chips and hot dogs—standard fare at our day care back home—crossed my mind. By now, I was starting to feel hungry, as North American dinnertime approached (despite the disapproval of my in-laws, we still persisted in eating at the barbarically early hour of 5:30 P.M.). So I eagerly began sampling, congratulating our hostesses in garbled French. A frown crossed the face of the woman holding the tray. Assuming she hadn't understood me, I repeated myself more slowly. But her frown only deepened. Puzzled, I looked around, only to observe that the other parents were dutifully feeding the treats not to themselves but . . . to their children.

As elaborate as they were, these weren't adult treats. "Those are for the kids," my husband whispered, explaining that the vegetable purees—beets, broccoli, and cauliflower—were intended to introduce the children to the day care's menu. They were being served at the traditional time for the French *goûter,* which roughly translates as "snack," but is a word usually reserved for children eating at this hour. Adults are expected to display restraint and wait until the traditional French dinner hour of 7:30 or 8:00 P.M. For the French, it was obvious: it was the children's snack time, not time for adults to eat.

Guiltily wiping the crumbs from my fingers, I watched the grinning toddlers—some of them almost toothless—munch their way through snacks that looked fit for a sophisticated cocktail party back home. Their obvious pleasure was met with murmuring approval from the adults.

Meanwhile, food—what kids liked, and what they were learning to like—was the focus of many of the conversations going on around us. As I later found out, this is not at all unusual. French parents spend a lot of time discussing food, and their children's eating habits are no exception. But these discussions are not anxiety ridden, as they so often are back home. Rather, French parents talk about their love of food: swapping recipes, sharing rituals. A small crowd had gathered around one dad, for example, who was explaining how he'd figured out a new way to serve artichoke hearts (a local delicacy) to his kids.

But I couldn't concentrate on the conversations around me. I was anxiously focused on Claire, who had just been invited to try one of the pastries. Aware that she usually greeted vegetables with clenched teeth, I offered her what I thought would be the most appealing color—pink.

I breathed a sigh of relief as she sampled the pastry and grinned, then cringed as she bit into the beet puree and immediately spat it out. Calmly, the tray swiveled away. As it retreated, I heard: "Don't worry, she'll learn to like it." And, within a couple of weeks, she did.

At the time, I realized that this was the start of my daughter's French education. Only later did I realize it was also the start of mine.

Another surprise at Claire's day care was the tidiness with which the children ate. This was, in fact, one of the first French children's eating habits I discovered. Seeing sixteen toddlers eating tidily with their cutlery and emerging spotless after their midday meal was a revelation. The children were simply not allowed to play with their food. Little fingers that dipped into bowls were kindly but firmly removed. Failure to cooperate (which was rare) was met with a gentle but firm response: plates would be removed. The message was clear: if you can't eat properly (which means eating tidily, even for toddlers), you won't eat at all. This was a stark contrast with how our older daughter had eaten: when she was a baby, Sophie smeared food on the highchair, the floor, the walls, even her hair. At the time, I was resigned to it; I had assumed that my mother-in-law was simply being unreasonable when she kept insisting that even very young children could eat tidily. After all, my parenting books said that children needed to play with their food; it was my job to get out of their way and to clean up after them. But now that I'd seen a French day care in action, I suddenly realized that my mother-in-law might be right: the ten-minute cleaning job I'd had after my first daughter's every meal might not be necessary.

Intrigued, I decided to follow their lead. At home, we resolved never to let Claire use her fingers (except for obvious finger food) and made sure to teach her to position her utensils and her body in such a way that crumbs or drops fell into, rather than beside, her plate. She always had a napkin (and we always had wipes) at the ready to wipe up spills. We made a point of praising her for eating tidily. It worked. Despite the three-year age difference, Claire still eats more tidily than her older sister.

This made Claire's transition into French life easier, because playing with your food is truly, deeply foreign to the French. "*On ne joue pas avec la nourriture!*" sums it up: "*WE* (the French) don't play with food." This phrase is much stronger than its English counterpart. "Don't play with your food" sounds feeble to French ears. Indeed, French parents equate their national identity with respectful food behaviors, and assert this to their children in a way that leaves no room for second thoughts. Children grow up assuming that no one who is *bien éduqué* plays with their food, under any circumstances. And because they never see anyone doing so, they don't think to question it.

Above all else, French children are never taught to view food as a reward. I learned this rule the hard way. Shortly after we arrived in France, I was standing in the checkout line at our local grocery store. I had just given my daughter a cookie, complimenting her on how well behaved she had been in the store. "But you'll spoil her appetite!" the cashier declared loudly.

Trapped in the line, with the evidence of my food crime visible on my daughter's crumb-smeared face, I cringed. Whereas I had seen my daughter behaving well, everyone else had seen *me* behaving badly. "Rewarding your daughter with food is a recipe for obesity," said an equally stern-faced mother. Nods of agreement came from the other equally stern-faced mothers in the line. I ran to the car, fumed all the way home, and threw all of my daughter's mini-snack food containers in the garbage. (Well, except for the one in my purse, in case of a real emergency.) But, later that night, I fished them out. What would I do without them the next time?

The "Supermarket Incident" (as I labeled it), provoked some serious reflection on my part. From the French point of view, I was committing many food faux pas. I summed these up with a second food rule:

French Food Rule #2:
Avoid emotional eating.
*Food is **not** a pacifier, a distraction, a toy, a bribe, a reward,*
or a substitute for discipline.

For the French, this rule is so obvious that it is never even spoken aloud. But for me, this rule was incomprehensible, at least at first. To accept it, I had to abandon the belief (widespread in North America) that it is normal to use food for purposes entirely unrelated to hunger or nutrition.

Food is a pacifier: we give kids something to eat when they're impatient, when they're tired, when they're whining, when we need just a few more minutes on the phone. This is a slippery slope. Kids (my own included) soon learn that whining works. For busy or distracted parents, this can result in an almost Pavlovian reaction: Kid Whines = Food, Fast. This often happens when we're on the run, or running late. But the danger is that it sets up a cycle in which snack food makes up the bulk of what kids eat, leaving them with little appetite for the more nutritious foods served at mealtimes.

For many parents, food is also a welcome distraction: we open the cupboards and look for something to eat when the kids are at a loose ends, or when they're bored, whether or not they're hungry. "Why don't we make some cookies?" I'd say to my daughters. "Or a cake?" At one level, this seems harmless. It can even be educational: teaching volume with measuring cups or learning manual dexterity with chopsticks. But the French feel that random snacking—even dressed up as math lessons—encourages a habit of impulsive eating that is hard to break later on. They love to invite children into the kitchen to cook (and even organize special cooking camps for them), but they make sure to organize this around scheduled mealtimes.

Food, in North America, is also sometimes used as a substitute for discipline. Parents withhold food as a punishment, and use the threat of withholding food to enforce good behavior: "Stop teasing your sister or you'll go to bed without supper!" Conversely, food is a bribe. "Do this and you'll get some ice cream!" Worst of all, food is a reward. One of Sophie's preschool teachers used to reward the children with candy for good behavior. French parents, as a rule, don't punish (or reward) with food, believing that this imbues food with emotional baggage—and that their children will, later on, attempt to deal with (or bury) their emotions through eating. This, in their view (which is supported by US and French research), has many negative consequences—not the least of which is disrupting children's ability to regulate their eating habits, increasing the risk of eating disorders.

Perhaps the deepest difference of all between North American and French parents is their attitude to playing with food. The parenting books I read after Sophie was born encouraged me to allow her to play with her food—to finger it, mouth it, even throw it. I patiently draped large sheets of plastic over and around her highchair, and let her go at it. (This was one of the practices that had my in-laws convinced I was truly an irresponsible parent.)

In fact, lots of toddlers that we knew played with food. Back home, before we moved to France, staff at Sophie's day care used to play the "farmyard" game. Cheerfully opening a box of Cheerios, they would scatter them on the floor and laugh with delight as the toddlers, cackling, pretended to be chickens, leaning over and pecking the cereal directly off the floor. For the French, who won't even *sit* on the floor to eat, this type of behavior is unfathomable. (Anticipating the reactions, I still have yet to tell this story to a single soul in France. It would be hard for them to comprehend that the staff were wonderful caregivers, despite this anecdote.)

Given this history, observing the second French Food Rule was a challenge for me: when we arrived in France, I was using food as a reward, a bribe, a toy, a distraction, and a substitute for discipline. The problem, from the French perspective, was that I was teaching my kids to use food as a response to emotional needs, which have little or no nutritional basis. When bored, our kids turn to food. When they're tired, they eat. When they're upset, they eat. A French child would never think to do this. They're just not programmed that way. French kids, like their parents, rarely eat for what psychologists and nutritionists term "non-nutritive" reasons. Rather, they have a deeply respectful attitude toward food.

This respectful attitude is taught to very young children in France, sometimes in the oddest (at least to my eyes) of places. The first time I went to a *restaurant gastronomique*, just before Philippe and I were married, I was astonished at the reverential atmosphere. Conversations were hushed, and long, appreciative silences followed the arrival of each course as we savored the new tastes and textures. The furnishings reflected the formality of the occasion: rows of heavy silver cutlery posed on plush red velvet tablecloths that looked more like rugs. Respectful silence greeted even the rituals that appeared, to me, to be slightly ludicrous—like the discreet sweeping of bread crumbs from the table with an intimidating-looking silver *ramasse-miettes* (literally, "crumb-picker-upper," an implement that looks like a tiny vacuum cleaner attachment that the waiter rolled across the table at regular intervals).

The food was superb: course after course of playful, sumptuous, and surprising tastes. But the most surprising thing of all that evening (at least to me) was the toddler in the high chair at the table next to us. He sat patiently as the meal progressed, eyes glazing over until he slumped over and fell fast asleep while his parents continued their meal unperturbed. Unhurried, they finished the dessert course only a few minutes before we did, just before midnight. When it was time to go, their child was woken up without ceremony. Popping his thumb in this mouth, he placidly allowed himself to be carried out of the restaurant without making a sound. No one batted an eye. (My children, who were not there, would have been howling the roof down.)

Looking back, this now seems less surprising. French children are exposed early on to elaborate meals and learn that their parents expect them to treat these occasions with respect. Their respectful attitude carries over into everyday meals, which have a slightly ceremonial feeling. The French never, ever, eat without putting a tablecloth on the table. They even have a special phrase for setting the table: *dresser la table*. (The word *habiller*, which is the normal French word for getting dressed, is also used.)

The image of a table getting "dressed" can still send my girls into fits of giggles. But it is actually an accurate description of how the French approach the dining table. They dignify the table, and themselves, through clothing it with the appropriate item to be worn for the most important moment of the day. Setting the table is a ritual that expresses the ceremonial and aesthetic aspects of French eating, at the core of which is the belief that eating is intensely social and that it rightfully happens around the table. This was as true for my in-laws' farming neighbors as it was for Philippe's university friends: everyone "dressed" the table with (at the minimum) a tablecloth, turning eating into a ritual that was about more than the mere physical consumption of food.

Preparing the table to receive the food in this way might seem a little old-fashioned. But it has a marvelous effect on children. They react as if a stranger in uniform has shown up at the front door: it immediately puts them on their best behavior. This effect is heightened by the rules concerning *how* the French eat. Food is never eaten standing up, or in the car, or on the go. Food is not eaten anywhere, in fact, but at the table. And food is only served when *everyone* is at the table. "*À table!*" is a summons that brings most French children running. Everyone waits for everyone else to be served, and for the ritual "*Bon appétit!*" to be said before beginning the meal. As children almost always eat with their parents, these habits sink in early.

So eating—even everyday meals—is treated like an occasion. And it is, above all, a social occasion. The French never eat alone (at home or at work) if there is someone else to eat with. And because French food tastes so good, it is an occasion to look forward to.

French food—even the simplest of foods—really does taste wonderful. I still remember the first yogurt that baby Claire ever tasted in France. We bought it at the local supermarket, so it was nothing out of the ordinary by French standards. Except that it was an extraordinary experience for Claire. Served in a little ochre-colored natural clay pot, capped with a crinkly gold wrapper embossed with a reproduction of Renoir's famous milkmaid, her yogurt looked like an intriguing Christmas present. Clutching her spoon, she peeled back the wrapping, dipped into the pot, tasted her first mouthful, widened her eyes, bent her head intently, and didn't look up again until every inch was scraped clean. Creamy, rich, tangy without being bitter, French yogurt is simply delicious. This is true for most of the food you find in France. So imagine how French kids feel about it. Food tastes great, is served with a sense of occasion, and is fun because it's social. The table is where parents and children relax together. It is where they appreciate not only food, but also one another. This makes the rigid approach to food education more bearable for children.

And food education is not something that most French parents view as optional. Because eating is so central to French culture, French kids have to learn *how* to eat the French way if they want to fit in. It is as important for a French child to learn the food rules as it is for an American teenager to learn how to drive. It's a rite of passage and a precondition for successfully navigating through society. So food, unsurprisingly, turned out to be our social entrée into village life.

When we first arrived, I would drive half an hour to the nearest large town grocery store to buy my groceries and do errands (*les courses*), comforted by the familiar act of rolling up and down the aisles with a grocery cart. But the aisles were empty, and the grocery store felt vaguely antiseptic and lonely. So after a couple of weeks, I became a faithful visitor to the village market, which was held twice a week in the cobblestone plaza in front of the church in the heart of the village.

I first had to overcome my resistance to shopping at the *marché*. My first impression was that the market was an incredibly inefficient way of shopping for a family. My mother-in-law, however, did all of her shopping there. Janine's typical *marché* visit would include purchases at the vegetable stall, the fruit stall, the cheese stall, the bakery, the fish stall, the butcher shop, and the honey stall (yes, there was a stall just for honey). She would spend, on average, between three and five minutes in each of seven or eight separate lines. At each stall, vendors would cheerfully greet each customer, meticulously choose their produce, carefully pack it, and slowly count out the change. I fretted and even pouted at waiting in line and longed for the online grocery delivery service that brought everything to our house back in Vancouver.

I also griped, at first, at how inconvenient it seemed to shop at the *marché*. Buying enough for a family of four for a week meant lugging heavy *paniers* (the straw baskets also used in supermarkets, as plastic bags have been banned in French grocery stores). Because the stalls spilled out into lanes and streets, cars were banned from the center of the village until the market was over around noon (in order to allow everyone to go home for their two-hour lunch, *bien sûr*).

This meant a long walk back home. At first, I struggled with my overloaded *paniers,* huffing and puffing back up the hill to our house—feeling slightly embarrassed as gray-haired grandmothers briskly sailed past me with their wheeled caddies. But lugging the bags provided some exercise, which I desperately needed: French women rarely work out (schlepping groceries being enough of a workout, apparently), and there was no gym within twenty miles of the village. And Janine taught me to buy smaller amounts and shop more frequently, as the French do. I even broke down and bought a caddy with a gaily-colored Scottish plaid motif that seemed out of place until my father-in-law pointed out that Brittany had actually been settled by Celts fleeing the invasion of Britain by the Anglo-Saxon tribes. (This gave me new insight into the French dislike of the "Anglo-Saxons," a category to which I apparently belonged, and into which Germans, British, Americans, Canadians, and even Australians are usually lumped.)

There was another advantage to buying food at the market. Food was fresher this way, Janine explained, because it could be purchased at precisely the right moment. This transformed what had been one of the most frustrating market rituals into one of my favorites: watching the fruit and vegetable vendors ask, "When do you want to eat it?" The customer's response would identify not only the day, but also the meal at which the item was to be consumed. "Tomorrow for lunch!" Or "Dinner on Saturday!" The vendor would then conduct a painstaking search (customers never being allowed to touch the produce themselves) through the avocados (or melons, or tomatoes, or pineapples, or whatever it was) until the perfect one was found. The logic of the long lines slowly became more apparent. If this much care went into planning every meal and choosing every item, no wonder it all took so long.

But there was another reason people liked the long and multiple lines: they were a core part of the village's social life. People didn't enter into idle conversations at the local café (as I discovered after a few cold shoulders). There were no chairs for sitting down in any of the stores. The village was too small to have a library. In fact, there was almost no common space anywhere in the village apart from the central square in front of the church that was used as a parking lot when the market wasn't being held.

Where, I wondered in the first weeks we were there, did people socialize? The market lines—which recomposed themselves rapidly as people moved from one stall to the next—provided, I discovered, one of the only opportunities for the normally reserved Bretons to banter and chat. If people were in a hurry, they'd come early (before the crowds) and be done in a few minutes. If they wanted to socialize, they'd come later.

By the end of the summer, I started coming later more and more often, as I learned so much from the conversations I struck up. These would often revolve around the food in front of us. How were the garlic shoots this week? What were the radishes like last week? Why were the local mackerel so small this season? Going to the market twice every week gradually introduced me to the local food culture. I had no idea that this variety of food could be available in one place. And I encountered lots of new tastes: *huîtres* (oysters, which I finally consented to eat, much to the approval of my father-in-law), *moules* (mussels, which soon became a favorite, cooked simply with white wine and a little parsley), and *cidre* (Brittany's famous apple cider).

Gradually, I learned that asking about food was a great conversation starter. I found that the best way to initiate conversations was to innocently ask: How do you cook this vegetable? (Or, more often than I'd like to admit: What *is* that vegetable?) A chorus of voices would respond, offering recipes, debating cooking times, suggesting spices. The ice would be broken, and we would move on to other topics.

The local fisherman was one of my first allies. By the time the market was setting up at 8:30 in the morning, he had already been up for hours, as the in-shore fishing boats left and returned before sunrise. But he had endless energy and a soft spot for kids. "Furr zee baybee" he would say smilingly, carefully filleting the fresh fish in front of us.

Everyone in the line discreetly listened to my answers to his gently curious questions about life "*en Amérique*" (English Canadians are, whether they like it or not, lumped in with Americans when abroad). Knowing that September was just around the corner, I would ask him questions about the local school, which his children attended—and where Sophie would be going. With Sophie hanging on every word, he would give upbeat answers with an encouraging smile. And no matter how much I insisted, he would never accept payment for any of the fish I chose for our daughters. He did this with all of the locals, but not the tourists who were still crowding the market, and I felt proud when I realized that this was a sign of acceptance.

The market was an education for the girls as well. At first, I tended to avoid the "messy" stalls if I had them with me. The butcher's stall—with the hanging pigs' heads and the decapitated still-furry rabbits—was a no-go zone. The *poissonnerie*—where the fish were beheaded, gutted, and de-scaled at the request of each customer—also made me nervous. So I made these rounds without the girls, usually entrusting them to my father-in-law, who would take them for a walk around the square.

But Jo soon grew impatient with my queasiness. One day, he gathered Claire in his arms and brought her over to the fish stall. Her eyes widened. Raising a chubby finger, she pointed at a particularly large specimen:

"*Poisson!*" (Fish!), she shrieked.

"*Coupe! Coupe! Coupe!*" (Cut! Cut! Cut!), she continued, turning her hand sideways and making a sawing motion in the air. By now, she had the attention of everyone in the line.

"Yum yum!" she gravely finished, pointing to her mouth to the sound of approving chuckles.

My daughter already knew, even better than I, how to make friends and impress people in France.

3

Schooling the Stomach

We Start Learning to "Eat French" (the Hard Way)

Mignonne,
Mignonne.
Si tu veux du pain,
Je t'en donne.
Si tu n'en veux pas,
Je te bâtonne!

Cutie-pie, Cutie-pie,
Oh so sweet.
If you want bread,
You'll get some to eat.
But if you refuse,
You'll get beat!

—Traditional French nursery rhyme

By the beginning of September, we were all looking forward to the start of the school year. No one had been awaiting *la rentrée* more eagerly than Sophie, who desperately wanted to meet kids her own age. So on the first day of school, we were there bright and early. Sophie walked clutching my hand, followed by my mother-in-law, while Philippe brought up the rear with Claire, dressed to match her sister (precious, but I couldn't resist). Janine had drawn my attention to the fact that French schoolchildren, even in a little country village, were much better dressed than their American counterparts—so Sophie had gotten a new outfit only days before. She looked adorable in a dusty rose shirt-dress with taupe leggings; I had judged earth tones—a popular choice amongst French parents—to be the safest bet for my kids (although lots of French children wear white, which mysteriously stays spotless).

Sophie and I had gone together in one of our first-ever mom and daughter clothes-shopping outings. On the drive home, I had reassured her that this year—her first in full-time school—would be just great. At the back of my mind was an image of eager village children being fascinated by *l'Américaine,* falling over themselves to befriend the new girl. But I had forgotten what kids could be like. And I had no idea what a small village could be like (having lived in big cities all my life). I soon learned: if you don't know the rules, you're the village idiot. As I was about to learn, my daughter didn't know the rules. And neither, apparently, did I.

The first inkling I had of trouble was the small white sheet posted on the front door of the school. The contents of the piece of paper were impossible for me to decipher. It was marked with today's date. It seemed like a list. It had lots of strange words that I couldn't recognize. But I did recognize the days of the week. Maybe it was a list of after-school classes?

Mais non! My husband said, laughing. "This is a menu."

I looked again and saw that he was right. Across the top of the paper, the days of the week were listed. Wednesday was missing, but that was normal, I reminded myself: French kids go to school only four days a week, with Wednesdays being devoted to sports and other extracurricular activities. Running down the left-hand side were the standard four parts of the French meal: *entrée* (first course), *plat principal* (main course), *salade* and *fromage* (cheese), and *dessert*. But I didn't recognize much else.

	Lundi	Mardi	Mercredi	Jeudi	Vendredi
Entrée	Endive salad with Emmental and croutons	Country pâté with pickles	No school	Radishes and sea salt	Beet salad bolognaise
Plat principal	Alaskan hake with organic pan-fried potatoes	Sauté de boeuf, sauce grand-mère with gratin dauphinois		Quiche provençale	Roast turkey with fine flageolet beans
Salade/ Fromage	Blue cheese	Tomme cheese		Edam	Goat cheese bûchette
Dessert	Plain yogurt, apricots in honey syrup	Fresh fruit cocktail		Chocolate éclair	Organic pear compote

This, my husband patiently explained, was the list of what the children were going to eat at lunch for that week in the school *cantine*. The meals were designed to be tasty, healthy, and varied. They were also inexpensive: on average $3, although children from lower-income families paid lower rates (the lowest fee at our school was less than a $1 per meal). The school posted the menu on each entrance door so that parents (and children) would know what was being served for lunch.

The *cantine* is a universal institution in France—found not only in primary and high schools, but also in many government buildings and private companies. The word is difficult to translate. The closest word in English is "cafeteria," but this incorrectly conjures up memories of the soggy pizza and overpriced French fries that were the norm at my high school. The best way to think about a school *cantine* in France is to imagine what your high school cafeteria would have been like if the food had been made by Cordon Bleu chefs-in-training, overseen by a nutritionist, and served to you at the table by maternal waiters (who were only too happy to cut up your meat if you couldn't quite manage it). The official term "*restaurant scolaire*" (school restaurant) sums it up perfectly.

Philippe and Janine scanned the menu, clucking cheerfully at their favorites. But the list struck me as ludicrous. Beets? Fresh fish? This sounded like a meal in a Michelin-starred restaurant, not food for five-year-olds. And certainly not for *my* five-year-old.

"Um," I said hesitantly, "something seems to be missing. There's only one choice every day." I was thinking of school cafeterias back home, where kids always had a choice, although one that was often admittedly dubious from a nutritional perspective: between strawberry and chocolate milk, for example, or between pizza and hot dogs.

"Everyone eats the same thing, *bien sûr!*" replied my husband. I had already learned that the phrase *bien sûr* ("of course") usually implied I had unknowingly committed some kind of social blunder about something that seemed blindingly obvious to the French.

"But what if the kids don't like what's being served that day?" I asked. This question gave rise to odd looks from the parents shepherding their children through the school doors.

"They go hungry!" Janine replied, looking impatient.

A story from *Tra la lire* (France's most popular magazine for preschoolers) popped into my head. In the story "La journée du NON!" (The Day of Saying NO!), cheeky little Michel is having a "NO" day. He says "NO" to getting dressed and goes to school in pajamas. He says "NO" to eating lunch at the cafeteria (radishes, sausages, mashed potatoes, and ice cream) and then goes hungry all afternoon. Michel feels sad, but his little friends (who ate all of their lunch) don't feel sorry for him, and neither do his parents. When I had first read this story, I had dismissed it as cruel and unbelievable. But I now realized with a sinking feeling that the French didn't see it that way.

"But this is ridiculous," I snapped. "Sophie only likes pasta for lunch. She'll be starving!" This was true. Despite my best efforts, Sophie refused to eat anything but pasta at lunchtime. And it had to be made in precisely the same way: with olive oil (definitely *not* butter) and liberally sprinkled with Parmesan cheese. The fact that the local grocery store did not carry Parmesan had not deterred me from continuing to make Sophie's favorite dish once we arrived in France. I was proud of my small triumph in charming the initially gruff grocer into placing a special order for "Sophie's cheese."

"School is about learning lots of things, including how to eat what is put in front of you," replied Janine. (Note to self: Next time, don't invite mother-in-law along for first day of school). I was cornered. The problem was that my husband and I had agreed that Sophie should eat lunch at school. This idea had originated with Janine. "Eating is central to French culture," she declared soon after we arrived. "And Sophie will not make friends unless she stays to eat at the *cantine*." So we had signed her up to eat meals there every day. At the time, it had sounded like a good idea. We had talked to Sophie about the *cantine*, and played it up: *think of all the fun you'll have with your new friends!* Now I was having second thoughts. But it was too late to back down.

We walked down the hallway to Sophie's classroom, where her teacher stood at the door welcoming the students. There was a long line, which moved slowly. As we got closer to the front of the line, I found out why. We watched as each child eagerly approached the teacher to be kissed on each cheek. Some of the parents kissed the teacher as well, whereas others shook her hand. This was accompanied by pleasantries about the summer holidays. After a few minutes, the child moved into the classroom and the parents gracefully retreated.

This was not an unusual scene in France. *Se faire la bise* translates as "to give a kiss," but a *bise* is really more of a delicate brushing of cheeks with a vague kissing action made in the air close (but not too close) to the other person's ear. I had a hard time with this, as I was brought up in a culture where your face was as private as your rear end: only a few very close family members have the right to touch it. But since everyone gives *les bises* every time they meet in France, I realized I had to start getting used to it.

Les bises made me nervous for another reason: they are unpredictable. When people meet one another in France, they may shake hands instead of exchanging *les bises*. Sometimes men kiss men, but sometimes they don't. On some occasions, I was expected to kiss people I was meeting for the first time (mostly family), but with other people (even those I saw frequently) I never got past shaking hands. In some parts of France, people exchange only one or two kisses, but in other parts of the country, people kiss three or even four times. Sometimes, people start with the left cheek, but sometimes with the right. All of these decisions have to be made in an instant, based on a complex calculation about the relationship you have with the person, the location of the encounter, their gender, who else is with you, how much of a rush you're both in, and some strange sixth sense about the social pecking order. I never quite figured out the logic.

All I knew was that you could get *les bises* really wrong. I had seen this with my husband. Soon after we met, we flew back home so that he could meet my relatives. My uncle John came to the airport to pick us up. In the arrivals hall, surrounded by people, Philippe did what comes naturally to French men: he gave Uncle John a big kiss on each cheek. John's stunned look was promptly misinterpreted by Philippe. "Oh," said my husband-to-be, smiling, "you must be giving three kisses in Canada!" As Philippe dove in to give another kiss, Uncle John ducked, and the two ended up in a locked-lip embrace.

Their relationship eventually recovered enough for Uncle John to give me away at our wedding. But *bises* still made me nervous. And they made Sophie nervous too; even with our relatives, she would balk, although she knew that refusing to give a *bise* is the gravest of insults. As her turn to meet the teacher approached, Sophie began to fidget. "*Bonjour!*" said Madame, smiling. Sure enough, Sophie hung her head, let go of my hand and slunk into the classroom. Madame frowned. Now was clearly not the time to mention my worries about food. But I worried all day. And it was a long day. French kids go to school from 8:30 to 4:30 (and many stay in after-school "study time" (*études*) until 6:30 or 7:00). Sophie's classmates would be used to this, as it was their third year in school (French kids start formal schooling part-time at two and a half, and full-time at three). They were *cantine* veterans, but Sophie was definitely not.

Sophie's face told me everything as she left the classroom. She bolted into my arms, wailing. When she calmed down, I heard the story. She had eaten nothing all day. Lunch was inedible (according to her). Unlike her day care, there was no morning or afternoon snack. And no one had allowed her to get a drink of water, even when she raised her hand.

Fuming, I put her to bed early and decided to show up at school early the next day with a packed lunch, water bottle, and some strong words for the teacher. I planned my comments carefully: "Sophie is having enough trouble adjusting to a new culture. At home, children can drink when they want to, even during class. Could she please bring her lunch from home until she settles in?"

Leaving Philippe to get Sophie ready for school, I rushed over half an hour early in order to get a chance to speak with Madame. But Madame was not impressed. Eyeing Sophie's lunch bag with suspicion, she sniffed, "I have to think of the entire class. We can't have special treats being sent from home, or special allowances made for anyone." Before I could stop myself, I blurted out my concerns. Would Sophie be stigmatized because she ate differently than the other children? Or wasn't as adventurous an eater? What would that do to her socially? And how would she ever learn anything if she was hungry and thirsty all the time? Seeing my worried face, Madame softened. "Come to see the *cantine* on your way out," she invited.

Our first stop was the kitchen, where the chef was already at work. Wielding a ladle taller than me, he stood on his tiptoes stirring onions in a pot that looked big enough to hold Sophie's entire class. Meals were made from scratch, he said proudly, pointing to the vegetables lined up on the chopping block. He tried to buy local ingredients whenever he could. And, he added, the government was planning to require 20 percent of the ingredients to be organic by 2012. Good food was not, he added, about spending lots of money; it could be simple, inexpensive, and tasty. I tried to look suitably impressed.

Not all *cantines* are lucky enough to have their own chef, I later found out. To cut costs, many have resorted to outside catering companies and started using prepackaged, preprepared ingredients where possible. In fact, one study released shortly after my visit suggested that up to half of France's *cantines* were not in compliance with the Ministry of Education's strict regulations. French parents were up in arms. One well-known chef, Cyril Lignac, even launched a reality TV show (*Vive la Cantine!*) where he played the role of "food savior" to kids in schools across France (much like Jamie Oliver's Food Revolution). Still, even the worst *cantine* meals in France were probably better than the average meals available at most North American cafeterias.

To understand the crucial role played by the school chef, it's important to know that the French think that lunch should be the biggest and most important meal of the day—representing about 40 percent of children's total caloric intake. Since vending machines are banned in all French schools, there is no place to get food except the *cantine*. A majority of students eat at school, and they are not allowed to bring their own lunches (unless they have serious allergies). So the *cantine* is the place where the majority of France's six million schoolchildren eat lunch every day. At Sophie's school, the chef was the undisputed master of the *cantine,* regularly walking around at mealtimes to ask the children what they thought of his dishes (and sometimes waving the ladle in the direction of unwilling eaters, Sophie later told me). Even without knowing all of this, it was clear that the chef took great pride in his work.

We thanked him and then moved on to the dining area. Proudly pointing out the cloth napkins and tablecloths (a significant expense for a small village school), Madame explained that the children were served the food by special staff who oversaw the meal (correcting kids' manners, sometimes not so gently) while the teachers had their lunch in a separate room. China plates and kid-size cutlery were waiting on the tables, lined up with the precision of a miniature military officers' mess. In spite of myself, I was impressed. This, she assured me, was standard for French schools.

Order was important, Madame noted, because (by government decree) the children spent a minimum of thirty minutes at the table. I thought of the older kids I knew back home, allotted ten minutes to gobble down a cold sandwich at their desks, but I said nothing. How could Madame possibly understand?

In French schools, continued Madame, mealtime is meant to allow students to socialize, to take pleasure in new foods and to discover them in a relaxed environment. Eating the same thing is also an important factor in diversifying children's diets. At school, under the influence of peers, children taste and eat things that would have them turning up their noses at home (peer-induced behavioral change is also confirmed by American research). The French system is actually a highly perfected peer-pressure-driven food diversification program. With a few hundred attentive kids watching, would *you* make a fuss over your food?

Teachers, too, played an active role in educating the children about food, explained Madame as we walked along the corridors to the exit. They had three key goals. The first was to protect children's health and support their academic performance by feeding them nutritious food. The second goal was to educate children: to cultivate their palates, teach them basic rules of food hygiene and nutrition, and open their minds to food as culture, art, and national heritage. And the third goal was to discipline their eating habits, setting up healthy routines for when, where, how, what, and *why* kids ate what they did.

At this point, I almost said something. Madame's approach seemed incredibly rigid, and I didn't think it was going to work with Sophie. But Madame was in full swing, and I decided to stay quiet.

Proudly, Madame quoted, from memory, the French National Ministry of Education: "School is a privileged place in which children are educated about good taste, nutrition, and food culture. Good taste must be taught and learned, and can only be acquired over time."

The exact approach to serving food, she explained, was governed by rules set out by the Ministry. Vegetables had to be served at every meal: raw one day, cooked the next. Fried food could be served no more than once per week. Real fish had to be served at least once per week. Fruit was served for dessert every second meal, at a minimum; sugary desserts were allowed—but only once per week. The rules even specified the quantities of nutrients expected to be in the average meal (if you're curious, these include 11 grams of high-quality protein, 220 milligrams of calcium, and 2.8 milligrams of iron for adolescents).

Meal planning was overseen by a nutritionist and a committee of parent volunteers. Parents were intensely interested in what their children were eating. That last part didn't surprise me: I had already heard parents greeting their children as they exited the classroom. Instead of the usual "What did you do in school today?" they all asked, "So how did you like your lunch?"

This reflected, I later learned, French parents' general lack of concern (at least to my North American eyes) with accelerating young children's intellectual development. No flashcards, no toddler violin classes, no Baby Einstein. In fact, French parents are puzzled by the intensity with which American parents try to stimulate intellectual precociousness in their offspring. (Flash cards? Really? You must be joking!) The French are deeply committed to formal schooling (which was more advanced than at home, as far as I could tell). But most parents believe that teaching reading and writing is a task best left to professional teachers. Instead, French parents focus on what they think young kids can and should learn: how to savor and enjoy food. All food. A typical question one French parent will ask another is: "So, what does she like to eat"? The other parent will proudly respond: "*Elle mange un peu de tout.*" (She eats a little bit of everything.)

Entire books on this topic are written for new parents, with tempting titles like *The Birth of Taste: How to Give Children the Gift of Enjoying Food*. In fact, French parents love to recount anecdotes about kids' first foods (much the same way North American parents share stories about first words). During our visits to village families with young children, we would almost invariably discuss what the children had been eating. Parents would share their children's food conquests in a kind of one-upmanship that North Americans usually reserve for sporting or academic achievements. Our friend Yves, for example, was incredibly proud that his nine-month-old daughter Nicole would eat Roquefort cheese (yes, the stinky green-blue moldy kind) and would excitedly offer little blobs to her in front of any and all visitors. I had to admit that Nicole did look exceedingly happy while gumming her cheese ("It's the salt," whispered my husband in an effort to console me).

So I knew first-hand that French parents thought variety was important. What Madame was saying made sense. But I hadn't known until now that the school played such an active role in educating children about food in the classroom. According to Madame, food education actually occurred through formal lessons. She gestured to a diagram on the wall that looked like a food pyramid. Edging closer, I noticed something curious. Instead of the regular food groups, there were nine recommendations, like rungs in a ladder. The food groups were there (fruits and vegetables; milk products; grains and legumes; and meat, fish, and eggs), but there were also recommendations, Madame explained, about limiting fats, sugar, and salt. The bottom row—the base of the pyramid—was devoted to drinking water. *Was this a food group according to the French?* I wondered.

But before I had time to ask, Madame had moved on to talk about her personal favorite: the lessons organized during "La Semaine du Goût" (Tasting Week), held every October in schools across France. Throughout the week, celebrity chefs (from top restaurants like the Ritz) visited classrooms charming young children as they cooked and tasted foods together. The online videos of their performances sometimes became national news stories. More humbly, local cooks, bakers, butchers, cheese makers, and assorted food lovers of all types visited classrooms and campuses, offering teachable moments like "Authentic Fruit Juice Workshops." Over 5,000 of these lessons had been organized across France the previous year. (Simultaneously, restaurants all over France offer special "Tasting Week" menus at affordable prices.) In spite of myself, I felt a skeptical look come to my face; I doubted that any gourmet chef, no matter how good, could convince Sophie to eat things she didn't want to eat.

But teaching kids about food didn't stop there, Madame continued. Great care was taken in teaching children how to eat well and wisely, and in "awakening their taste-buds," as she poetically put it. The school followed the teaching method developed by the national French Institute of Taste (no, I am not making this up). Each year, teachers began with simple lessons on the senses that encouraged children to develop skills of introspection and verbalization. Through exploring how food experiences are composed of taste, vision, smell, touch, and hearing, children learn to explore food through their five senses. This "taste training," as it is commonly known in France, is based on lots of fun games. A favorite teaching tactic for Sophie's age group is the *sac fourre-tout*. Children take turns reaching into a small hole in this "stuff sack" (which is filled with fresh vegetables and fruit), handling and describing what they find, before seeing its contents. In another lesson, children are given trays with many small pieces of different foods and asked to classify them into categories like salty, sweet, acidic, and bitter. Later on, they're blindfolded and asked to taste, describe, and identify a piece of food they are offered. The goal is to encourage children to develop a sensory appreciation of food, using all five senses. That, I admitted, sounded like something Sophie might like.

Madame looked encouraged. She referred enthusiastically to French research on "sensory appreciation" and its importance for healthy eating habits. Schools, she proudly noted, used these research results in their curriculum. In classroom lessons, students learned to reflect on food and to speak about their thoughts and feelings. Once this happened, she continued, children began to develop richer ideas about food. The same food—avocado, for example—might be prepared three or four different ways and offered to the children, who would learn about the different culinary expressions and about their own sensory skills. Spices were introduced in older grades, where children were also asked to critically analyze media messages about food, and learned about France's *patrimoine culinaire* (culinary heritage) as part of their social studies lessons. That even sounded like it would be useful for me.

The lessons then moved on to introduce complex aromas, explore food preferences, and prepare dishes (usually regional specialties), finishing with Tasting Week's grand finale: a *repas de fête*. This is a difficult concept to translate but is best understood as a celebratory meal at which eating is the primary vehicle for celebrating. All children had to go through this process together, Madame insisted. For those really interested, special after-school classes were available (like the summer cooking camps that our older nieces and nephews attended). The local government had even organized a field trip the year before, to the Epicurium—the world's first museum dedicated to fruits and vegetables—in the heart of the southern French city of Avignon.

"So," concluded Madame triumphantly, "Sophie will have a wonderful time eating at school, just like everyone else." I didn't know what to say. All of this sounded like fun, but I still didn't think it was going to change Sophie's mind about beet salad.

"That does sound wonderful," I stammered, feeling as if I was on thin ice. Gathering my courage, I insisted: "I don't think this will work for Sophie. She needs to eat well in order to learn well. She needs to snack at least twice a day. She can't concentrate when she's hungry. And I'm not sure she'll be able to handle the food in the *cantine*. Could she not bring her own lunch, or at least her own snacks?"

"NO!" came the reply. It was clear there was no room for negotiation. "Snacking provides poor nutrition, which doesn't help children learn," said Madame, with a firm tone. "It's my job to teach healthy eating habits to *all* of my students." For Madame, it was clear that learning to eat the French way was mandatory.

I must have looked mutinous because Madame stopped at the exit to add a couple more points. Throughout the year, Sophie would come home with fun ideas about food, Madame promised. The children would grow their own vegetables in special plots set aside in the schoolyard. The class would go on field trips to the local market, which was only a five-minute walk away. And they'd blend studies of food with other subjects, like science, particularly in their module on snails.

Madame must have noticed my reaction at her mention of snails, for she stopped her monologue to suggest that if I had any other questions I should perhaps see the school's psychological counselor.

I froze in alarm. "Isn't Sophie a bit young to see a counselor?" I gasped out weakly.

Silence.

"The counselor would be for *you*," Madame finally said before turning away to welcome the arriving students.

My husband laughed when I told him this later. "French people don't get anxious about food," he said. "Most believe that children's eating problems are due to the parents." I found this insulting. Did he think that *I* had caused Sophie's eating problems? It turns out he did (sort of), and we ended up having one of our first big fights of our year in France.

"I'm not anxious," I told him. "I'm simply protecting Sophie."

"From what?" he replied. I didn't have a good answer.

The bell rang, and the students streamed into class towing Sophie in their wake. I was left clutching her brown paper lunch bag and wondering what would come next.

The answer was: nothing. No special allowances would be made for Sophie, who would have to adapt, and the sooner the better. The purpose of school was to educate Sophie, in spite of me. No one would pander to her or to her parents. Or, in my case, to her anxious foreign parent.

None of this made me feel very comfortable. But, as I quickly learned, French schools are not interested in making parents feel comfortable. They have a punitive model of education (which applies equally to both parents and children who get out of line). When I learned that one of Sophie's classmates was getting detentions because she didn't finish her in-class work fast enough (in kindergarten!), I started to realize what we were up against. But I felt powerless to do anything about it.

"Why do they have to be so rigid?" I later asked my husband.

"Why do you think I left France intending never to come back?" was his reply. It was true: my husband didn't cope well with the many rules and routines of French society.

But he also pointed out something really important about the French schooling system: by making food education mandatory, the government ensured that healthy diets would not be restricted to the elite. In countries where food education and nutrition are not mandatory at school, children from wealthier families with higher levels of education tend to eat much more healthily. In contrast, our village school—which included families from all walks of life (from farmers to pharmacists, fishermen to factory workers)—had a mission to teach everyone to eat well, supporting what children learned at home. And low-income parents had more help, I knew, than did North American parents, through tax breaks, reduced fees for all sorts of things (even train fares), and government-subsidized day care and after-school care. The French approach levels the playing field (although the exclusion of Muslim children due to the lack of halal foods is a longstanding issue).

So, like many other things, good food is democratized in France. As a result, there is much less difference between the tastes of different income groups than in the United States. Philippe's family was a perfect example: Janine was (as she put it) from very humble origins. But while she and Jo had both stopped school at sixteen, they could hold their own in any five-star restaurant. So I had to admit that Madame's claim that food education was a social equalizer made sense. Providing proper food to *all* children, and teaching *all* children how to eat properly, is, for the French, an important expression of their national motto of Liberty, Equality, Fraternity (the former constrained by the latter, I thought to myself a bit sourly).

This explanation made Madame's adamant attitude—that every child must participate—seem more reasonable. The French approach to food is about much more than nutrition or the satisfaction of physical needs. Rather, learning to eat well is also about learning how to eat well *together.* "Taste training" for French children is really a form of citizenship training, because all children have the chance to be exposed to good food, and good taste, in school. Eating at school is a shared rite of citizenship. If Sophie didn't participate, it would affect her socially (and, later, professionally).

And more than this: Sophie's entire education would be enriched. French children learn to listen to their senses, and their bodies, in interacting with food. Food is a subject of scientific study, but it also has an affective, intimate dimension, as children learn to think about their self-image, and family life, through exploring what they eat at home and at school. The terms used to describe this process, such as "gustatory awakening" (*l'éveil gustatif*), suddenly seemed less pompous. Children, I realized, were not just learning to eat; they were also learning to be curious and thoughtful. And they were not only taught about good nutrition, but also encouraged to develop a sense of critical judgment about food.

This sounded promising. So, in spite of my reservations, I agreed that we would gently, but firmly, insist that Sophie continue going to the *cantine.*

Predictably, Sophie reacted badly during the first weeks of school. The first words out of her mouth every morning, barely awake, were a despairing howl: "Maman, I *don't* want to go to school." I forced her to go and forced back the tears. After all, she was only in kindergarten. Admittedly, the days were long. But kindergarten is still kindergarten, I thought. How stressful could it be?

It was only later that I began to realize why she had such difficulty. She spoke French, but was definitely *not* French; bilingual but not bicultural. She suffered from a complete lack of *éducation* as a result of her North American upbringing. Even the playground games were different: Sophie had to translate the unwritten rules of "What time is it, Mr. Wolf?" into "1 2 3 Soleil," and to transform "Duck Duck Goose" into "Le facteur n'est pas passé." Even hopscotch was different.

So she didn't fit in, and she learned the hard way; or, rather, was taught the hard way. At first, her classmates' favorite playground tactic was one of those innocuously malicious rules that sends a *Lord of the Flies* shiver down parents' spines: "Everyone gets to play except the new kids." Except that my daughter was the only new kid in the school. So Sophie was very alone for the first month; hence the tears. But I only found out about this much later, in part because of the code of silence in the French schooling system (in which parents are treated as interlopers at best). And, if I am being honest, because I didn't really want to listen. Having dragged my family to France, I was determined that we would be happy, even if it required a lot of pretending.

This led to months of frustration. To disapproving glares from the other parents, Sophie would sob in my arms every day as I left her in the classroom. "I know this is good for you," I would tell her. "I would never put you in a school that was bad for you." But silently I wondered whether we were doing the right thing.

One of the most difficult things—for me as well as for Sophie— was the lack of choice about when she could eat during school hours. The primary way in which French parents control their kids' access to food is through strictly scheduling mealtimes. The French do this as a matter of course with children, toddlers, and even babies. Food is not provided on demand. Food is provided when adults decide it should be provided. This is not simply because of some autocratic wish to control when children eat. The French believe that scheduling meals leads to more balanced eating habits and a healthier digestive system. I summed this up with the following rule:

French Food Rule #3:
Parents schedule meals and menus.
Kids eat what adults eat: no substitutes and no short-order cooking.

I could see the logic in this. But I didn't think it would work for my kids. And, in fact, this is one of the rules to which both my children had the hardest time adapting. One day, I arrived unexpectedly at Claire's day care just before noon. When my husband had dropped her off that morning, he had forgotten to tell the staff that I would be picking her up early to take her to a doctor's appointment. I opened the door to see Claire, red-faced, standing in the middle of the room. Her mouth was open in a long, drawn-out O shape that meant only one thing. Sure enough, her crying soon picked up where it had left off. She was so angry she didn't even notice me standing in the doorway. All of the furious attention bundled up in her little body was directed at the children who were eating and the people who were feeding them.

Four toddlers were seated primly in low-slung high chairs, aligned in a tidy row. Four staff, one per child, were seated facing them. Each of the women had an apron, a tray, a dish, a spoon, and a smile. They were all steadfastly ignoring Claire.

"She is hungry, but she is still learning to wait her turn," remarked one woman, while slowly scraping the last bit of puree from a bowl. I bit my tongue, reminding myself that North American frankness was not appreciated here. Controlling my urge to stuff something, anything, into Claire's mouth, I took her into my lap, sat down, and waited. *I'm not leaving until she gets something to eat,* I thought, forgetting all about our doctor's appointment.

As Claire (and I) slowly calmed down, the meal quietly continued. The children were served the traditional four courses—*entrée, plat de résistance, fromage,* and *dessert.* Portions were relatively small.

The children had to do their best to finish them and were given lots of time to do so. One by one, the chairs were liberated, and the next four children settled in. Again, an adult sat in front of each child, slowly offering food, smilingly accompanying them right to the end of the meal. Considering that the day care had sixteen kids, this seemed incredibly labor-intensive. But every child left the table full and happy. Even Claire: when it was finally her turn, she sat with the other little children and smiled delightedly as the first mouthfuls of food came her way. She finished every morsel and had a long and delicious nap after our delayed visit to the doctor (who, by the way, was completely understanding about why we were late: "The most important meal of the day!" he said, smiling).

What a contrast with Claire's day care back home, where kids would sit at their tables, open their lunch bags, and eat what they could in ten minutes. Most food was served cold and eaten with fingers and hands, and lots of leftovers came home every night. It was the children's responsibility—even as toddlers—to feed themselves. In fact, the ability to feed oneself is viewed, in North America, as a major step toward independence. Food is also a matter of individual choice and preference. Early on, children are given lots of choices. Most American parenting books suggest that kids get to decide whether, what, and how much to eat. Others go further and suggest that kids should also get to decide when they eat. In practice, most families give a high degree of choice to children. And processed foods enable this, as even fairly young kids can find ready-made food in the pantry, or heat it up in the microwave.

Choice is important for North Americans because it is about one of their most dearly held values: individual autonomy. Even young kids have control at the dinner table, and over the dinner menu. Sophie was already used to this, which is why she found it so difficult to have no choice about when and what to eat. So, unsurprisingly, the lack of choice at the *cantine* also bothered me. I thought that the food itself seemed both tasty and healthy. But I worried about Sophie's refusal to eat it, and I worried about the effects of suppressing her autonomy about something so important.

My husband thought this was funny. "My autonomy isn't too suppressed," he joked. "After all, I married you even though my mother was totally against it!" This was true, although my mother-in-law had long since reconciled herself to her foreign daughter-in-law (or so I could convince myself on my good days).

"And besides," he said to me one night, "if the food is delicious, why do you need to have a choice?" This was a good question, and I didn't have a good answer. The best response I could come up with was that choosing made me happy. But the French don't see it that way. And, thinking about it, I could see their point. The *cantine* didn't allow choice, but as a result, kids ended up with a highly varied diet. So French parents didn't mind the fact that the kids didn't have choices about food—they didn't think they were ready to handle it.

But the different views on choice held by Americans and French run deeper than this. A simple example of this is their response to the following question (used by scientists in the largest-ever comparative survey of French and American eating habits):

"You have the choice between two ice cream parlors. The first offers fifty different flavors. The second offers ten. Which one would you choose?"

Thousands of people in France and the United States responded to this question. The answers were complete opposites. Nearly 70 percent of French people chose the store with only ten flavors. But 60 percent of Americans preferred the store with fifty flavors.

As a very unscientific test, I asked this question of all of my in-laws. Unsurprisingly, they answered just like an average French person. When I asked *why* they'd answer this way, their response was straightforward: "If someone is only making ten flavors, they'll put more care and attention into making those the very best quality. If they're making fifty, the quality will probably be lower."

Aha! I thought. For Americans, having lots of choices is synonymous with quality; it makes us happy. But for the French, choice doesn't mean better quality—in fact, just the opposite. Too much choice is (potentially) a symptom of lower quality, which certainly wouldn't make the French—who have such high standards for everything—very happy.

This new perspective on choice seemed to make sense. And that's exactly what I told Sophie. "They're only making one thing because they want it to be absolutely delicious. And it is!" I'd say firmly but cheerfully, as she balked every morning in front of the menu posted on the school door.

In addition to encouraging her to adapt, I also plotted to help her resist. But it wasn't very successful. Secret snacks in Sophie's pocket promptly resulted in a warning. So we found other strategies. We checked out the menus in advance and discussed them, so that Sophie at least wouldn't be surprised by their appearance. And we started giving her bigger breakfasts to tide her over until lunchtime. We also asked one of the sympathetic servers to keep an eye out for Sophie. Initially suspicious, she soon warmed to her special duty (slipping Sophie extra pieces of bread if a meal looked like it was too much to handle). And we told Sophie to try to find a "buddy" to walk into the *cantine* with, to make lunchtime more bearable.

That is how Marie and her family entered our lives. Sophie and Marie started playing together in the playground after school, and I eventually worked up the courage to introduce myself to her dad, Eric. Our first few conversations were formal and polite, but upon learning that we lived just up the road, he immediately (and unusually, for a Frenchman) invited us over to their house, which turned out to be a small farm (the sort that is the envy of English tourists), with a sandy courtyard surrounded by long, low stone buildings covered with vines. Chickens, ducks, geese, and children roamed in the fields. The vegetable garden stretched down to a pond, around which Marie would ride her pony, Fastoche, after school.

In his day job, Eric was a carpenter. But his real calling was training horses for jumping competitions: the herd currently consisted of several fillies, a few foals, and a rambunctious stallion. Marie's mom, Sandrine, was a nurse. On sick leave, but always smiling, she defiantly refused to wear a wig over the tufty thatch of hair that had stubbornly resisted her cancer treatment. We studiously avoided talking about her illness, and I wondered whether our arrival in the village was a relief: new faces, with no history.

Marie and Sophie would spend hours grooming Fastoche, wandering the fields, and running down to the sea and back. Sophie charmed the entire family with her stories (all entirely made up) about bears and wolves and whales back home. Marie became a regular visitor at our place, which helped give Sandrine some much-needed rest. The girls' visits were a welcome distraction for everyone, and Marie and Sophie soon became best friends.

Reassured, Sophie finally began settling into school. It helped that her French speaking skills (like Claire's) had improved dramatically. In fact, both of our daughters had almost forgotten how to speak English. This was partly our fault: to help the girls adjust, we had agreed to speak exclusively French to them. But this had worked better than we expected: by late fall, Claire refused to speak English (and scowled when I tried to speak it to her). Sophie wasn't much better. One day, she innocently looked up at me and asked one of those questions that make you realize how young your children still are: "*Maman, pourquoi on parle Anglais?*" (Mommy, why do we speak English?). When she would consent to speak her native tongue, it came out with a strong French accent—she rolled her *r*'s—and she stumbled over her words.

Although things were better, they were far from perfect. Despite having made friends, Sophie still complained about the food at the *cantine* (although now she did it in French, which for some strange reason I found less irritating). Without fail, she would always tell me that she was *affamé* (starving) when I picked her up after school. Guiltily, I would stuff snacks into her as soon as she jumped in the car. French people, of course, don't eat in their cars. So our crumb-filled backseat became a bit of an embarrassment (and, I suspect, the subject of scandalized village gossip). I would dart out of the classroom with Sophie, jog to the car, strap her in, and drive home. Not a great way to make friends with the other moms.

Still, by early November, Sophie had stopped crying in the mornings when I dropped her off at school. We had reached a new equilibrium, and I began to relax. But then we got our first dinner invitation.

4

L'art de la table

A Meal with Friends, and a Friendly Argument

La nourriture des enfants n'est pas un carburant.
Elle est constituée de culture, de paroles, et de plaisirs partagés non mesurables
en même temps que de calories et de vitamines.

Children's food is not fuel.
It is made up of intangible culture, words, and shared unquantifiable pleasures
as much as calories and vitamins.

—Dr. Simone Gerber, French pediatrician

To understand why a simple dinner invitation could make me nervous, a bit of background is necessary. When we first moved to France, social gatherings involving food made me anxious, mostly because I was afraid that I'd have to eat new things in new ways. I might have to wield nutcrackers to extract every last bit of meat from lobster claws. Or I might be asked to use a thin metal toothpick to extract slimy things (whose names I couldn't remember) from slimy shells. And then eat them—gracefully.

So it felt like an exam every time I sat down for a meal with other people, which was made all the more excruciating because the meals could last for two to three hours, or even more. The other thing that I found overwhelming about French meals was that several conversations would be going on at any one time. The French don't really have a linear approach to dialogue at the dinner table. The only rules seem to be that

(A) more simultaneous conversations are better than fewer; and
(B) clever interruptions—particularly to make a sardonic joke—score you the most points.

The uninhibited interweaving of multiple conversations seemed to contradict the rigidity of the French approach to eating (I realized later that for the French, conversation and food go together like beer and sports do for North Americans). I found it intimidating and often simply couldn't keep up, much less get a word in edgewise. It didn't help that my French was far from perfect. I could carry on calm one-on-one conversations, but although I had a good accent, I still sometimes garbled longer sentences and was stumped by translations for complicated words. The pained, confused expressions on people's faces would bring me to a stumbling halt.

Admittedly, this wasn't only an anti-French feeling; I felt the same way about fancy meals anywhere. I remember one miserable meal at

Oxford very clearly. I had been invited to sit at the High Table with the dons and found myself sitting face to face with one of the world's top experts in my area of study. He proceeded to grill me about my interests and background while I squirmed in my chair. Almost everything about the setting made me uncomfortable. For starters, there were way more forks, spoons, and knives surrounding my plate than I knew what to do with. Bewildered by the choices, I simply sat still while everyone else started eating. An attentive neighbor must have noticed my lost look; suavely, not missing a beat in the conversation, he reached over and briskly tapped the fork that I was meant to pick up. Grateful yet embarrassed, I started eating.

But my sense of relief didn't last long. We had been served green peas, my nemesis. My neighbors were deftly maneuvering them onto their forks and eating them without a second thought. I, on the other hand, tried to spear them with what I presumed was mannered delicacy (at home I would have used a spoon). But the peas (undercooked in a way only the British could manage) resisted, and I had to chase them around the plate. One vigorous swipe with my fork, and a particularly large pea gave a mighty jump across the table and landed on the plate of my interrogator, bringing our conversation to an abrupt halt.

Memories like these were hard to erase. So when our first dinner invitation came, I wasn't at all eager to accept. Virginie and Hugo, Philippe's old university friends, were organizing a reunion dinner. Half a dozen couples were invited, some of whom Philippe hadn't seen in years. My first reaction was, predictably, anxiety: passing muster at a dinner with old friends was not something I was looking forward to.

In fact, I knew that I probably wouldn't pass muster, at least not through engaging in rapid-fire, witty conversations around the dinner table. In desperation, I picked up a book on French etiquette that was intended for Americans living in France. As I read with a sinking feeling in my heart, Polly Platt's sage advice (based on decades of living in Paris) was to pretend to be a piece of furniture—an elegant chair, to be precise. That way, she advised, you wouldn't feel the need to speak, you wouldn't make everyone squirm (listening to your mangled French), and you wouldn't feel bad when no one spoke to you the entire evening. *This is going to be awful,* I thought.

To be frank, I was also worried that the dinner would be an occasion for Philippe's friends to evaluate me rather than befriend me. The question would apply to my children as well. Were they *bien éduqué*? This upped the ante because I knew that Sophie and Claire were simply not ready to eat the way French children did. Even if I managed to get through a meal without mishap, they probably wouldn't. They would whine (a serious faux pas), react negatively to the food being served (even worse), or refuse to eat (perhaps the worst offense of all).

My reaction spurred the second big fight of our year in France. I didn't want to go, and I certainly didn't want to bring our daughters although all of the other couples were apparently doing so. I didn't really understand why it was so important that we all go together, but it was clear that it was important to Philippe.

"We could leave the kids with your parents," I suggested to my husband one evening.

"But all of the other children will be there, and they'll miss out on the fun!" protested Philippe.

"We won't start eating until really late, we'll finish way after midnight, and the kids will be exhausted! You wouldn't ask them to run a marathon at this age, so why ask them to stay up all night just for a dinner?" I retorted.

"Because!" snapped my husband, fuming. "That is how *I* was raised! And that is how French children *should* be raised!"

I realized I didn't really have an answer to that one. That *is* how French children are raised. From quite a young age, they accompany their parents through long dinners, which sometimes start very late by North American standards. And in France, get-togethers with family and close friends, especially meals, are often multigenerational affairs. In this case, everyone was not only welcome, but also *expected* to come. From my husband's perspective, it would be rude not to bring the entire family, as well as unfair to Sophie and Claire to exclude them. "Plus," he argued, "how do you expect them to be able to handle long dinners well if they don't start now?"

I realized that he also had a point here. French kids have more stamina at the table than do most North American adults. I remembered our wedding: dozens of children had come, and they had all sat patiently throughout the entire meal. As we danced until the wee hours, they gradually disappeared without fuss. I later found that their parents had been discreetly bedding them down on a pile of coats and sweaters in a corner, where they slept blissfully while we danced right alongside them.

In contrast, many of my relatives began retreating before the night was over; they couldn't quite believe that the eight-course meal started at 9:00 P.M. and still wasn't finished by midnight. Some of them missed dessert, and quite a few missed the dancing. One of the few exceptions was my eighty-nine-year-old grandmother, who had a strict sense of duty and a secret love of glamour that belied her staunchly Calvinist upbringing. She sat proudly upright in her chair, nodding approvingly as Philippe and I moved onto the dance floor for the opening bridal waltz (one of the few "Americanisms" that I insisted on), and then surprised everyone by spryly accepting her own turn on the dance floor.

Thinking about the French kids at our wedding, I began to change my mind. It's true, I thought. Sophie and Claire need to be able to keep up with the other children if they're going to fit in to French society. Philippe had won the argument.

Although I didn't want to admit it, part of me was looking forward to the reunion dinner simply because I was feeling lonely. I hadn't made many new friends in the village yet. Most people kept their distance.

True, Philippe had met some old acquaintances. One night when we were out for drinks at the local brasserie, the burly bartender thrust out his hand in greeting. It turned out that he was Philippe's "cousin" (although that term seemed to be used very loosely in Brittany to refer to any blood relation, no matter how distant). One mother in the schoolyard turned out to be the daughter of one of my mother-in-law's childhood friends. Another turned out to be the nurse who had given my husband his vaccination shots as a teenager ("and not in the arm," he grinningly told me). And there were some other faces I recognized, like the mayor's deputy (charmingly named Madame L'Amoureux) who had signed our marriage certificate a few years back. But we never got beyond formal, guarded conversations with people, whether old acquaintances or not. The casual complicity between neighbors that we'd had back home just didn't seem to be happening. French people, I was learning, were not open to divulging much to people with whom they didn't share a long personal history.

Another reason I wasn't meeting many people was the fact that the weather had changed. Strong winds whipped dark dense clouds across the bay, and stinging rain and fierce squalls were interspersed with the sunshine. At first, this was exhilarating; a welcome contrast to Vancouver, where low, gray clouds could stack themselves up against the mountains for months on end, and where the winter rains were like an endless, cold monsoon. But as the days got shorter, the sun disappeared. Autumn storms whistled through the house, sometimes so strongly that the walls shook and the wooden beams moaned. We stuffed small rolls of newspaper and rags in the cracks. Mold grew on the doors, the walls, even the windows. We wore wool hats at breakfast. The romance wore off fast. Our friend Andy had stuck to wandering in southern France for good reason, I realized. In the village, windows were shuttered, and there were fewer and fewer people outside. The charm had even worn off of Radio Bonheur, as by now I had reached my lifetime dose of chirpy accordians.

It wasn't just the weather, however. I had to admit that I didn't have much in common with the villagers. This particular corner of Brittany is extremely traditional, rural, and Catholic. The French have the largest families in Europe, and the Bretons lead the pack. Most families had at least three children. The record-holder in our village was a woman who looked about my age and was the proud parent of fourteen children. Never raising her voice, and never smiling, she drove around town in a school bus with her alarmingly well-behaved offspring—the girls immaculately dressed, like their mother, in twin-set sweaters and sober skirts. Our Dennis the Menace children were not on their list of approved playmates.

"Maybe," I said brightly to my husband, "they just don't have time to socialize."

Apart from Eric and Sandrine, the only other friendly acquaintances I had met were at the local farm where we had started buying most of our food. Sandrine, who was a close friend of the owners, had brought us there one day. The farm, a short walk from the village, had never been "modernized." On a picturesque plot of land overlooking the river, they raised cows, pigs, chickens, geese, turkeys, and ducks, plus market garden vegetables. This enabled a steady flow of goods for sale throughout the year, as well as a relative degree of food self-sufficiency. Hubert and Joseph—two shy, sweet, bachelor brothers—seemed amused by the fact that their previously "backward" farm had now been labeled "organic." But they were savvy too; the farm had become a distribution center for organic produce from across the region. And the food they provided was incredibly fresh, and surprisingly diverse: cheeses, vegetables and herbs, fruits, fresh bread, dairy products, dried sausage, and homemade jams were all apparently being grown, picked, caught, and made within a twenty-mile radius of our house.

Our visits to the farm soon became a weekly routine that made me feel slightly more at home. So, too, did participating in village rituals. We faithfully brought Sophie and Claire to the regular *Fest Noz* (night parties) held on the quay of the small village fishing port, where old and young danced together to traditional music and ate *galettes* (Brittany's regional specialty, a savory crêpe made of buckwheat flour).

We also wandered the seashore, just like the locals. Brittany has the highest and lowest tides in Europe, and some days the water would draw back well over a mile from shore. We'd pull on boots and wade through the barnacles, rocks, and algae, surrounded by villagers—from toddlers to grandmothers—furiously scraping and whacking rocks or digging and poking the muddy bottom for local delicacies like *bulots* (whelks, a kind of mollusk) and *coquilles St. Jacques* (scallops). We even went to the annual *bénédiction de la mer,* clambering along with the villagers up a rocky headland to watch the village priest (in full vestments) gravely step into a local fishing boat, head out into the bay to bless the waters, and pray for all those who had lost their lives at sea.

Thanks to my in-laws, we attended these events. But I was still very much an outsider, a spectator of village life. In my eager North American way I'd introduced myself to all of the neighbors and parents at the local school, but they were stiffly polite, seemingly uninterested in any social contact. The French, I found out, do not make friends easily and definitely do not like to socialize with "new" people, much less outsiders. The fact that I spoke French and was married to a "local" didn't seem to change my status: a foreigner.

I had been looking forward to the start of school, I admitted to myself, because *I* wanted to make friends with the other moms. But school had started months ago, and I wasn't making much headway aside from some polite chitchat once in a while. So I felt more and more lonely as the weeks went on. Now that the weather had gotten bad, our stream of visitors had tailed off. My father-in-law was one of the only people who would drop by the house regularly. He came most mornings, usually when Claire (who had taken to getting up well before the crack of dawn) was almost ready to be put down for her early morning nap. I would rush out the door to take Sophie to school and often return to find Claire fast asleep in Jo's arms. He'd sit quietly with her until she woke up, sometimes waiting for over an hour, biding the time by watching the fishing boats trawl back and forth across the bay. Often, he was the only adult (besides Philippe) with whom I had a proper conversation all day.

To be fair, the French don't easily make friends with other French people either. For the French, friendship is a deep, intimate, lifelong commitment—one that is made cautiously and rarely after one's mid-twenties. Eric and Sandrine were, I learned, exceptions that proved the rule. Even Philippe's friends had been slow to warm, giving me the cold shoulder for years until we really got to know them. "Why are they so mean to me?" I once asked my husband. "They're not being mean! They just aren't comfortable talking to you because they haven't gotten to know you yet," he replied, bewildered. "*But we've been together for three years!*" was my exasperated response.

Philippe's friends had eventually warmed up to me after our wedding. In fact, Hugo and Virginie turned out to be the most loyal, warm, wonderful friends. They'd remember our birthdays or surprise us with lovely cards or little gifts for the children, sometimes out of the blue. Their kids really connected with ours, to the point that they felt like cousins. This was the upside of friendship in France—once you made friends, they truly were friends for life and shared an intimate complicity that was lacking, Philippe felt, with most of our friends back in Vancouver. So, as the date neared, I discovered that I was secretly looking forward to dinner, despite dreading difficulties about feeding my overtired kids and anxiety about meeting a bunch of new people. I expected to be both scrutinized and ignored (that "elegant chair"). But what I didn't expect was that this one evening would turn me into a convert to French food culture.

The evening started with a misunderstanding, followed by a friendly argument.

We had arrived the expected fifteen minutes *after* the time for which we'd been invited (the French make a point of never arriving earlier than this on the theory that you don't want to embarrass your hosts by arriving before they are completely ready). Other families were arriving at the same time, and just getting through the doorway took several minutes, with all of the *bises* that were being exchanged.

A beautiful table greeted us as we followed Virginie into the living room. Lovely place settings were aligned on top of a creamy linen tablecloth: pale moss-colored plates nested in bigger white plates, cutlery intertwined with sprigs of dried lavender, napkins nestled in wine glasses next to ceramic bowls on which were perched bird-shaped puff pastry crackers. It looked typically French—at once rustic and sophisticated, formal yet festive. The kind of look I knew I could never pull off at home.

The other children were already gathered around the table, at a slightly respectful distance. Their eyes were on the crackers, but no one dared touch them. They all knew that it was considered very rude for children to help themselves without being asked, even if food was within reach. I always marveled at the self-control evident in even the youngest of French children, which mine certainly didn't display.

An anecdote I later heard from one French friend hinted at how this self-control is achieved. Starting at the age of three, all of the children at her *maternelle* (preschool) had to sit still with their hands on their knees while the lunchtime dessert was served to *all* of the children. Only when everyone had been served, and the *maîtresse* gave permission, could they begin to eat; anyone who gave in to temptation had their dessert promptly taken away.

Anticipating that some sort of situation like this would arise, I had briefed my daughters in the car. I had learned this technique from watching my sister-in-law, Véronique. Just before guests would arrive, or they would arrive at someone's house, she would take the children aside and firmly remind them of the rules. "No touching any food before the adults invite you to start." "Only take one of what you are offered, or you won't get any more." But somehow my messages about manners didn't seem to have sunk in, and my girls hadn't had the benefit of training at the *maternelle*. Sure enough, before we could stop her, Claire rushed over and grabbed a cracker from the table, crowing with delight as she stuffed it into her mouth.

I chided her gently. "That's the adults' table! Don't be rude!"

"*Mais non!*" replied Virginie, smiling. "That's the children's table!"

I looked more closely and saw that she was right. The wineglasses were miniature versions of adult ones, as was the cutlery. And there were more than a dozen place settings, whereas only four couples were coming to dinner. The table had been so beautifully set that I hadn't imagined it was intended for the children.

But then I remembered the attention that Philippe's family would pay to setting the table at home. Even my adventurous, no-nonsense, outdoors-loving, holes-in-his-socks husband would carefully smooth the wrinkles out of the tablecloth before lining up the cutlery and plates just so. If we were going to be late coming home on an evening when we had dinner guests, he would set the table in the morning before going to work.

This was one of the apparent paradoxes that so intrigued me when I first met my husband. How could someone who worked in war zones and loved adventure sports like sailing and mountaineering be so *finicky*? But the answer was obvious, at least for the French, for whom a carelessly laid table is an example of one of the worst sins imaginable: an offense against good taste.

Embarrassed by my mistake, I followed Virginie and Philippe into the salon, where the separate table for adults was to be found. We sat down on the sofa and chairs, and started with *l'apéritif*: the "meal-before-the-meal" of finger foods and cocktails eaten in a casual setting before dinner. Small, thin glasses filled with multicolored layers emerged from the kitchen: *les verrines* (melt-in-your-mouth layered confections eaten with dessert spoons). Mine had a layer of *avocat, fromage blanc,* and *saumon fumé.* Philippe's *tomates confites* were topped with a layer of *mousse au chèvre frais,* decorated with tiny wisps of *ciboulette.*

In the meantime, the children were invited to their table. Worried about leaving Sophie and Claire alone, I started to get up, but my husband gently steered me back to my seat. "Leave them alone. They'll eat better without you there." And, out of the corner of my eye, I saw that it was true: my daughters were pulled irresistibly along in the wake of the older children, who were settling themselves in at the table. Tiny *verrines* were waiting for them too: bright red beet and green zucchini *mousse* in thin layers that mimicked candy canes.

The *verrines* didn't last long, and even Sophie and Claire joined in. But as the first course arrived, I cringed: grated carrot salad with vinaigrette (a French kids' favorite). Barely able to watch, I saw Claire staring at Jacqueline, an older girl who clearly fascinated her. Jacqueline had taken Claire under her wing, helping her into her chair and sitting next to her in the lovely, slightly proprietary way that older French children often adopt with younger children at the table.

Into Jacqueline's mouth popped a spoonful of carrots. Claire fidgeted, her hands in her lap. Jacqueline helped herself to an even bigger spoonful. Gingerly, Claire put one strand of carrot into her mouth, munching distractedly, as another girl leaned over and began telling her a story. Claire listened, wide-eyed, while eating one mouthful, and then another. By her fifth mouthful, I began to relax. Even Sophie had started nibbling on the skinniest morsel of carrot she could find on her plate. Maybe I didn't need to hover over the children's table after all. Plus, the conversation around me was getting interesting.

The guests were in heated conversation about an announcement earlier in the week by France's president, Nicolas Sarkozy. At the annual Paris Agricultural Fair (a big event in France), he had held a press conference to announce that he would be launching a national campaign to lobby UNESCO (the United Nations Education, Scientific, and Cultural Organization) to place French cuisine on its official World Cultural Heritage list. If successful, French cuisine would join other globally recognized cultural treasures like Spanish flamenco and Japanese silk making.

The president had ignited a furor in France and abroad: Could food really be "cultural heritage"? The French government seemed to think so. To make it clear, they had even set up a Mission for French Gastronomy and Patrimony to launch the campaign.

To me, this sounded a bit silly. "Do you really believe that French food is the best in the world?" I asked one of my neighbors. "What about Italian food?"

Looking annoyed, he responded: "*Mais non!* It's not about French cuisine being the best in the world. *Gastronomie* is an important part of culture for *all* French people."

"But how can *eating* really be called cultural heritage?" I asked. Heads started to turn in my direction.

"It's not the *act* of eating, but rather the *approach* to eating that is the most distinctive element of French culture," responded my neighbor.

"Still," I argued, "it seems sort of elitist to me. Why are you all obsessed with food?"

This got a strong reaction. Amid the din of voices, Hugo's voice was the loudest.

"French *gastronomie* is not for the elite, it's for everyone in France!" he insisted. "Sarkozy is seeking recognition for the art of everyday eating. Everyone in France learns this art and celebrates it!"

"*Il faut manger pour vivre, et non pas vivre pour manger* (one should eat to live, and not live to eat)!" he concluded, triumphantly. I must have had a blank look on my face; under his breath, Philippe explained that it was from a play by Molière (who I knew was roughly the French equivalent of Shakespeare).

"But you *do* live to eat," I responded. "Just look at what we're doing tonight!" I added.

"Art means using your imagination, being skillful at something," explained Hugo patiently. "You can approach lots of things like an art, like setting the table beautifully," he said, nodding at the table next to us.

"It does look lovely," I offered, hoping to sound conciliatory. Virginie beamed. I gathered my courage: "But isn't eating like this a little, well, bourgeois?"

"*Mais non!*" Hugo protested. "My father was a bus driver! I work for a telephone company. I grew up in a very ordinary family. We all did," he said, gesturing to everyone around him.

At this, the other guests gradually stopped talking among themselves; one by one, they followed Hugo's lead in an attempt to prove that good eating was not the sole preserve of *la bourgeoisie*. I had to admit that they seemed to have a point. Virginie was a nutritionist, and Chloé worked in a factory, organizing logistics and deliveries. Antoine ran his own small business, providing marketing advice to small companies. Frédéric, an engineer, worked as a manager for a big concrete company, but—like most of Philippe's friends—came from "modest origins." And I knew that Philippe's parents had left school in their teens and gone to work in the shop owned by Philippe's grandfather. His maternal grandmother had been a washerwoman for a hotel, lugging loads of heavy laundry in big *paniers* on her back, and washing, drying, and ironing them by hand.

I realized, wilting, that my comment had been inappropriate. But before I could get a word in edgewise, Virginie jumped in. "Actually, Americans are the elitist ones, the snobs!" she argued. "Only the middle class and the wealthy have access to good food and eat well. No one else! In France, everyone eats well—good food is for everyone, no matter rich or poor. We're actually much more egalitarian than you are," she concluded triumphantly.

This statement ignited all of my pent-up frustration about Sophie's experience at school. Before I could stop myself, I retorted, "But few people are really that interested in eating such fancy food. And it's a terrible idea to make everyone eat the same way. People should be allowed to choose what they want to eat!"

"But choose what?" said Antoine, Philippe's closest friend, with a smile. "Sure, Americans are free to choose, but they end up making terrible choices. They have no standards for what, when, or how they eat. And they often eat alone. We all know the result!"

I paused at this, in part because it was so hard for me to translate

Antoine's comment. What he'd said was: "*N'importe quoi, n'importe quand, n'importe comment, et souvent seul.*" The French phrase *n'importe quoi* is hard to translate, as it is a dismissive term that can be used in a variety of ways. French people often use it to mean "whatever" (like American adolescents), or "nonsense," or even "garbage." So Antoine's comment implied that Americans eat poor-quality food, at all hours of the day, with no thought given to manners. This felt a little too close for comfort as I remembered the snacks Sophie gobbled in haste in our crumb-filled car after school and the pasta we served night after night at home.

Meanwhile, Antoine's comment had sparked a small tsunami of remarks. The French have a love-hate relationship with Americans, and something had been unleashed by our exchange. As so often with the French, this took the form of escalating sequences of witty one-liners and wordplays (the kind I often had trouble understanding, much less inventing).

"Americans think food is just a commodity; a matter of convenience (*une commodité*)," sniffed Frédéric.

"But they usually treat eating like it is inconvenient (*incommode*)!" said his wife, Chloé, laughing. (I had figured out by now that she was my husband's ex-girlfriend, and I permitted myself a small evil-eye glare directed her way.)

"Americans think that money spent on food is wasted because it goes in one day, out the next," said Inès, laughing.

"The real problem is that Americans eat like children. American food is *infantile*," said Virginie gravely. She had spent several years living in the States and worked as a nutritionist at the local school board.

"Americans behave like two-year-olds at the table!" she continued, getting into her stride. "They are impulsive eaters: they snack all the time! They have no self-control: they don't know when to stop eating. And their servings are much too large! They have childlike tastes: they love to eat fatty, sugary foods—exactly the kind of thing kids love." She finished, damningly, with "Americans have no taste! Just compare a croissant to a doughnut!"

This, of course, met with approving nods, as well as a few blank stares ("What's a 'doo-not'?" I heard one husband whisper to his wife).

As the target of all of this, I didn't know what to say. But I felt that I had to say something. I summoned up my courage, and croaked out, "I think your approach to eating is way too fussy and regimented. How can you expect *everyone* to eat like this?" My comment was met with silence. Luckily, Philippe came to my rescue. He had left France nearly fifteen years ago and had lived all over the world. So, more than anyone in the room, he had a balanced view. "Both cultures have good aspects," he said mildly. "French people do eat better than Americans, and their approach makes sense. But you can't impose a uniform way of eating in a country as young and diverse as the United States. They'll have to evolve their own food culture, but it will take time, just as it did in France."

Before anyone could object, everyone's attention was diverted by the main course, which had just arrived at the children's table. Hugo had prepared a fish dish: *dorade à la provençale,* served with rice. Everyone got up to watch the children eating (a favorite pastime of French parents). Distracted, I watched the adults watching their children savor the food. Not hovering too close, they kept a discreet eye on the table, allowing Hugo to orchestrate the serving, which was met with an enthusiastic chorus.

By now, Claire and Sophie seemed to be thoroughly carried away by the festive atmosphere. Claire, still dazzled by Jacqueline, ate everything on her plate. She even took a nibble at the bizarre-looking side dish: crosnes, a form of tuber that closely resembles waxy caterpillar larvae. Sophie, however, didn't do so well, cautiously eating some rice, refusing to touch the fish after one tentative taste, and quickly hopping out of her chair with a mutinous look when the crosnes appeared on her plate. Being told that they were a French delicacy didn't help, and for a few cringe-inducing moments she refused to return to the table. But after some coaxing, she reluctantly sat down. The adults moved back to their seats. Out of the corner of my eye, I saw that Sophie still wasn't eating much, but Philippe motioned to me to say seated.

"Don't make a fuss," he said to me quietly. "You'll only make it worse. Just wait and watch." He was right. Within a minute or two, Sophie relaxed, and even ate some more fish—having figured out that it was delicious. Meanwhile, I was mulling over everyone's comments. I knew that Antoine was right. What French people ate at ordinary meals wasn't so different, at least in spirit, from what was served in high-end restaurants. I thought of my in-laws' neighbor Bernice, who had almost never left the village and still talked about how happy she was when they tiled the dirt floor of her family home (in which she was still living). Of modest means, Bernice sat down every day to a three-course meal that didn't differ that much, at least in spirit, from what we'd be eating this evening.

Suddenly timid, I turned quietly to Virginie. "Where I come from, only a few people are interested in *gastronomie*. Why is it such an obsession for the French?"

"It's a pleasure, but not an obsession!" she said, laughing.

"Good food was democratized a long time ago," added Sylvie, overhearing us. "It's because of the French Revolution: the aristocrats no longer had a monopoly on the best food and the best chefs. The revolutionaries made French food culture accessible to everyone."

"Not just that!" interrupted Hugo. "It's economic! Paris was Europe's first big city with a middle class that had enough disposable income to eat at restaurants. Cooks couldn't depend on aristocratic patrons any longer, so they opened restaurants and had to compete for customers and public opinion. French food is about capitalism and competition leading to better food for everyone!"

"Actually, it's really about religion," offered Sylvie. "Catholic countries have always been more interested in food. French *gastronomie* is like a secular communion, like a sacrament or a ceremony."

By this point, I was completely lost. Maybe I was misunderstanding the word "*gastronomie*." For me, it meant elaborate, expensive, indulgent meals that had little to do with what interested me about food: nutrition, health, and price.

"Maybe it would help if I understood how French people learn to eat as they are growing up. Why don't you tell me the most important things that French children learn about eating?" I ventured.

This got everyone's attention. "Knowing how to enjoy food," said Sylvie.

"And knowing how to talk about it!" added Hugo.

"How to behave at the table, and to enjoy good meals with family and friends!" said Olivier.

"It's part of French culture," someone else chimed in, "that children should learn to eat well!" This got the most enthusiastic nods.

In the meantime, the children had moved on to salad and cheese, and to my quiet delight I saw Jacqueline feeding tiny bits of goat cheese to Claire who, as the youngest child at the table, was the focus of enthusiastic encouragement from the older children. Sophie, not one to be left behind by her younger sister, was making a tentative foray into the salad, although I noticed she was picking out the smallest leaves, and not even this level of peer pressure could make her change her mind about the cheese, which sat untouched on her plate. I had to admit that the scene—the children gaily eating, with parents looking on approvingly—seemed idyllic.

Having finished their main course, the children were dismissed until it was time for dessert, and ran off to play. It was the adults' turn to eat. Conversation turned to critical scrutiny of the entrée—*soufflé à la bisque de homard* (lobster bisque soufflé). The French love to talk about food in concrete terms. But soon my question had sparked a more abstract discussion. *What, exactly, was French food culture? And how could you explain it to the average American?* By the end of the evening, they had their answers pinned down.

French food culture, it turns out, has three core principles. Over the perfectly cooked *bar de ligne* (European sea bass), we hashed out the first and most important principle: *convivialité* (conviviality, which for the French means something like "feasting/socializing together"). For the French, eating is inherently social. People of all ages tend to eat together, whether at home with their families or at work with colleagues. This is so socially ingrained that people can't think of doing otherwise. In fact, French people never, ever eat alone if they can help it; people eating together are often called *convives* (which means "table companion," but translates literally as "living together"). So whenever I explain to the French that North Americans often eat alone in their bedrooms watching TV (even if there are other family members in the house), or alone at their desks at work, they are truly astonished.

Convivialité is also one of the primary sources of the pleasure that French people associate with food. Why? Because the French make a point of having *fun* while eating. Pointed jokes, witty repartee, critical appreciation of the food: the French zest for life is perhaps no more apparent than at the table. This is one of the main reasons that French children learn to eat so well (and spend so long at the table, uncomplainingly): the table is a place of emotional warmth and connection. It is also a place where they learn not only about how the world works (from listening to their parents talk), but also about conversation skills (how to interact with adults, how to argue without offending someone, and how to listen well).

Another aspect of *convivialité* is that people are not only expected to eat together; they are expected to eat the *same thing* together. Meals are about the collective enjoyment of a set of dishes, not individual choice about what to eat. (The French sociologist Claude Fischler calls this the "communal" approach to eating together, in contrast to the American "contractual" approach). This is a great way to teach children to eat new foods; scientific studies have shown that they are much more likely to try something new if an adult has tried it first.

This was another finicky French food habit that I had trouble getting my head around. And it was one that often led to disputes. The night before, I had suggested to my husband that we phone Virginie and Hugo to explain to them what our children liked (and didn't like) to eat. From my point of view, this was polite, because it would allow everyone to avoid embarrassment at dinner. But for Philippe, this was the height of incivility. My in-laws happened to be over as we began our exchange (Note to self: Never make controversial suggestions to your husband in front of your mother-in-law). Philippe's mother couldn't resist jumping into our debate.

"Guests," said Janine, with a severe look on her face, "have an obligation to please their hosts. Telling people you dislike food, especially food they might prepare for you, is simply bad manners." She used the term *mal éduqué* to drive her point home; as soon as those words were out of her mouth, I knew I'd lost the argument. Pointing out that this would trample my individual autonomy, or that I considered forcing someone to eat something they didn't like to be bad manners, would have no effect. I might protest, but Philippe's mother's belief in the supremacy of the French worldview was unshakeable.

Next, over *fromage* and *salade,* we moved on to the second principle: *le goût.* Virginie began by explaining why *le goût* (which roughly translates as "taste") is so important. For the French, it is very important that things taste good, and people spend a lot of time making sure they do, even for the smallest of children. Taste, in this sense, is about more than the physical sense of tasting things. Rather, it is a kind of savoir faire transmitted by shared experience, and embedded within a broader culture. For French people, *bon goût* really matters.

This focus on *bon goût* is of supreme importance in French culture. It isn't really a form of snobbery (although there is certainly some of that). Rather, *le goût* is a shared social identity, which is bound up with French culture. It's the primary thing that matters to French people when considering how much they like or enjoy something. The equivalent principle for North Americans would be price, or choice. Good taste (and thus good food) isn't something complicated and reserved for gourmets—it's for everyone.

It was sometimes hard for me to take the French attachment to *bon goût* seriously. But the intensity with which Philippe's family and friends would utter the ritual phrases condemning bad taste—*"c'est du mauvais goût"* or *"ça fait mal aux yeux!"* (literally, it hurts the eyes)—made me realize that the French take the issue of taste very seriously indeed. This has its downsides: French people are very sensitive to questions of *goût* and, as a result, tend to focus on the negative. They always seem to be complaining about what they don't like about something (or someone). They even have a word for the kind of complaining harangue in which the French specialize: *râler,* which roughly translates as "loud, sustained grumbling and complaining." (I think of it as the adult version of whining, and have still not, after all of these years, gotten used to it.)

There is one positive effect of this, though: there is a constant one-upmanship embedded in French culture; people aren't afraid to tell each other how they could improve or what they aren't doing right. This is one of the main reasons, I came to realize, that everything in France is so beautifully done: people are openly demanding of the very high standards associated with their understanding of *bon goût.*

The third principle of French food culture is the one that I'd already started learning the hard way: food rules. In France, Hugo explained, eating is governed by shared social norms (*les règles,* or rules) about when, where, how much, and how food is consumed. These rules are some of the first things that French children begin learning—before they learn to read, or even to walk and talk. The rules gently guide all aspects of eating and create a set of shared food rituals across all of France. In fact, the word *gastronomie* literally means "rules of the stomach" (from the Latin *nomos* [rules] and *gastro* [stomach]). But these are not ironclad, oppressive regulations; they are more like habits. And (after much debate), the dinner guests agreed that the most important rule—the one that enabled all of the other ones to be maintained—was the following:

French Food Rule #4:
Food is social.
Eat family meals together at the table, with no distractions.

This rule seems to turn North American understandings of food on its head. It's really about *how* to eat, rather than *what* to eat. Of course, this rule (and I encountered lots of variations) has a host of implicit subrules that most people back home would be familiar with. "Don't eat on the run," for example. Or "don't eat standing up." Even worse: "don't eat in the car." These are rules that Americans observe only in the breach.

Absorbing these explanations, I began to understand why adults and kids gather at the table so naturally in France. As a happy by-product, French kids learn how to eat well, for the rules governing eating are more easily reinforced when eating together with adults every evening.

By now, it was nearly midnight. I hadn't seen Sophie and Claire for hours, although I could hear chatter and laughter from another room. My husband peeked in at them and assured me that all was well. Then all the children came running back to the table at the mention of dessert: a simple *mousse au chocolat* with a raspberry sauce that induced a sweet silence for five full minutes.

Sipping coffee and enjoying a few *mignardises* (little round, hard cookies often served at the end of a formal meal), I watched them eat and marveled at how well the evening had gone. I'd never seen a group of children eat so well, or so happily. Even Sophie and Claire had tried new things with much less complaining than usual. The most surprising thing was that everyone thought this was *normal*. Not once during the entire evening did I see a parent force, threaten, or cajole a child into eating anything. No fuss, no resistance, no coercion, and no whining.

It was now, I suddenly realized, well past midnight. I was feeling slightly woozy owing to the late hour, and also perhaps owing to the *chouchen* (sweet Breton apple mead) that had been served after dessert. But I was still excited enough about the ideas I'd been hearing to have a flash of insight. Eating well *and* eating together, for the French, is the cultural equivalent of saying the Pledge of Allegiance, or watching *Hockey Night in Canada*. It's a daily, lived expression of their cultural identity.

"I get it!" I said cheerfully to my hosts. "If asked which inanimate object best represented their culture, many Americans would probably say the car. But most French people would probably say the dining room table!"

This met with approving chuckles. We grinned around the table at one another, our earlier tension forgotten. My hosts and their guests were happy: they had succeeded in explaining French food culture to the satisfaction of a foreigner. And I was happy too, mostly because I had succeeded in making a funny remark (one of my first-ever successes at being witty in French).

Given how easy it all seemed that evening, I felt more confident than ever before about the wisdom of the French approach. What had seemed overwhelming a few months ago—teaching my children how to "eat French"—now seemed manageable. If there were food rules for adults, there must be food rules for children too, I reasoned. I would just have to figure them out and apply them to my own family.

I couldn't wait to get started.

5

Food Fights

How *Not* to Get Your Kids to Eat Everything

Dans un petit jardin, tout rond, tout rond, tout rond,
Il y a des poireaux, des carottes, des radis, des tomates, des pommes de terre,
Et une petite rivière qui coule, qui coule, qui coule!

In a little garden, round and round and round,
I see leeks, carrots, radishes, tomatoes, and potatoes,
And a little river that runs and runs and runs!

—This traditional nursery rhyme is the French version
of "Round and round the garden, like a teddy bear"

There was one downside to the French approach to late-night dinners: my kids' internal clocks didn't have a "sleep-in" option. Claire and Sophie had gone to bed well after midnight but had woken at seven in the morning. Lack of sleep seems to have an opposite effect on adults and children: whereas I was groggy, they were wired and excitable.

The day stretching out before us seemed very, very long.

Sitting in our cold kitchen with damp air wafting from the stone walls, I had one of my (many) moments of doubt about our French adventure. Everything had seemed so simple the night before. Learning about French food culture had resolved many of my criticisms and questions. Full of enthusiasm, my resolution about changing my children's eating habits had been heartfelt. I had even shyly shared my idea with Philippe's friends, and they'd sent us home with an armful of cookbooks and warm words of encouragement.

Things seemed different in the pale, gray morning light. All I could think of were excuses and objections. *I don't have enough time. It's too expensive. It won't work: the Americans and the French are just too different!* My energy and enthusiasm waned away.

In the meantime, Sophie and Claire had gotten their hands on the cookbooks, spreading them out on the living room floor. They soon found a favorite, and I peered over their shoulders. The recipes were intriguing: yogurt and avocado smoothies, oven-baked parsnip fries, tomato-strawberry tarts. There was even a baby section, with simple soup recipes designed to be drunk in baby bottles. "My First Red Puree" featured tomato and fennel, followed by "My First Yellow Puree," combining corn and chicken. My favorite was "My First Green Puree": peas, mint, and a handful of baby spinach leaves.

The photos were clever too. The authors had figured out something basic about kid psychology: children love to look at real-life pictures of other children. Images of happy kids eating (and cooking) appeared on almost every page. And the photos of the dishes were whimsical and funny. Vegetables and fruits were arranged in a series of faces and shapes, by turns grotesque or coquettish. Tiny little figurines floated in soups or perched on pastries in a *Where's Waldo* style. Claire figured this out quickly: scanning each page, she would search until she found a little *bonhomme,* pointing her pudgy finger with pride. The pages that attracted her most avid attention were, naturally, in the sections on *goûters* and *desserts.*

"Which one is your favorite?" I asked. Sophie finally settled on *palets choco-raisins:* lacy dark chocolate wafers daubed with dried apricots, slivers of almonds, raisins, and hazelnut chunks. Given her aversion to all nuts and seeds, this surprised me. Claire surprised me too, by picking an old French favorite: *gâteau au yaourt* (yogurt cake), a sort of sponge cake with a slight tangy flavor. The recipes actually looked easy: I knew my mother-in-law could whip this cake up in under ten minutes.

I promised the girls that we'd make their chosen desserts later that afternoon. In the meantime, I extracted a promise from Philippe to take them over to play with Marie. I needed some time to think.

After they had gone, I sat down with a cup of strong coffee and went through the books one by one. Some of these were cookbooks, which I put to one side. I was more interested in the books *about* children's food. Virginie and Hugo had also lent me a few books written by doctors, nutritionists, psychologists, and sociologists. As I leafed through them, one term kept appearing that intrigued me: *aliment.* This was a new word for me. I headed to the dictionary in hopes of finding some enlightenment.

Aliment, it turns out, doesn't translate directly into English. Both *aliment* and *nourriture* are translated as "food," but these two words do not have the same meaning in French. *Nourriture* is the easy one to define, as it corresponds to the English meaning for food: something you ingest. But *aliment* is more complicated.

Searching for an explanation, I came across a quote from one of the best-known French nutritionists of the twentieth century, Jean Trémolières. He argued that an *aliment* is more than just a nutritious foodstuff. It is also something that can satisfy both emotional and physical appetites; it nourishes both physically and psychologically. In fact, a better translation of "*aliment*" would probably be "a nourishment."

Somewhere in my head, a light bulb went on. *Aliments* are more than just food. *Aliments* are cultural definitions of things we find nourishing and appetizing. Something that is an *aliment* in one country may not be in another. (Think frog's legs.)

This reminded me of a comment made at dinner the night before, one that I hadn't understood at the time. In the midst of our discussion, Virginie had remarked: "When you go into a supermarket in the United States, there is hardly any food!" At the time, I thought it was a ridiculous comment. Now it started to make more sense. There was not a lot, in most American supermarkets, that most French people would consider (traditionally at least) an *aliment*. This was a bit like the Puritans who nearly starved their first winter in the New World because they couldn't (or wouldn't) recognize the edible things all around them. For Virginie, the processed and prepreared foods that filled up the aisles in a North American grocery store weren't real food because, although they were edible, they weren't nourishing.

The realization slowly dawned on me. Learning how to eat like the French was not just about my kids eating vegetables. It was about changing how we *nourished* ourselves, and about changing our psychological and emotional relationship to both cooking and eating. This was a bit of a shock. I had thought I would be fighting to change my children's eating habits. Now, I realized, I'd also have to fight my own ingrained eating *and* cooking habits.

This was going to be challenging, because I simply didn't enjoy spending time in the kitchen. Years of scrambling to prepare dinner after getting home from work meant that I had a harried, stressed feeling whenever I thought about cooking. This was a drastic change from life before kids, when I actually had liked to cook (although I admit that my total cooking repertoire was well under a dozen dishes). Somehow, the stress and chaos of having kids had worn me down, and I fed them a much more limited diet, and cooked much less, than my preparenting self would have believed possible. The thought of learning new dishes and organizing myself to change our family's approach to food seemed daunting. My doubts began to resurface. I started to pile the books in a corner and decided to get on with my day. Everyone, I hoped, would forget about my rash suggestion to teach my kids to "eat French."

It was not to be. The phone rang before I even finished my pile. It was Philippe's mother.

"How did your dinner go last night?" she asked. I didn't know what to say, but as it turns out I needn't have worried. Without waiting for a reply, Janine carried on. "I just talked to Philippe, and he told me that you had some *fascinating* conversations about food. He asked me whether I had some cookbooks that I could drop off. I've got a *great* one that I used when he was a baby." (Note to self: Remind husband not to confide in mother-in-law before consulting with wife.)

"Great!" I said, forcing myself to sound enthusiastic. "I'd love to see them."

When I hung up the phone, I was feeling anxious and cornered. Family pressure had been mounting since we arrived. Philippe's parents were *not* happy at the way their grandchildren ate. Our most recent restaurant outing with my in-laws had been a disaster. We arrived at 7:30 P.M. (early for the French) in order to get a table with a view at the only seaside restaurant in the village. Both tired and hungry, the girls whined and bickered, provoking glowering looks from my in-laws, the adults at the next table, and even the waiter. Philippe's mother insisted on ordering fish for Sophie (although I also quietly ordered a plate of plain pasta, just in case). Luckily, the pasta arrived first; I studiously avoided everyone's gaze when pulling the Parmesan out from my purse. *I* knew that Sophie wouldn't eat her pasta without it, but I also knew no one else would think this was appropriate. When the fish arrived, Sophie pursed her lips, turned red, and looked as if she was about to cry. I quietly asked the waiter for ketchup, ignoring his disdainful look. Smearing it on Sophie's fish had the desired effect; she started to eat. But Philippe's mother clearly voiced her disapproval. "Humph," she snorted loudly. "*La méthode américaine.*" Labeling something the "American method" was, for her, a grave insult. Coating something in ketchup was bad parenting, a concession to a childish caprice. Even worse, it sullied Sophie's emerging taste buds. It was clear what they were thinking (even the waiter): *How would these children ever learn to eat properly?*

Something had to change about the girls' eating habits. They were old enough to start feeling everyone's disapproval, even if they couldn't understand it. And I realized that they needed to learn to eat like other French kids. If we decided to stay in France, they would be negatively affected socially and professionally if they couldn't eat well. The high value that French people placed on food made me feel responsible, as never before, for how my children were eating.

I was even more eager to do this because of the reading I'd been doing about the links between nutrition, school performance, IQ, and health. Kids who ate more vegetables and had a more balanced diet did better at school. They had higher IQs. They were less likely to be overweight, so they would live longer and have fewer health problems as adults. Reading all of this made me even more convinced that I had to do something about how our kids were eating.

Plus, things had been going better at school and at day care. Both Sophie and Claire were eating more and trying more new things. In fact, they would eat things at school and day care that they refused to eat at home. Claire would almost always eat everything that she was offered at day care, the staff happily reported. And at school pick-up, Sophie had adopted the French habit of telling me what she had eaten at lunch. She would happily chat about things like grated carrot salad (although items like radishes, another school favorite, still wouldn't pass her lips). And her visits to Marie's house had also widened her repertoire. Seeing Marie eat things like lettuce and lentils had a magical effect, and Sandrine was gentle but firm in encouraging Sophie to eat what everyone else was eating when she stayed for dinner.

We were ready, I thought, to try changing our family food culture. Christmas was just a month away, and I wanted it to be a positive experience. French families look forward to the Christmas family meal the way many North Americans look forward to the Super Bowl: it's the big event of the year. Plus, I knew that there would be at least thirty people for dinner, many of whom would travel from across France to be there. I wanted Philippe's extended family to have a good impression of our children, which meant that I needed to train them to eat like French children.

The problem was that I didn't know exactly how to go about doing this. No one had taken the time to explain the rules to me, and no one I'd asked had a handy list. *Maybe I'll find a list in one of the books?* I thought. American parenting books were often full of long lists of recommendations (that I never managed to stick to). By early afternoon, I'd gone through all of the books borrowed from Hugo and Virginie, looking for a list of rules. But there was none. The French "rules" that I'd noticed were probably so universally understood that no one had ever thought to write them down.

I was going to have to make my own plan. And I was going to have to test it the hard way, through making mistakes, and through breaking the unwritten rules that govern food in France for even the youngest of children.

"The Plan," as I labeled it, took several days to craft.

First, I reviewed what I had learned. There were general rules, I decided, that were useful in understanding French attitudes. But they weren't actual, practical tips. They were more like principles, or habits. Still, I thought, it would be worth noting down the rules at the start of The Plan, as a reminder. I took a clean sheet of cardboard paper from the kids' art box and sat down with a few precious Crayola washable markers (they apparently don't have the washable kind in France, and I'd had to ask my sister for an emergency shipment soon after we arrived).

One by one, I jotted down the food rules I'd learned.

Rule #1:

Parents: You are in charge of your children's food education.

Rule #2:

*Food is **not** a pacifier, a distraction, a toy, a bribe, a reward, or a substitute for discipline.*

Rule #3:

Parents schedule meals and menus. Kids eat what adults eat: no substitutes and no short-order cooking.

Rule #4:

Food is social. Eat family meals together at the table, with no distractions.

This was a pretty good summary of what I had learned so far. But there was another issue that had been nagging me: the connection between kids' eating habits and parenting styles. French parents seemed to exercise a natural authority around their children that I, and most of my friends back home, lacked. This was evident in many ways. French children sat patiently, waiting until everyone was served before starting to eat. French children compliantly tried new things with a sense of open-minded curiosity. French children didn't have tantrums at the table. And, most amazingly, they were taught not to interrupt adults. When we sat at the table in France with our children, the adults could actually carry on extended conversations.

Some of this authority was imposed through an old-fashioned, authoritarian-style parenting that didn't fit with my approach. I remembered one unhappy incident with Sophie earlier that year. We were having a small family gathering at my in-laws, and the *apéritif* had just been served. The children had gathered round, hovering expectantly, not daring to touch the treats that had been put out on trays. Sophie couldn't resist and grabbed a cracker. And then another, and another, stuffing her mouth. Spying her out of the corner of her eye, my mother-in-law gave her two verbal warnings, and then (when Sophie didn't stop) a hard slap on the hand, in full view of everyone. Sophie retreated in tears and was politely ignored.

As far as I could tell, most people thought that this was appropriate: Sophie had broken a food rule, and it was Janine's duty (as she happened to be the closest adult, as well as the hostess) to bring her back into line. When the French reprimand their children in public, this is not seen to be humiliating (although I certainly felt this way, and Sophie did too). Rather, they are committed to instilling discipline in their children (and they assume that the adults around them will be sympathetic). Firmly disciplining your children in public in North America is, I somehow felt, politically incorrect (and, in some cases, physical "discipline" is against the law)—but in France, it's almost the reverse. Even total strangers might let your child (and you) know their disapproval of public misbehavior; as a concerned adult, they are just doing their duty.

I was astounded at the contrast. Many North American parents feel a sense of panic when one of their children starts misbehaving in public. We are often deeply embarrassed and are driven to end the behavior as quickly as possible. In my case, I was always fearful of making a scene because I didn't want people to think I was a mean (read "bad") parent. So I ended up giving in to my kids when sometimes I shouldn't have. French parents, on the other hand, feel obliged to discipline their child in public—with the full support of onlookers.

Elise, a French friend of ours in Vancouver, once described the first time she realized that the French parenting style wasn't acceptable in North America. One day at the playground, soon after they had arrived in Canada, her six-year-old boy kept trying to interrupt her while she was speaking to another mom. Elise turned around and berated him soundly, lecturing him on his impolite behavior. "I felt," she later recollected, "an icy silence all around me. I looked up, and all of the parents in the playground were staring at me. It was then that I realized that what French parents might view as normal discipline, North American parents might not."

Yet most French parents are not overtly forceful. They're loving while being firm. And somehow, magically, the children we met were often devoid of the impolite behavior and stubbornness that I saw in my own kids and in so many of their North American friends. This was, I began to realize, not just an issue of differing food cultures. It was also an issue of parenting styles.

French parents were in charge. This impressed me, because in our family I sometimes wasn't sure who was in charge. The symptoms were obvious. I cajoled. French parents did *not* cajole. I wheedled. French parents *definitely* did not wheedle. I begged, threatened, and bribed my kids. French parents did none of these things (at least as far as I could tell). They calmly and firmly (but usually gently) told their children what was expected, and let their kids know (in no uncertain terms) who was boss. And their children seemed to miraculously comply.

How do French parents achieve this? Well, they demand more of their children, are stricter, and are less indulgent. They do not romanticize childhood. And they have little affection for that early phase of childhood that North Americans idealize as a time of innocence and creativity. Imagine a nation full of unapologetic tiger mothers dedicated to producing well-behaved children rather than violin prodigies, and you would have more or less a good idea of how French parents think and behave.

From the French point of view, the world is made by adults and for adults. Few concessions are made to children. Their children dress like little adults: mostly pastel and matte colors, and no more pink on the girls than you would see on their mothers. The furniture in kids' rooms is usually a miniaturized version of adult furniture (no princess loft beds with slides, thank you very much, and no princess potty thrones either). Children are expected to be quiet (*tranquille*) in public. They are not placed on a pedestal and are not expected to be at center stage in a gathering.

My mother-in-law's views are fairly typical. From Janine's perspective, children's primary job is to behave, and parents' primary job is to help them behave. Some of this is generational: for example, the idea that children should be "seen and not heard." But even mothers my age expected their children to be *sage* (which literally means "wise," but when used with children means "discreet" and "well-behaved"). This is, above all else, a rule to be followed at the table, as suggested by the highest compliment my mother-in-law could pay to my children at the end of a family meal: "We didn't hear a single word out of you!" Older children would be welcome to speak, but only if they had something interesting to say. Their interventions weren't tolerated just because they were kids.

Before we moved to France, I had dismissed this behavior as old-fashioned. But after several months of living in France I realized that the passionate belief that the French have in the need for *éducation* stems from a completely different view of childhood. This really hit home after I started searching for children's books in French for our daughters. I imagined snuggling up on the couch with Claire with the equivalent of *Peter Rabbit* and *Winnie-the-Pooh*. And I couldn't wait to start reading classics with Sophie. What, I wondered, would be the French equivalent of *Anne of Green Gables,* or the Famous Five—books that were my favorites when I was young?

But the books that family and friends suggested to us were much less innocent in tone. *Le Petit Prince* was above the girls' heads. *Babar* scared them (with the mother elephant being shot in the first few pages), and its colonial story was, in my opinion, racist. Many of the other books that we were offered had incidents that I considered too cruel or macabre for our children. *Barbapapa* became a favorite, but that wasn't the sort of reading repertoire I'd hoped for.

Determined to find the French classics that I was sure existed, I went to the village bookstore. The puzzled bookseller wasn't much help. Having cleverly consulted Philippe beforehand, I knew enough to ask for *les grands classiques* and *les contes de fées* (fairy tales). But I was offered Hans Christian Andersen, the Brothers Grimm, and *Pippi Longstocking* translated into French. There wasn't even an equivalent of Mother Goose; French children sing nursery songs instead. Listening to Claire sing "Frère Jacques" in an off-key chorus with her cousins was, I had to admit, very cute. But this didn't satisfy me as a replacement for reading the sort of books that I identified with childhood.

I tried explaining this to Philippe's father one evening. "Back home," I said cautiously, "childhood is viewed as a really innocent time. There are lots of books about magic and make-believe. The French don't seem to have the same sorts of books."

"Kids aren't innocent," snorted Jo, in an uncharacteristically direct tone. "They're like little animals. If they aren't disciplined, they'll never learn to behave!"

This meant that there were some real differences in how I parented, as compared to the other parents in the village. At the homes we visited in the village, there were far fewer toys than back home (and certainly fewer than in our basement playroom, stuffed from floor to ceiling with kiddie paraphernalia). And French parents didn't really involve themselves in kids' playtime as much. I saw this at the local village playground, but also in Paris when visiting my sister-in-law, Véronique. Whereas parents back home would follow their children around, at a discreet distance, helping them clamber and climb if needed, grinning all the while, French parents would more often than not settle onto one of the benches with an uninterested look on their faces. Some even brought magazines or newspapers. Clearly, kids' play was not for them.

In fact, getting *too* close to your kids was frowned upon. A common criticism I heard from the other mothers in the village (and one that I was sure was directed at me behind my back) was that someone was "a slave to her children." Philippe's relatives were surprised (and, to be honest, a little concerned) about how attached I was to Sophie when she was born—holding her too much, breast-feeding her on demand, and even (the ultimate no-no) sleeping with her.

However, I saw lots of French parents express their love in other ways. They spent a lot of time with their children—in the evenings and on weekends. Families seemed to socialize together a lot more—a dinner invitation would be for everyone, from the youngest to the oldest member of the family. And most of the moms we knew prepared homemade food for their children every day, even if they worked full-time. I marveled at how some of them produced amazing meals in a matter of minutes, dashing around their (by my standards) tiny kitchens. They never seemed to be caught off-guard (as I often was) at dinnertime. Because food was a priority, they were organized, and because they were organized, making good food from scratch was relatively quick and painless. They thought creatively about offering new types of food to their children, exposing them to lots of flavors. Training their children to "taste everything" was one of the most important priorities for the French mothers I met—just as important as reading, talking, or giving the baby toys. This was supported by a loving but authoritative parenting style.

The French approach, I began to realize, is a very good way to behave if you want to prevent food from becoming a power struggle between parents and kids. At first glance, their methods seem coercive because there are so many rules and limited choices. But in fact the opposite is true. Because there are fixed rules and routines that everyone (including the parents) respects, there is no negotiation and no power struggles. French kids, in general, thrive within this structured approach to parenting. And French parents also make sure that food is fun and tasty, which helps kids look forward to eating. As a result, their kids are usually happy to come to the table.

In our house, on the other hand, we had few routines and fewer rules. I wasn't sure why I behaved this way, never having articulated my parenting style to myself. The fragments of ideas I remembered from the books on "attachment parenting" were the closest I got to a parenting philosophy. *Children need to form an emotional bond with their parents. Anything that threatens the parent-child relationship is a threat to their long-term psychological health.* Now, I began scrutinizing these ideas. In practice, I began to realize, *my* attachment to these ideas had translated into my not wanting to argue about food (or lots of other things) with my kids, because I didn't want to screw them up, or weaken our attachment. Admittedly, once written down, this does not seem entirely logical. But in the sleep-deprived state that lasted for years once the kids arrived, logic wasn't always my strong point.

Maybe, I decided, I'd have to rethink my "attachment parenting" approach. Part of this would involve rethinking the way that we handled "why" questions with the kids. At the heart of my vague definition of attachment parenting was a commitment to getting kids to think critically. Sophie's first "why" was met with praise. We encouraged her curiosity, and she began asking endless questions. At times, this stretched my mother-in-law's patience very thin.

"*Why* does she ask 'why' all the time?" Janine once exclaimed.

"I'm teaching her to negotiate, and to think critically," I responded, wondering where this was going.

"But children shouldn't be negotiating with their parents!" she snapped, clearly exasperated. "Some things should be so routine that they don't even ask questions! Especially about eating!"

I shrugged it off at the time, but I later began to wonder. Maybe Janine was right. I had encouraged my children to express their individual views, and to use their questions to dispute parental orders, allowing them to exert control where they could. One of the places where they did this, early on, was at the table. Meals at our house were usually rushed, as we were either herding the children out the door in the morning or rushed getting home after work. Hurried and harried, I'd usually accept the kids' rejections of my cooking and meet their demands for substitutes. Bread and butter, or pasta, became our routine. My kids learned that they—not I—decided what to eat.

From the French perspective, this was not attachment parenting. This was indulgent parenting. Traditionally, the French believe that children who have not yet reached the age of reason (*l'âge de la raison,* which the French believe occurs at the age of seven) shouldn't be allowed to decide about many things, most certainly not what and how they eat.

This made me wonder why I caved in so easily to my children's demands. Was I really being "child-centered"? Or was I just being a distracted wimp?

The potential flaws in my "child-centered" method were driven home by the experience of acquaintances of ours, British expats who'd bought a crumbling country château nearby and were spending their summers fixing it up. They'd allowed their four-year-old son to eat what he liked, on the assumption that some internal wisdom would guide him to eat a balanced diet over time. After some time spent subsisting solely on dairy products and white bread, he developed anemia and had to be briefly hospitalized. Although he quickly recovered, the story soon made the rounds of the village gossips and seemed to reconfirm French people's views about the mysterious, even sadistic refusal of English-speaking people to eat real food.

Thinking about all of this made me exhausted. I'd started off simply wanting to get my kids to eat better, but I had gotten caught up in a conflict between American and French ways of *being:* of parenting, of nourishing, of caring. And I kept coming back to the same question:

Did I need to behave like a French mother in order to get my children to eat like French kids?

I wasn't sure that it would work. But I decided that it was worth a try. Proudly, I pasted my rules to the fridge door. Later that night, my husband read them with raised eyebrows.

"What's this?" he asked.

"Don't you remember that dinner party?" I reminded him. "I'm trying to figure out how to get the girls to eat like French children."

"This sounds a little bit too strict," he protested, clearly dubious.

"But France is like that!" I protested. "There are strict rules for everything!"

"I want to enjoy my meals, and I think the girls do too. Are you sure you want to apply all of these rules at once? Food is about pleasure, not about being strict," he persisted. His comments made me wonder whether I was on the right track. But Christmas was only a month away. I had decided that the girls' eating habits needed to change, and fast. So, undeterred, I turned to developing the next part of The Plan. I needed to find out how French kids eat, and how they think and feel about food.

Luckily, I was spared the necessity of having to do my own research. Philippe's cousin Christelle was a *puéricultrice,* which is something like a cross between a pediatric nurse and a kindergarten teacher. I called her up one evening and explained what I was interested in. She was intrigued and had lots of great suggestions. There was abundant research, she explained, because France had been a pioneer in developing *puériculture* (the science of childrearing) in the nineteenth century and was still a world leader.

She told me, for example, about the French researcher Claude Fischler, who had spent thirty years studying eating habits and food preferences. Together with an American researcher (Paul Rozin at the University of Pennsylvania), he had surveyed 7,000 people in France and the United States about their eating habits. And he had done detailed studies of French children and parents. Perfect!

Reading this research confirmed the ideas I'd developed: by the time they were school-age, French kids liked eating a variety of foods, and their love of variety made them more interested in vegetables. I also gleaned some important principles from reading the survey questions that Fischler had asked when trying to probe how well French children understood habits of healthy eating. Interestingly, these included some sayings that my in-laws were fond of repeating, like "One must eat a bit of everything," and "Eating unhealthy foods once in a while is not a problem." The French children in the surveys, I also learned, had a very good understanding of which foods were healthy (and unhealthy) and why. So although—just like kids everywhere—they loved things like pizza, soda, sweets, and ketchup, they ate these in moderation, as did their parents.

Fischler's work on adults also confirmed my impressions. Americans tend to be anxious about food and to identify health, nutrition, and dieting as the key issues they associate with eating. The French, on the other hand, almost never mention any of these topics when asked for their thoughts about food. Rather, they talk about pleasure, tasty food, socializing, culture, identity, and fun. In one of the most revealing studies, Fischler showed a picture of a chocolate cake to both American and French people and asked them for the first word that popped into their head. For Americans, the most common word was "guilt." For the French, the most common word was "celebration."

How do French kids learn these ideas? Part of the explanation is the amount of time they spend at the table with their parents, where (naturally) the conversation focuses on food. The tradition of the family meal is alive and well in France, where the entire workday is structured around mealtimes. Stores shut for one and a half or even two hours between noon and 2:00 P.M., so that everyone can go home for lunch. In repeated surveys of French families, nearly all the kids eat a traditional, sit-down, three-course lunch *every* day. More than half of them eat at school: French schools have a two-hour break at noon in order to allow kids the time required to eat (at least thirty minutes) and to properly digest their food (during the sixty- to ninety-minute recess that follows lunch). As a result, school finishes later: usually at 4:00 or 4:30 P.M., which is when the traditional *goûter* is eaten. Shops close at 7:00 P.M. in order to allow everyone to get home in time for dinner at the traditional French hour of 7:30 or 8:00 P.M. By 9:00 or 9:30, most kids are in bed.

So more than 90 percent of French kids eat their evening meal at home every day, with all of their family members. In contrast, only 40 percent of American adolescents and 55 percent of kids under eleven eat dinner with their families every day. And one in three eat with their families less than three times per week.

But French families do eat together, and most do so every day of the year. This provides ample opportunities for teaching kids about food. And one of the most important things French children learn at these meals is that "new is normal." French adults love variety and will eat varied diets as a matter of course. Naturally, their children grow up to do the same. This was even evident in the comments people made in passing about food choices.

"I had an apple yesterday, so I'll have a peach today," my mother-in-law would say, when considering which fresh fruit to pick for dessert at lunchtime. Or, when discussing at breakfast what we should eat later that day: "We already had chicken this week, so we shouldn't have that again."

Thinking about Janine's example led me to write down the fifth French Food Rule:

French Food Rule #5:
Eat vegetables of all colors of the rainbow.
Don't eat the same main dish more than once per week.

This French habit of varied eating is pervasive. French parents will scrutinize the school menus at the start of every week—not only to see what their children are eating, but also so that they can avoid serving the same dish at home that week. (In Paris, my sister-in-law told me, the schools actually send home suggestions for evening meals.) When Philippe's parents visited us before we moved to France, I learned that they would expect a different dish at every meal (my record is three weeks of new dishes, which more than exhausted my repertoire). The only exception seemed to be breakfast, which was almost invariably the same: juice, coffee or tea (milk for the kids), white baguette, butter, and jam or honey. I had trouble reconciling the French approach to breakfast with the healthy approach to eating the rest of the day, but I had to admit that starting my morning with fresh baguette smeared with butter and honey did wonderful things for my mood.

Variety and trying new foods were probably the most difficult things for my kids to handle, I realized. And because of their resistance, I'd fallen into bad food habits. Before they were born, my diet had been much more diverse. When I had started university, my culinary skills were limited to reheating frozen dinners in the microwave, boiling eggs, and cooking pasta, but I soon branched out to salads and comfort foods like chili. But with the arrival of kids, our family eating habits had fallen back into a narrow rut, with little variety and almost no novelty.

After more than a week of research, I decided I had enough information to create the next phase of The Plan. I wanted to create a set of personalized routines that would help us to improve our eating habits. They had to cover what, how, and when we ate. So I decided to include issues like scheduling, parental discipline, and variety.

In order to keep things organized, I decided to write everything up in a simple table. In the left-hand column, I would write down the new, specific rule that we would adopt. In the right-hand column, I'd write down what we had to change in order to be successful with the new rule.

THE PLAN	
Our New Food Routines	**What We Have to Change**
Eat four meals per day: breakfast, lunch, after-school goûter, dinner.	No more random, extra snacks, especially bedtime snacks.
Eat only at the table.	No eating in the stroller, car, or anywhere else.
Eat slowly.	No gulping or gobbling. Every bite has to be chewed slowly.
Children eat what they are served. Adults, not children, decide what is served.	No substitute or replacement dishes, and no extra "fillers" like bread and butter.
Kids eat what adults eat.	No special dishes for the kids.
Don't eat the same dish more than once a week.	Stop relying on pasta and bread.
Eat processed foods only once a week.	Shop only at the local market. No ketchup, except on hot dogs and hamburgers.
No complaining about food.	If you complain about something, you have to eat a second serving.

I pasted The Plan on the fridge, next to the list of French Food Rules. Written down, it seemed more impressive. It also seemed more and more unlikely that this was actually going to work. How could I force my kids to start behaving like this? I'd have to have a strategy, I decided. This too got written up in markers and posted on the fridge:

The Strategy

1. *Explain the rules in advance.*
2. *All rules must be obeyed.*
3. *Once introduced, stick to the new rules. Absolutely no backing down.*

I would start, I decided, with the first three routines together: no more snacks, no eating in the car or the stroller, and eating slowly. This would get us off to a good start. Plus, both the car and the stroller were full of crumbs and spills, so dirty they were embarrassing. I'd give them a thorough cleaning and then announce the news to the girls.

I anticipated that there would be lots of objections. So I also came up with some simple Smart Things to Say when my kids objected (as I knew they inevitably would).

If you eat well at mealtimes, you won't be hungry in between.

You're still hungry? I guess you should have eaten more at your last meal.

Or, on a more positive note:

You're hungry? Great! You'll really appreciate your next meal. It's in only . . . [fill in blank] hours.

I even got Philippe to help me translate "You get what you get, and you don't get upset!" into French. Primed with these Smart Things to Say, I thought about when to initiate The Plan. It would make sense to start on a Monday: new week, new beginning. Philippe would be out late at work, but I decided it might be better if I handled things myself.

So on Sunday evening, I carefully explained to the girls what was happening. I showed them the rules and routines taped on the fridge. Claire nodded solemnly and stuck her thumb into her mouth. Sophie stamped her foot in protest but then soon lost interest in the abstract discussion.

Still, I told myself, they knew what was coming. But, unfortunately, I didn't.

When I picked Sophie up from school on Monday afternoon, the first words out of her mouth (as on every school day) were: "I'm hungry!"

Already prepared, I quickly replied:

"Great! I've got a nice *goûter* waiting for you at home. We just have to pick up your sister at day care, run a few errands, and then head home."

"But I'm *huuuuungry!*" wailed Sophie.

"I made homemade blueberry muffins. Your favorite! And look how clean the car is! I spent an hour and a half cleaning it today. You wouldn't believe all of the stuff I found. Look, here's that plastic fairy you thought you lost," I carried on, hoping that Sophie would be distracted. Not a chance.

"I'm *really* hungry!" she whined.

I tried a different tactic. "French people don't eat in the car, and don't forget you're half French," I said sternly.

"Then I should be able to eat in the car half the time!" snapped Sophie.

With that, I ran out of things to say. But I held firm. Sophie kept whining in protest as we drove to the day care, the grocery store, the dry cleaner, and the post office. Claire, equally used to eating when she got in the car, joined in the chorus.

Deafened and irritated, I drove straight past our last stop (the village bakery) and headed home. This added insult to injury. Claire's favorite treat was fresh baguette, which I'd normally buy for her every afternoon as we drove home from day care. She even had a preference for bread from one of the three bakeries in town (the bakers, fiercely proud of their recipes and methods, produced very distinctive baguettes). Normally, this treat was the highlight of her afternoon: lining up in the bakery, gravely handing over the money, and clutching the still-warm baguette in her hands. So when she saw the storefront go by, her face crumpled. Her whining had been tailing off, but now it returned and soon escalated into full-force crying.

By the time we got home, she was too overwrought to eat. Sophie gobbled down three muffins and two glasses of milk and left the table with a happy look. But Claire launched into a full-scale tantrum. I knew my daughter: if she got sufficiently hungry, she got too worked up to eat. Despairingly, I tried stuffing tiny pieces of blueberry muffin into her mouth, with no luck.

I felt a bit frantic. This was only the first day of The Plan. As a last resort, I rummaged in the cupboard, found an old baby bottle, heated up some milk, and poured it in. Success: her belly full, Claire calmed down (except for the occasional shuddering hiccup) and consented to sit on my lap while we read a story. After all of the fuss, I was feeling as if I could do with some warm milk myself.

Dinner was the next hurdle. I had prepared something I knew the girls liked for dessert: *mousse au chocolat*. But I had also prepared things I knew they would not be so happy about. At the market that morning I'd picked up some fresh fish (local sole), squash, and potatoes.

I congratulated myself on a smart move: serving the mashed potatoes first—and letting them make their "volcanoes," which involved shaping the mashed potatoes into a conical mound, making a hole in top, and popping a dab of butter in, then sitting back and watching it melt. This was as satisfying as I knew it would be, and I even got Claire to take a few mouthfuls of potato (normally something she refused to eat).

But then the fish and the squash came out, and their defenses went up. Claire, still upset from her missed snack, burst into tears. Sophie put down her fork, folded her arms, and scowled. I picked up one fish-laden fork in each hand, determined that they wouldn't get the better of me on our first day.

But I had forgotten another obvious food rule (one that applies anywhere). It's no use forcing children to eat. If kids really don't want to eat, they will—at some point—simply clench their teeth. And they egged each other on. I now realized my mistake: they had probably had enough mashed potatoes that they didn't feel hungry any more. And Sophie's three blueberry muffins earlier on hadn't helped either.

Desperate, I thought of my secret weapon: dessert.

"If you don't eat this, you won't get dessert," I said firmly. And I pulled the chocolate mousse out of the fridge, placing the bowl on the table in front of them.

Bad idea. Claire cried louder. And Sophie was furious.

"I want mousse!"

"If you don't eat your fish, you won't get any mousse!"

"I *hate* squash!" yelled Sophie, echoed by her little sister. "*Me too!*" wailed Claire.

"No complaining about food," I snapped. "If you complain, you get a second serving!" And I plopped another spoonful of squash on Sophie's plate.

"Fine," responded Sophie, after a few back-and-forth rounds. "I won't eat *anything*." And, pushing back her chair, she left the table. Claire glanced at both of us with that wary, appraising look that second children often have (*Can I get away with that too?*), and quickly followed suit.

Fuming, I put the mousse away. I had forgotten Rule #2: Food is not a punishment, or a reward.

Somehow, I knew the evening was going to continue to go downhill. Gritting my teeth, I got them upstairs, and we started our bedtime routine: bath, pajamas, brushing teeth, tucking in, and story time. Telling stories was a precious ritual with the girls. In the first few weeks and months in France, when they'd been most unsettled by our move, I'd created an imaginary fairy friend for each of them. "A Fairy Story" had become so much a part of our routine that Sophie and Claire refused to go to sleep without one. Even babysitters had to be briefed on the story line that had to be strictly followed to avoid a bedtime mutiny.

Just as I was leaning over Sophie's bed to start the story, she abruptly spoke up.

"I'm hungry! I want a bedtime snack!"

Smiling smugly to myself, I replied with one of my Smart Things to Say.

"If you're hungry, it's because you should have eaten more at dinner. But don't worry, you'll have a great breakfast," I said in a cheerful voice.

Sophie mustered up the worst insult that she was capable of: "You're not my friend anymore! You're *mean*."

"Sophie," I said gently, "I'm your mother, not your friend. Now, do you want your fairy story?"

"*No!*" replied Sophie, rolling over to face away from me.

"Don't you want a hug?"

"*Go away!*"

As I left the room, I heard quiet sobs. And I was barely holding back the tears. This was the first time in her life that Sophie had refused a bedtime story. Meanwhile, Claire was crying in her bedroom. Giving up, I heated up another bottle of milk, hoping it would induce her, at least, to fall asleep happily.

I felt sick to my stomach. Neither of them had eaten well. Sophie had gone to bed hungry and angry. Claire had reverted to the feeding habits of an infant. We'd had the worst fight we'd ever had. I realized that I'd made things worse, rather than better. The Plan wasn't going to work. This wasn't the way to get children to love food.

Not for the last time, I bitterly regretted having moved to France. We had few friends, the girls were miserable, and we were living in a house that was little better than a moldy wind tunnel. We'd left friends, great jobs, and a fun city to move to a village where people thought Parmesan was exotic. And they wanted *me* to change *my* eating habits?

Luckily, Philippe's train was delayed, so the girls were asleep before he arrived home. When I debriefed him later that night, his response was thoughtful. (One of the things I love about my husband is that he never [well, almost never] says *I told you so*.)

"The French way of eating *is* better for the kids, and for us," he gently insisted. "But you can't do this through punishing them," he said. "The rules are a good idea, but you're not going to convince the kids to love food by being too strict with them. It has to be enjoyable. Not necessarily loads of fun, but simply pleasurable."

Philippe had put his finger on where I had gone wrong, I realized. I thought that I had been trying to create a new routine. But I had made my routine into a power struggle. I had been too literal about the rules. If badly applied, food rules can be a form of emotional violence that shows a lack of respect for the individual.

I remembered one of my favorite parenting books: Jane Nelsen's *Positive Discipline*. My mistake, I decided, was that I'd been too permissive in the past, but had now overcompensated by being too authoritarian (strict, controlling, punitive). What I needed instead was to be *authoritative* (firm, but kind, and gently supportive).

Looking back, I also realized that I had forgotten about the two other "pillars" of French food culture: making eating a source of social pleasure and making things taste good. I probably shouldn't have served squash on our first night. And I probably could have been a little more flexible.

There was a reason that the French food rules weren't written down, I reflected. After all, they are habits and customs rather than *regulations*. I remembered what Madame had said at school. Rules are not (or don't need to be) about suppressing individual preferences but rather about fostering individual taste. Just as kids need a well-rounded education, they also need a well-rounded palate. I wouldn't achieve that by forcing my children to eat large servings of every vegetable they hated. The Plan had failed.

After the dismal start to our food experiment, I gave up. Christmas loomed, but I just didn't have the energy to try again. My mood matched the weather: cold, rainy, miserable. I was terribly lonely and regretted having decided to move our family to France. What had I been thinking? It wasn't even snowing: we were going to have a wet, rather than white, Christmas. I spent long hours on the phone with my sister in Montreal, who tried in vain to cheer me up.

The only bright spot was the girls' enthusiasm for their first family Christmas in France. Before we moved, we had never managed to come for Christmas: flights were too expensive, and neither Philippe nor I could get enough time off work. The girls were thrilled at the thought of all their cousins gathered around the table. They wanted to help prepare food for the big dinner that Tante Monique was hosting (our contribution to this seven-course meal was a few hors d'oeuvres) and happily accompanied me on our last-minute market outings. They even came with me on our last pre-Christmas visit to the farm. As usual, they ran to visit the animals as I picked up our baskets of food. Their favorite was Arthur the Pig, who had sadly disappeared ("Gone on a holiday to Canada," Hubert the farmer told them with a twinkle in his eye).

Even without snow, Christmas did seem magical. Gorgeous lights went up in the village, and the shops were full of intricate, intriguing window displays (watching the girls stick their noses up against the windows made me understand why window-shopping in France is called *faire du lèche-vitrine*—literally "licking the windows"). The girls even got to visit with Père Noël, who arrived by boat every year a few days before Christmas. The village children waited in a little huddle at the port on the edge of an old stone walkway. As Père Noël rounded the corner in a skiff, they walked down the cobblestoned quay to meet him, confessing their sins and demanding their gifts with wavelets lapping their boots. Then Père Noël sailed off around the rocky headland. Sophie and Claire came back glowing from this encounter, which seemed much more magical than the shopping mall scene back home.

So, when Christmas Eve arrived (the traditional time for family dinners in France), I was feeling slightly (but only slightly) reconciled to being there. But I was still anxious about how the girls would behave, knowing that we'd be up well past midnight in the presence of almost every member of the extended family. Philippe tried his best to gently encourage me as we drove over to his aunt's house.

"Try to relax," he said. "If they see you being anxious, they will be too. If they see you trying new foods, they will too. And if they see their friends and family enjoying new foods, it will be that much easier."

I tried to take his comments to heart. It was easier than we had expected as we arrived at the already-full house, where animated conversations were in full swing. With thirty people there, the obligatory greetings and *bises* took us at least half an hour, during which I had already lost track of Claire and Sophie, who had been taken under the wing of older cousins and chaperoned to the children's table. I decided I would not let myself worry too much about what or how they were eating. People didn't seem to be that focused on it—there were simply too many children to keep track of (another advantage of large families, I decided). Plus, the *mises en bouches* were already circulating: *carpaccio de St. Jacques,* smoked salmon (with little morsels cleverly perched in tiny little white ladle-like spoons, surrounded by creamy lemon sauce), and tart *verrines aux agrumes* (tiny glasses filled with citrus mousse).

In the end, the dinner went more smoothly than I could have hoped. Meals at the *cantine* and *crèche* had apparently taught the girls more than I had been able to teach them at home; they proudly sat in their chairs, "just like the big kids," right through dinner. And although both Claire and Sophie politely refused the foie gras (which I couldn't bring myself to eat either), they devoured the melt-in-your mouth *pintade de Noël* (guinea fowl) with gusto. They didn't eat much else, but nobody seemed to notice.

Just as at Hugo and Virginie's, the children ran off to play, leaving the adults to enjoy their conversation. After a *plateau de fromage* worthy of the Ritz (Monique actually wheeled the tray around on a cheese trolley, with a specially made cheese knife), everyone came back together for the *bûche de Noël*—the traditional Yule log cake, complete with bark (chocolate buttercream), holly leaves and berries (marzipan), and snow (powdered sugar). As the youngest person still awake (the babies having been put to bed), Claire got the first piece—and clearly reveled in every second of the attention she was getting.

In fact, I had expected Claire to break down in a tantrum by 10:00 P.M., but she just kept going. It helped that new things to eat, each more delicious than the last, kept emerging from the kitchen. It also helped that her cousins were behaving as if this was all perfectly normal. By midnight, I was wondering aloud whether I should put her and Sophie to bed. But my apparently Puritanical fanaticism about the girls' bedtime was firmly overruled several times by the extended family (*"Why, you can't put them to bed now! They would miss all the fun!"*).

So Sophie and Claire managed to stay up well past the champagne at midnight (only one sip!) and, in the end, put themselves to bed. One after the other, they curled up (Claire on the sofa, Sophie in a carpeted corner with pillows) and contentedly drifted off to sleep. After sitting at the table for more than five hours, I blearily longed to join them. When it was time to go, after 2:00 A.M., Philippe and I picked them up and put them over our shoulders, just as we'd seen with the French toddler in the restaurant (it seemed like ages ago). And just like that toddler, Claire popped her thumb into her mouth and placidly allowed herself to be carried out of the house without making a sound.

On the drive home, I mused about how well the dinner had gone. Philippe was right, I admitted. French families encouraged their children to eat well, but they did this largely without direct conflict. Rather, parents created good routines early on, and the kids absorbed good eating habits by osmosis, by seeing and copying other kids and adults around them. I'd have to treat the rules more like habits, or like long-term goals. And I'd have to include other people in the kids' French food education, starting with myself. I had been wrong to try to change my children's eating habits without changing my own. I'd have to reform my own eating first. I'd have to make eating fun. Luckily, something I had recently read gave me the perfect idea for how to go about it.

6

The Kohlrabi Experiment

Learning to Love New Foods

En voilà un qui coupe la soupe	This little one served the soup
En voilà un qui la goûte	This little one took a sip
En voilà un qui la trempe	This little one dipped in the cup
En voilà un qui la mange	This little one ate it all up
Et voilà le petit glinglin	And this little mate
Qui arrive trop tard	Arrived too late
Et ne trouve plus rien	And found nothing to eat
Et qui fait couin couin!	And squeak squeak squeaked!

—This traditional French version of "This Little Piggy
Went to Market" is counted by an adult
on the fingers of a child's hand.

My New Year's resolution was simple. By March, the kids should be eating ten new foods—and loving them. Christmas dinner (and an equally lavish New Year's dinner that had followed it) had inspired me to try again. But this time, I'd be more strategic. The kids would learn to eat new things, I told myself, even while learning how to make eating fun—for the whole family. I would (temporarily) give up on strict scheduling and on eating slowly. And I would relax my strict snacking regimen. For the moment we'd simply focus on developing the kids' ability to eat, and enjoy, a variety of foods; we'd move on to the other food rules after that.

My resolve was strengthened by some scientific research that I had stumbled across in my late-night Internet searches. A decade ago, two American researchers designed a novel experiment. It was based on decades of research showing that children's food tastes and habits begin forming in early childhood. The experiment was simple, but ingenious. Nine day-care programs were chosen to participate, involving nearly 120 children between the ages of three and five. The scientists divided them into three groups: A, B, and C.

On the first day of the experiment, children in all three groups were served vegetables as a snack, and their eating choices were recorded. One of the choices was a vegetable deliberately chosen to be unfamiliar: kohlrabi, served whole and sliced. After the snack, each child was interviewed, but not a single one could identify the target vegetable. (If you don't know what kohlrabi is, don't worry: I didn't either. A main constituent of the national dish of Kashmir, it's a member of the cabbage family that looks like a hairy turnip on steroids. But its sweet, mild taste belies its Frankenstein appearance: the hearts of young kohlrabi plants can be as juicy and crunchy as an apple.)

On the second day, a university student came in to read a picture book to each group just before snack time. Group A heard a story about a young boy going through his grandfather's garden and discovering that he liked vegetables, with the exception of kohlrabi. The book was modified so that the boy's refrain—"at least I didn't have to eat kohlrabi"—was mentioned on every page. Group B heard the same story, but with a positive refrain: "almost as good as kohlrabi." Group C was read a book of similar length, but with no reference to food.

After the story, the children were again interviewed. Two-thirds of the children in Group B (the "positive message" group) could identify the kohlrabi correctly. All of the children were again invited to taste the kohlrabi. The only children who refused to do so were in Group A (the "negative message" group). And more than two-thirds of the children who tasted the kohlrabi said that they liked it.

This is admittedly a quirky experiment. But it demonstrates an important fact: kids' food tastes are more adaptable than many of us would believe. Even more important, this experiment shows how simple it is to cultivate kids' love of food. If adults joyfully and mindfully incorporate positive messages about food—*all* food—into everyday life, then kids will learn to eat all sorts of things. And peer pressure works: if other kids and adults eat these things, even the most unwilling kids will probably do so too.

France, I realized, was a country where the kohlrabi experiment has been running for hundreds of years. By the time they are three years old, the only things that most French children have yet to taste are alcohol and offal (organ meats), a French delicacy that most will soon learn to love. Of course, the French are not unusual. Back home in Vancouver, we saw this all around us. The kids in the Indian family across the street loved *dahl* (lentil soup) and spices like turmeric. Sophie's Mexican friend loved hot sauce. Claire's Polish friend brought sauerkraut in her lunch. Kids' food preferences are, in other words, more malleable than most American parents would believe.

Of course, French kids—like kids anywhere—sometimes tend to be uncomfortable trying new foods. From chatting with Philippe's cousin Christelle—who now ran a day-care program in the French city of Lyon—I learned the scientific word for the fear of new foods: neophobia (literally, fear of novelty). Neophobia, she told me, usually appears at about the age of two (more or less the age at which children start feeding themselves). According to her, scientists disagree about why it arises. It may be a protective behavior: young children who are afraid of eating new things are less likely to poison themselves. It may have an evolutionary basis: in nature, the foods that are sweet, fat, or salty tend to have the highest nutritional value and are the least likely to be poisonous. Or it may be primarily psychological, appearing as kids enter a developmental phase of opposition to their parents (the infamous "terrible twos" and the dreaded "No! phase"). And some experts also believe that neophobia may be related to kids' developing taste buds, which lead them to reject bitter tastes (often found in vegetables) and favor sweet, fat, and salty tastes as more innately pleasurable.

Whatever the explanation, Christelle told me, French experts agree on two things. First, although there is a genetic, biological component to food dislikes, there is also an important cultural component. Kids *learn* what to like or dislike. And this starts early; some research suggests that flavor experiences in the first year of life can influence food acceptance, and even food preferences, later on in life. Second, neophobia is a developmental *phase,* not a lifelong condition (although it can develop into a personality trait if badly handled by parents).

My conversations with Christelle gave me hope. Her ideas corresponded with what I'd heard from French parents. According to them, neophobia (although they didn't call it that) is primarily a psychological condition. French parents expected that children might refuse new foods, but they viewed this as both normal and temporary. When I asked, most parents thought that their kids were testing limits rather than really expressing a true dislike of the food offered to them. And they insisted that it was important not to enter into a power struggle: if their kids refused food, their parents would simply take it away, with little fuss. But no substitutes would be provided—and parents held firm to this rule.

This quote from a French parenting book is typical: "Opposition to food can't persist if there is no opponent. In the face of a child's refusal to eat, the best parental response is serene indifference. Parents should remind themselves: 'I know this will pass. My child will not continue refusing to eat if I simply refuse to react.' " Indifference and serenity were not attitudes I had been cultivating, but I had to admit this sounded much less stressful than my usual approach.

French parents also believe that there are very few foods that truly taste bad. So their view is that most kids are capable of eating most things. Of course, some foods are likely to be distasteful—like the strong taste of raw garlic. But most of the foods that kids won't eat (like broccoli) don't actually taste objectively bad. From the French point of view, most of kids' aversion to food is psychological, rather than physiological.

The French have internalized these ideas in their everyday parenting culture. They believe that kids are inherently curious about food, that most foods are an acquired taste, and that it is the role of parents to help children. So educating their children to enjoy a variety of foods is one of the most important parenting tasks in the toddler years. To do this, the French parents I knew tried to develop what they saw as their babies' innate curiosity about (and love of) trying new foods. In fact, a little more digging on the Internet turned up some scientific research that backed them up: infants are consistently interested in trying new foods (just as they always prefer the new toy in the room). And tasting new foods when kids are still young can influence food preferences later on. That's not all: the French studies that Christelle sent to me suggested that many children (about one in four) have little or no neophobia; if parented appropriately, they will happily continue trying new things and will never develop aversions to new foods.

The priority that French parents give to eating as pleasure also means that French parents are not overly controlling with their children. They instinctively know that parental anxiety and pressure can backfire. Feeding children is not about forcing children: often, this means they eat less cooperatively (as I found out the hard way before Christmas). So punitive rules aren't applied. Rather, rules are about positive discipline, combined with unquestioned routines that make it seem entirely natural for French children to try new foods. This reduces pressure on kids—and on parents. One example is the helpful rule that French parents use to get children to try new things:

French Food Rule #6a:

For picky eaters: *You don't have to* like *it, but you do have to* taste *it.*

The girls' Papi (grandfather) is a master at applying this rule when introducing children to new foods. The trick is to get the kids to take the initiative rather than forcing the issue. For example, he might pick his moment while everyone is enjoying an *apéritif* before dinner, which involves drinking some sort of cocktail and nibbling on salty snacks like olives, crackers, pâté, or nuts. French children adore *l'apéritif,* perhaps because of its informality; it is the only socially sanctioned snack that French adults eat. And it's the only time when the family doesn't eat at the dining room table; *l'apéritif* is taken seated comfortably in the living room. For the children, for whom eating standing up (or anywhere but at the table) is strictly forbidden, *l'apéritif* has a slightly Carnavalesque feel—a ritualized way of breaking the rules that feels festive and fun.

So, when Papi asks them to try something new during *l'apéritif,* our kids are usually happy to accept. An olive might be casually offered. If the child resists, a gentle murmur of encouragement arises from the adults and older children. *Vas-y!* (Go ahead!) But the child is not forced to do anything. Adult conversation continues, and no great fuss is made.

Usually, our children cautiously test the food, most often when there are no eyes on them. Their reactions (whether pleasurable or not) are met with calm acceptance. A child might politely respond, "*Non, merci.*" "Didn't like it? That's okay. You'll try again later." Or, "Great, you liked that olive? Try this one." And a new bowl holding a different type of olives slides across the table. This happens over and over again, at regular intervals, over a period of a month or two. Eventually, the child usually starts eating the new food.

Papi's technique displays a key element of the French approach to children's eating habits. They don't fuss. They don't hover. No one is anxious. Parents are cheerful but matter-of-fact. Above all, if the child refuses to eat, the parents simply take the food away without too much comment, without providing substitutes. And because of the "no snacking" rule, they know that their child will be hungrier at the next meal, which will work to their advantage.

As a result, food never becomes a power struggle. Rather, food is part of a routine. It's a fun routine with lots of novelty and socializing, but it is still a routine. Children unquestioningly come to the table, accept that their parents choose what they'll eat, expect to be pleasantly surprised, and, for the most part, enjoy every mouthful. There is a kind of innocence about this that always amazes me. It simply doesn't occur to most French kids to resist.

How do French parents do this? Part of the answer is the fact that they assert authority over the scheduling of feeding when their children are still very young. I saw this for myself when Sophie was a baby. Like most babies we knew, Sophie was breast-fed on demand, which meant three hours (or often less) between feedings. At eight months of age, Sophie's eating schedule looked something like this (although it changed every day):

1:00 A.M. ~ breast-feeding
4:00 A.M. ~ breast-feeding
7:00 A.M. ~ breast-feeding
8:30 A.M. ~ baby cereal
(20-minute nap)
11:30 A.M. ~ breast-feeding
12:30 P.M. ~ vegetable puree, baby crackers
(20-minute nap)
2:30 P.M. ~ breast-feeding
(20-minute nap)
5:00 P.M. ~ breast-feeding
6:00 P.M. ~ fruit compote, or yogurt
(20-minute nap)
9:00 P.M. ~ breast-feeding
(in bed for the night)

If this sounds exhausting, it's because it was. My husband and I would exchange grim looks as we headed to bed, hoping against hope that Sophie would sleep through the night (she was fourteen months old the first time she did so, and I still quietly celebrate that anniversary every year). She was getting thirteen hours of sleep, and we were averaging less than six, broken up by the 1:00 A.M. and 4:00 A.M. feedings. I was a zombie.

This drove me into a bout of the "baby blues" (although not full-blown postpartum depression): between sessions of sleep-deprivation–induced crying, I frantically read any book on children's sleep that I could get my hands on. I tried the No-Cry Sleep Solution. I tried attachment parenting–style rocking to sleep. Finally, in desperation, I tried Ferber-ization (otherwise known as "crying it out"), but I broke down after about a minute and a half. Nothing worked. Sophie woke up like clockwork at 1:00 A.M. and 4:00 A.M., and went back to sleep only with a contented belly full of milk. My milk.

One of the things that made this somewhat bearable was my assumption that this was the fate of all mothers. But then we went to visit some of my husband's old friends—French friends. The couple had an eight-month-old baby, and I figured I could commiserate with a similarly frazzled new mom. Except that she wasn't frazzled at all.

At eight months, baby Clément's eating schedule looked like this:

8:00 A.M. ~ wake up, 240 ml milk
(2- to 3-hour nap)
12:30 P.M. ~ Vegetable soup, fruit puree, or yogurt
(2- to 3-hour nap)
4:30 P.M. ~ 240 ml milk
(1-hour nap)
7:00 P.M. ~ 250 ml milk with dissolved baby cereal
(in bed for the night)

The first day of our visit, I watched in amazement as little Clément—who was understandably hungry at mealtimes—guzzled his milk, devoured his purees, and contentedly napped for hours after every meal. He slept soundly through the night, every night of our visit.

Clément's four meals were served at precisely the same time every day. Meals were never served early, not by even five minutes. In between meals, he was given only water. Clément quickly learned that adults decided what he ate, where he ate (only in his highchair), and when he ate. His patience was astounding: he never, or very rarely, cried out of hunger. In fact, given the quantities of food he ate at his meals, I wondered whether he ever felt very hungry.

Most French children are raised like Clément (who, by the way, has grown into a happy, healthy eater-of-everything). By the time they are toddlers, French children have learned that their parents are in charge of their eating routines. This means that they are fairly willing to accept that they have to taste new things. And, once they have gotten used to this idea, French parents take the next step:

French Food Rule #6b:

For fussy eaters: *You don't have to* like *it, but you do have to* eat *it.*

French parents apply this rule with familiar foods that their children are usually happy to eat. This rule had a magical effect on my kids (and on me). Before, when my children would say, "I don't like it," when I served things they usually liked, I would immediately get worried. I'd try to change the taste of whatever they were refusing (More butter? More salt? What about a bit of soy sauce? Ketchup?). Unwittingly, I ceded the decision-making power over eating to my kids. Looking back, I realized that I was caught between my desire to support my kids' individual choice and autonomy (refusing this food is okay), and my desire to get them to eat good food (refusing this food is *not* okay). In North America—a culture that prizes individual choice—kids don't have to eat what they don't like. But parents worry desperately that they are not eating well. This sets up a vicious cycle: we feel anxious about food and, sensing this, our children often eat less well.

French parents don't give their children as much choice. Being able to eat well is a social survival skill, at school and in the workplace. Expressing a personal food preference in public is viewed as a sign of bad manners, which is not viewed lightly in French culture. If children have already eaten something in the past, and liked it, then a random caprice about that particular food is not tolerated. They're simply told, gently but firmly, to eat it. And, for the most part, they do. (The odd French child will refuse to eat. But true *refus alimentaire* is a relatively rare medical phenomenon that doesn't affect most children.)

French parents are also told something else that many North American parents don't learn. French pediatricians warn families about neophobia, telling them that children's appetite diminishes and becomes more fickle somewhere between the ages of two and four. This is in part physical (as kids' growth rate slows down), and in part psychological (French children go through a "no" phase, just like kids everywhere). The French even have a formal term for this: *la phase d'opposition.* They know that they have a limited time frame to introduce new tastes, flavors, and textures, and to build the foundation for healthy food habits. So they focus on introducing a large variety of foods in the first two years of a child's life.

I have to admit that I am still sometimes baffled by the "logical" order French parents follow for introducing new foods to babies and toddlers. Soft cheese comes before hard cheese, for example, because it is easier to chew. So Roquefort might be offered to a baby at nine months (typically, they love the salty taste and tangy texture), but Cheddar will be offered much later. Whatever your opinion about their logic, the goal seems sensible enough: to train children's food tastes, experiences, and preferences. The goal here is to help children develop a love of variety.

But the French understand variety differently than North Americans do. Our parenting books (and parents) tend be focused on micronutrients, like omega-3s, or iron. The French, in contrast, tend to spend less time on micronutrients. Rather, French advice focuses on teaching young children to get used to variety in taste, texture, and color, for example. So the advice French parents get is not solely focused on which specific foods contain which particular nutrients; rather, it is focused on how specific tactics (like varying the colors of the purees at each meal) can help instill an expectation of novelty. And by giving their kids lots of vegetables, unprocessed foods, and high-quality treats, they train their kids' palates to enjoy "real" food.

In fact, many French people are still relatively unused to processed "convenience" foods of any kind. I realized this soon after I married Philippe, when he came to me late one evening with a strained look on his face.

"What was in that ice cream you bought?" he asked rather queasily.

"We don't have any ice cream in the house," I responded, mystified. "We finished it last week, and I haven't bought any more yet."

"But there's a big tub in the freezer," he replied. "And it tastes, well, a bit odd."

"Let me look," I suggested, worried that some forgotten tub of ancient ice cream had given my newly wedded husband a case of food poisoning. Visions of him on his deathbed flashed through my head. I ran to the freezer and rummaged maniacally through the various plastic pots and tubs.

To my relief, I was right. I was *sure* there was no ice cream in the house. But what had Philippe eaten?

I ran back to the bedroom to find him lying down clutching his stomach.

"There *is* no ice cream in the freezer! What did you eat?" I asked, trying to keep the worried tone out of my voice.

"Of course there is!" my husband snapped. "It's in that big white plastic tub!"

I ran back to the kitchen and pulled open the freezer door again. Was I going crazy? There was a white plastic tub, but it was full of raw, frozen chocolate chip cookie dough—the kind I bought at the supermarket, to make "fresh" cookies as a treat. Grabbing the tub, I ran back to the bedroom, where he was looking even worse.

"Is *that* what you ate?" I asked him in disbelief, bending over to wave the tub in front of his half-closed eyes. Seeing the look on his face, I tried to sound calm. "This isn't ice cream—it's cookie dough!"

It was his turn to look shocked. "Is *that* how you make cookies? I've never heard of such a thing!"

"How much did you eat?" I demanded, astounded that a spoonful of cookie dough could have given him a stomachache.

"Well, a bowl full," he admitted. "It did taste a little odd, but I thought that this must be a new American flavor, and I didn't want to waste it, so I ate it all."

This, I realized (after several minutes of hysterical laughter, which Philippe sadly couldn't share), was one of the potential downfalls of French food training: years of rigorously enforced messages about *not* being fussy might lead people to politely consume inedible foods, even against their better judgment. But from my husband's perspective, the problem was not with his taste buds, but rather with my shopping habits. It took a long time before he forgave me for buying such a "fake food" item.

This is the other critical half of the French food equation for parents, and it boils down to something pretty simple: give your kids mostly unprocessed, nonindustrial, homemade foods, and this is what they'll learn to love. This will become their comfort food. So the French are not primarily concerned with policing their children's food intake, or banning all "fake foods." Rather, their goal is to train their children to eat a balanced diet and to realize how much healthier they feel if they eat mostly "real food."

The results—in terms of vegetable and fruit consumption by French children—are impressive. Before I allowed myself to be truly convinced of the French approach, I actually looked up the statistics. The French recommendation is that kids eat five portions (about two and a half cups) of fruits and vegetables per day. Just under half (42 percent) of French children achieve this. And many of the rest were pretty close. In contrast, only about 10 percent of American children and adolescents (and 20 percent of toddlers) are estimated to consume the American government's recommended daily two and a half cups per day of fruits and vegetables. The most popular "fruit" in North America is actually fruit juice (just under half of fruit intake in toddlers). And the most common type of "vegetable" consumed by American kids is the french fry (up to one-half of all vegetables consumed, in some studies), which doesn't qualify as a vegetable in the French statistics.

I know what you're thinking. I had the same question. *How do French parents actually get their kids to eat all these fruits and vegetables?*

A big part of the explanation lies in how early kids are introduced to a variety of foods, and with what intention. First of all, it's important to understand that French parents aren't solely focused on getting kids to eat their fruits and veggies. Rather, they're interested in training their kids' appetites. The French understand "appetite" as a psychological state, which primes you to eat (and be satisfied) by certain foods. So, for the French, an appetite is not just a measure of an empty stomach; it is also a state of mind. If eating is something that someone *does,* then appetite is what he or she *feels* like doing. This depends on many things: the time of day, your desire to eat, how you feel about the setting, and so on. The French deliberately train their kids' appetite, emotionally, psychologically, and physiologically. And they do this very differently than North American parents do.

In North America, parents tend to start with a very few foods, and introduce them very slowly. Beyond that, little guidance is given. As the American Academy of Pediatrics (AAP) informs parents on their parenting website: "For most babies it does not matter what the first solid foods are." *Food Fights,* a book written by doctors and published by the AAP (and promoted on its website), devotes an entire chapter to ketchup as kids' condiment of choice. The book contains some views that would make French pediatricians wince (notably, using ketchup to encourage children to eat vegetables doesn't have long-term implications for their future acceptance of new foods and flavors).

The French equivalent of the AAP is the Société Française de Pédiatrie. The longest section of their publication on infant and toddler nutrition is titled "food diversification." It does not mention ketchup. Reading through this (and other texts published by French pediatricians) provides some fascinating insights into how French parents approach variety in babies' diets. First of all, they are very precise about ages and stages for introducing new foods. Cookbooks (and baby food websites) will typically be divided into the following categories: 4 to 5 months, 6 to 9 months, 9 to 12 months, 12 to 18 months, and 18 to 36 months. Each phase has new types of foods, with the goal of children eating pretty much everything adults do by the age of three.

The French also differ in terms of what they feed their children. At four months, the first food for French babies is not necessarily cereal (as is usual in North America), but rather a thin vegetable puree or soup. Standard advice from pediatricians is to dilute this with milk, and serve it in a baby bottle. On Day 1, a dollop of soup (say, leek soup) in their milk introduces them to the taste. On successive days, the amount of soup is increased (and the amount of milk is decreased). Within less than a week, baby is drinking vegetable soup rather than milk for the main meal of the day. The next step is to gradually thicken the soup, moving to a sippy cup, and then to a spoon. By the time babies are developmentally ready to learn to eat with a spoon, they've already learned to like their veggies.

Fruits are started shortly after vegetables and are usually given at the afternoon *goûter*. Anticipating that French parents will be eager to introduce as many tastes as possible, French pediatricians gently caution, "It is preferable to introduce only one fruit per day, in order to allow a child to learn to appreciate the specific taste of each fruit."

By nine months, the options have expanded dramatically. By now, baby is eating a wider range of vegetables. For some, these still come as a brothlike soup in a baby bottle; others have graduated to being fed with a spoon (the preferred method for breast-fed babies). On the menu are carrots (but not too many, in case of constipation), green beans, spinach, zucchini, baby (white) leeks, baby endive, baby chard, and squash. Again, parents are encouraged to give only one vegetable per meal, to foster the baby's budding taste buds. Cereals are not offered, except for a tablespoon or two stirred into the baby's milk for the morning and the evening bottle-feeding. (I don't agree with everything in the French model: despite all of the research demonstrating the advantages of breast-feeding, France has some of the lowest breast-feeding rates in the industrialized world. And if French mothers do breast-feed, they typically stop at two months.)

A second, more advanced phase of diversification starts at one year, and lasts until about three—the crucial period in which the French shape (some books even use the word "construct") their children's tastes. The preferred vegetables they use are often curious choices, at least to American eyes. My mother-in-law was surprised, for example, that I started my daughters off with green peas—because she felt that their taste and texture was "too strong." In fact, the French (somewhat haphazardly, at least in my opinion) classify vegetables into "mild" and "strong" categories, according to their taste. As she explained to me, "mild" vegetables (like baby leeks) should be given before "strong" ones like cabbage, turnip, onions, tomatoes, peppers, eggplant, and parsley. Our friend Laurence, who lives in the south of France, started off serving simple zucchini puree to her babies, then added parsley and tomatoes a few months later. By the time baby Antoine was a year and a half old, eggplant and peppers had been added, the texture had gone from smooth to lumpy, and Antoine was eating something that closely resembled ratatouille.

This list of "strong" vegetables would be daunting to most American parents, but French parents will usually feed these "unusual" vegetables to their children without a second thought. Ever heard of cardoons (*cardons*)? Neither had I (they're a kind of artichoke). The Society of French Pediatricians puts them on their recommended list, and you can find them in most French markets. Salsify also features on their list. I had to look this one up too, only to learn it was a plant called Jerusalem star (or vegetable oyster) that I'd never even seen, much less thought of giving to my children.

One thing that is not on the Society of French Pediatricians' list is a mention of the standard North American protocol:

> *Start these new foods one at a time, at intervals of every 2 to 3 days. If symptoms such as diarrhea, vomiting, or rash develop, stop immediately and contact your doctor.*

When I was a new mom, this kind of statement terrified me. Giving my baby food could cause diarrhea and vomiting? Yikes! As a result, I was extremely cautious. By the time she was one year old, Sophie had been introduced to a relatively small number of vegetables (yam, green peas, potatoes, squash, and carrots), and her diet was heavily reliant on cereals (buttered bread and crackers).

Her cousins, meanwhile, had graduated to leeks, zucchini, and much more. This is typical. By the time they are a year old, French kids are eating a lot of vegetables. They are offered grains and cereals at every meal, but these make up only a relatively small part of their diet. By the time they are two years old and likely to show signs of neophobia or oppositional eating, most French kids have tried (and eaten) more foods than many American adults. This continues into their teens. In the research reports that Christelle sent to me, there were also studies by French nutritionists of food *dislikes*. I read these with a growing sense of astonishment, as I couldn't believe how many foods French children had apparently tried. In the Top 20 on the list of "foods I dislike/hate" were things like oysters, beef tongue, cooked endive, turnip, liver, brain (source unspecified), tripe, creamed chestnuts, and kidney. Now, with the possible exception of turnip, many American parents (including me) have not tasted most of these foods, much less introduced them to their children. But French kids are regularly served all sorts of foods and see their parents eating and enjoying them. That's how they learn to believe in the Golden Rule of French Food: *Il faut manger un peu de tout* (One has to eat a little bit of everything).

Reflecting on all of this, I became more and more worried. It was now mid-January, and weeks had passed since I had initiated The Plan. My failure had made me feel pretty helpless. For Sophie, in particular, it felt like it was too late. I worried that she was too old (although she had only just turned six). She already hated trying new foods. And I could relate—I didn't particularly like trying new foods either, despite knowing that expressing a personal food preference was, for the French, the height of bad manners.

Sandrine consoled me by pointing out that Sophie was eating well at the *cantine*. It was true that lunchtime meals were sometimes the highlight of her day. The week before, just after school had started again after the Christmas break, Sophie had come home from school with her face glowing. "Maman, I got the *fève*!" (I got the bean!). Seeing the puzzled look on my face, she laughed and explained. The *cantine* had served a special dessert: the *galette des rois*. A tiny figurine was hidden in one—but only one—piece. One lucky child at each table would have the piece with the figurine and be the *reine* (queen) or *roi* (king) for the rest of the day. Sophie showed me her paper crown and, clutched tightly in her hand, the *fève,* which was not a bean at all, but rather a tiny porcelain figure of a little queen, complete with crown. Of course! It was the *Fête des Rois* (the Christian feast day of Epiphany), when children across France eat a special cake served only on this day and delight in the role reversal that accompanies it.

Thinking of Sophie's story, I realized Sandrine was right. She *was* ready to start adapting to French Food Rules at home. But I wasn't sure if *I* was ready. I still felt overwhelmed. On top of parenting and working full-time, I had to plan my children's dietary diversification as if I were grooming them to be Michelin-starred chefs? My first thought was to rebel. But the cookbooks were so enticing that I kept opening them. Paging through one of the baby cookbooks one day over my morning coffee, I suddenly thought: *Why not take them back to the beginning? They hadn't tasted all these vegetable purees, but why couldn't they start now?* The more I thought about it, the more excited I got. I would serve the purees as soups. This would eliminate my daughters' most frequent objections to the new foods: their appearance and texture. Once they'd learned to like the taste of something new in a soup, I could gradually move on to introducing it in other forms. After all, that's exactly how French babies learned. In fact, *la soupe* was still a favorite evening meal for the French.

It will be a kind of "food rebirthing," I thought (although this was so hippie-sounding that I kept the term to myself). We'd pick a dozen vegetables and reintroduce them over a month. This would be our own family version of the kohlrabi experiment. I found inspiration in a cookbook by Cyril Lignac, the *cantine* crusader I had heard about from Sophie's teacher. I had brought one of his cookbooks home from the library and enjoyed reading his astute sayings, which summed up the French philosophy nicely. My favorite was "In order to like a food, you first have to *tame* it." I liked this idea, which suggested a gradual process of getting to know one another, of becoming intimately acquainted with something. As I read in another book that Christelle had sent to me (*La naissance du goût* [*The Birth of Taste*] by psychologist Natalie Rigal), this involved exploring new food with all of the senses—sight, smell, touch, taste, and even hearing.

This gave me some interesting new ideas about how to deal with potential refusals to eat the new things I'd be preparing. We'd try taste training, just like at school. If the kids didn't want to taste the food at first, I could ask them to smell it, or describe it. They'd still be encountering the new food (and making progress, from the French perspective).

But I had also learned from my research that actually getting kids to taste the food (even a little bit) was the trick to teaching them to like it. So by the third time it was on the table, the kids would *have* to taste it. But they wouldn't have to eat it. As per the French approach, I wouldn't provide substitutes, but I wouldn't force them into eating either.

Poring over the cookbooks, I enthusiastically drew up our week's "tasting menu," as I decided to call it. I'd introduce one new vegetable per meal, in soup form. It would be served as a starter. After a little bit of hesitation, I picked leeks and spinach. They were both "mild" vegetables, according to the French, and the bold green colors would make it a challenge. I added red pepper because it was one of my favorite things to eat. And I included a simple red lentil puree, so that at least one of the soups would have a denser texture. For familiar comfort, I also chose carrots, hoping they'd be an easy winner.

The soups would be simple, I decided, and would be the same consistency as baby purees. Each would have only one or two primary ingredients, so that the tastes of the vegetables would come through. None of the recipes would have salt or spices (except for a bit of salted butter dabbed on top). Once the girls liked it, the food would reappear in a main dish (or in its raw form) later that week. And once they had learned to get used to new tastes every night, I'd start introducing the other French Food Rules, like banning snacks. But first we would make new food fun.

These ideas were inspiring, but one thing made me hesitate. The mess and extra work of making purees was not something I had been looking forward to. But once again the French proved their ingenuity when it comes to anything culinary. Some smart person had invented precisely what I needed—and what many French parents rely on. The "BabyCook" (*beebee-kook*, as my husband charmingly pronounced it) made a proud appearance on our countertop. Shaped like a little chopping machine, but with a unit on the side that you could fill with water (like the coffee makers in hotel rooms), the BabyCook would steam, blend, and puree your vegetables to the perfect consistency, all in one container (and reheat or even defrost them later if necessary). *Voilà!*

We were now ready to start off with Phase One of The Plan (version 2.0). Proudly, I pasted my menu on the now-crowded fridge.

Lundi	Mardi	Mercredi	Jeudi	Vendredi
Creamy Carrot Soup	Lovely Leek Soup	Pleasant Pepper Puree	Yummy Lentil Soup	Special Spinach Sauce

It was my husband's idea to feature fancy names for each dish. It didn't matter that the kids couldn't read yet: we read the names out to them, and everyone had agreed that they sounded more appetizing (or at least funny). Philippe got the idea from the *cantine* at the local school, which had menus that sounded more appealing than even fancy restaurants back home.

"It's all in the marketing," he told me one day, having driven Sophie home after listening to her talk with Marie about the beet salad they had eaten at lunch. "Half of it is in the visual presentation—the tablecloth, the cutlery, the napkins, the serving dishes—but half of it is in the names. Even young kids feel more interested if something has a nice name."

At the time, I didn't really believe him. But it was the first voluntary contribution he'd made to The Plan, so I decided to humor him. I remembered something I'd read in an in-flight magazine about marketing food to your kids—something about placing fruits and vegetables in attractive bowls, and giving things fancier names. The French call this *l'art de la présentation:* the art of presenting food.

Our French friends were only too happy to make suggestions, especially about making the kids feel that the table was a special place. Buying cute cutlery sets for the kids was one suggestion. We put out a request, and the girls soon had Babar, Barbapapa, Tintin, and the Petit Prince to choose from. Mamie brought over small bowls with little hand-painted scenes of children dressed in traditional Breton costumes; they had been personalized, with the girls' names embossed on the outside of each bowl in a lovely cursive script. Placemats covered with horses appeared in the house—a gift from Papi, who loved taking the girls for pony rides. These, I hoped, would make the introduction of new foods a lot more fun for the girls.

Still, I was hesitant about actually reinitiating The Plan. What if it failed? A week passed, and I kept putting it off. Part of the reason, I had to admit to myself, was that I myself was rather picky. As a child, I tended to eat just a few favorite things (McChicken sandwiches, grilled cheese with ketchup, and applesauce). As a teenager, I usually microwaved myself some dinner and ate it alone at the table. Our parents ate later, sometimes in front of the TV. Everyone spent a lot of time in separate rooms. I got an after-school job at McDonald's and later at the local drugstore (but kept eating at McDonald's). So it was no surprise, I reflected, that I hadn't introduced the girls to much variety. I didn't tend to eat a varied diet myself. But the problem was that Sophie and Claire were likely to become hardened neophobes if they didn't start eating new things, especially given the fact that they hadn't had the benefit of exposure to eating new things when they were younger.

Nearly a week passed by, and I hadn't made a single soup. Finally, Janine took matters into her own hands. Unannounced, she showed up late Friday afternoon at the house with a *panier* full of groceries. "I'm here for dinner!" she said gaily. "Go finish what you were working on!" she insisted, gently shepherding me from the kitchen. A few minutes later, the smell of frying onions wafted from the kitchen. Like most French women, Janine is an excellent cook. What surprised me most about her everyday cooking was how few flavorings, herbs, and spices she used: onions, parsley, garlic, white wine, salt and pepper. With this, Janine managed to produce a miraculous array of dishes, usually in less than half the time it would take me. And both she and the kitchen were always immaculately clean. I envied her no-fuss, no-muss approach and found it slightly mystifying. How could something so simple to prepare taste so good?

Our kids also loved her cooking. "*Mamie, ça sent bon!*" Sophie exclaimed when I brought the girls home from school. Their *goûter* was a real treat: Mamie's favorite. Fresh, still-warm baguettes were sliced into five-inch-long pieces and then slit open lengthwise. Keeping the baguettes almost closed, Mamie spread the insides with salted butter from our local farm (which changed color almost every week, depending on what the cows were eating). Then she took a bar of dark chocolate and split the pieces into little chunks, tucking them one by one into the slit. One end of the baguette was wrapped with a paper towel (so little hands stay clean) and handed over to the eagerly waiting children. *Yum!*

The trick with this snack, Mamie explained, is that (like a lot of traditional foods served at the *goûter*) it feels like a treat while actually being quite healthy. Dark chocolate has lots of minerals (like magnesium), and plain bread and butter provide the carbohydrates that active kids need. Importantly, the children weren't allowed seconds. The relatively high energy density of the food meant that they left the table feeling satisfied, but they'd still be hungry for dinner.

She was right, in part because she waited for two hours before calling them for dinner. Just before 7:00 P.M., the girls were summoned inside. One "*À table!*" was all it took to bring them running in from the garden.

While they had been outside playing, Mamie had been strategizing about the evening meal. The table had been set with napkins, cutlery, and the girls' special bowls (the first time they'd seen them). Little menu cards appeared at each place setting. *Special Spinach Sauce*, I read out loud to the girls, who were looking very curious.

The meal started with the two small bowls appearing on the table, each with a little plate acting as a lid. Sophie leaned closer.

"What's inside?" I asked, leaning over to take a look. Mamie gently blocked my hands as I reached for the lid. "Let them do it!" she cautioned.

Under the lids were small servings of what looked like dark green sauce with tiny dabs of butter slowly melting into little transparent pools. Whiffs of steam curled up. The girls stared, and then laughed as they realized that the bits of butter were artfully arranged in happy faces, complete with teeth.

"Quick! Let's eat them up before they disappear! What would you like to eat first? An eye or a tooth?" said Mamie.

Claire went first. Into her mouth popped a buttery eye with a dab of green goo. No reaction. After a moment, out popped a clean spoon. Sophie went next. In popped two buttery teeth with a spoonful of green goo. She hesitantly tried a second spoonful. This time, the clean spoon came out a little faster. Soon, the happy faces had disappeared, and both girls were rapidly digging their way to the bottom of their bowls. As they scraped the bottoms clean, two smiling rabbit faces appeared. They nodded silently and held out their bowls for more.

Mamie's visit had gotten us off to a good start. "Festive and fun," I would remind myself, as dinnertime would approach every day. "The table should be the happiest place in the house," my husband would remind me whenever I got tense about food. And I did get tense, as preparing the meals was an extra effort at what I always felt was the most stressful time of day—late afternoon (what Philippe and I called the "arsenic hour," and with good reason). Luckily, we were a lot less busy than we would have been back home. Lessons for French kids don't tend to start until age six or seven. So there were few after-school activities to sign up for, and we were home early enough every day for me to have time to throw something together, with the miraculous B.B. Kook (as we'd now rechristened it) as my mainstay.

I also planned some new Smart Things to Say, but I made sure that they were encouraging rather than frustrating for the kids.

> *"You don't like it? That's because you haven't tasted it enough times yet. Maybe next time!"*

> *"You don't like it? That's okay, you'll like it when you are more grown up."*

> *"You're hungry? That's fine. You'll really appreciate your [insert next meal]. We're having something really yummy: [insert name of dish]."*

In spite of my stress, and to my amazement, The Plan continued to work. The girls didn't try every soup the first time. But after two or three weeks, they had tried everything on my list. This was an-other thing I learned from the parenting books: assess the quality of a child's food intake over a period of a week (or weeks) rather than demanding a completely balanced meal every time they sit down.

I made a point of leaving the food in front of them even if they didn't want to taste it while Philippe and I ate our servings. After seeing us eat, the girls would usually be convinced to put a tiny bit in their mouths. Sometimes, though, we'd have to wait until the next ap-pearance on the menu. Unsurprisingly, Claire was an even more avid taster than Sophie (who usually had to be convinced to follow her younger sister's lead).

From my research, I had learned that "peer-to-peer marketing" works too. The funniest experiment I found was one where scientists created a new blue-colored food for kids and tracked whether positive or negative messages from fellow students would increase or decrease consumption. The results were predictable: peer pressure works. But what was fascinating was that kids who had received positive peer messages about the new blue food were more likely to try another new food the next day, even when on their own.

After reading this (and thinking about "positive messaging"), we also tried to change our language. I avoided saying that foods tasted "bad" or "good." I used only positive words, such as "good" or "tasty." If I thought something wasn't healthy, I said so, and explained why, using the word "unhealthy" rather than "bad." And the girls, in turn, were encouraged to use this language.

To convince the girls to move on to eating the vegetables in their more adult version (and to make sure I got even with my brother-in-law, who had been teasing me about my "liquid diet fad"), I made sure that the vegetables turned up in solid form—both raw and cooked—within a week of being eaten in a soup. This was less complicated than it sounded once I had planned the menus out in advance. I just put aside some of the vegetables before making the purees, and pulled them out of the fridge a couple days later. Chopping them into thin strips and serving only a few small, lightly steamed pieces made it easier for the girls to eat them. "The point is that they *taste* these things," I reminded myself, "not that they *eat* a whole bunch." Small servings took the pressure off me and off them too. And I made sure to serve the new vegetables with something they liked, so pasta appeared on the menu more often than I wanted in those first few weeks. But when it did, vegetables and pasta were served tossed together, and we all—even Philippe and I—followed the "one piece of pasta, one bite of vegetables" rule. Philippe soon had the girls laughing with his mock attempts to sneak extra bites of pasta, and his good-humored willingness to be "caught" made it easier for the girls to follow the new rule too.

Most important, my husband and I made sure that at least one parent sat down to eat with the kids. Our usual pattern was for one of us to be at work, with the other running around the house (doing laundry, cleaning, sending emails, opening mail) while the kids ate. Now, we took the time to sit down with them. We ate exactly what they ate, because I had also learned through my research that what parents themselves eat in front of their children (rather than what they *tell* their kids to eat) is the best predictor of kids' eating habits.

In line with our theme of "festive and fun," I had also decided to do away with punishments. But there were, Philippe's mother explained to me, natural consequences that flow from the French approach to eating. Most important, meals are eaten in a logical sequence: *entrée, plat, salade,* and then *dessert.* If you don't follow the order, you've broken the rule, and there is a consequence: if you don't eat your *entrée* or *plat,* then no *dessert.* I explained this sympathetically to the girls, and they accepted it more quickly than I did. I was helped by the fact that lots of French kids' books seemed to carry this message: there was Michel the "naughty" mouse, who tried to eat his dessert first, or Amélie, the little girl who didn't get dessert because she said "*non*" to her carrots. A little propaganda couldn't hurt my cause, so we made sure to read these stories regularly.

Sophie, however, tended to complain at every meal, and the effect on Claire was immediate. When simple encouragement didn't stop Sophie's complaints, I implemented Mamie's approach: if you complain about the food, no dessert. Sophie didn't quite believe me, but I told her in advance, and she only tested the new rule once. It was, I told her firmly, not a punishment, but simply a logical, natural consequence of her behavior: I worked hard to prepare nice meals, and her complaints (along the lines of "ooh, gross") felt like insults. Instead of complaining, we offered, she could simply say, "*Non, merci.*" I think the parenting lingo went straight over her head, but it worked nonetheless. After being deprived of dessert once (with the resulting storm of tears, stamping of feet, and full-scale meltdown tantrum), she adjusted quickly to the new rule, which worked like a charm. At the same time, we encouraged her to say positive things at the table. "What do you like about this meal?" I'd ask her; to my initial surprise (and even hers), she usually did have nice things to say. Everyone felt happier as a result—even Sophie.

The "variety" phase of The Plan had now stretched into a second month. But I had now learned enough to be patient. Plus, Philippe and I found an unexpected pleasure in sitting down and eating the soups with the girls. We had planned to make a point of tasting everything for *their* benefit. But we actually found that we ended up enjoying the new tastes too. And the requirement that the vegetables reappear in "adult" form in menus later in the week pushed me to be more creative than I'd ever been about cooking.

Dinnertime now took a little longer—in part because it did sometimes take more time to cajole the girls into trying the new things. But we were also having more fun at the table. We invented a few new rituals around the theme of "tell me about your day": the best thing, the worst thing, a funny thing, something I learned, something I did to help someone else. Claire would make us all laugh by taking a bite of food and saying, "Look, my hair grew!" (As she was self-conscious about still being nearly bald, I told her that the only way to grow the full head of hair sported by her older sister was to eat vegetables with lots of "vida-meens," as she called them.)

We also told more stories around the table. Sophie's personal favorite was an anecdote about when she was young. From about the age of two onward, she decided that she didn't like anything pale and cold. This included cheese, yogurt, sour cream, cream cheese, whipped cream, and even ice cream. Even at birthday parties, she'd turn up her nose at dessert if she thought it might contain one of these ingredients. By now, she'd learned to like ice cream. But she would still react violently if cheese—even something as mild as Cheddar—appeared on the table. To make the point about how silly this was, we'd use the ice cream anecdote whenever Sophie was being difficult at the table.

"Remember how you didn't like ice cream?" we'd ask her. This would usually result in a drawn-out, reluctant, "Yeeeaaah . . ."

"Well, this is just like ice cream. Before, you didn't like ice cream, and now you do. You just haven't tasted [insert name of new thing] enough times to like it yet." That usually got a smile, and hence an open mouth, into which a bit of food would be quickly popped. Eventually, this usually led to a grudging (and sometimes enthusiastic) acceptance of whatever new food was on offer. Sophie still vehemently refused to eat cheese, but we were making progress.

My in-laws, after an initially enthusiastic bout of advice, had said nothing for several weeks. I took this as a sign of approval.

"Isn't it great that the girls are eating so many new things?" I said to Janine one day in the line at the market. I couldn't contain my pride any longer.

I knew when she started her sentence with "*Oui, mais* . . ." (Yes, but . . .) that I wasn't going to get the answer I was hoping for. "Children should eat what adults eat," she gently chided me. "You're spending a lot of time catering special meals. It would be much simpler if they ate what you ate, when you ate, and as you ate, right from the start."

Hurt, I didn't have much to say. It was true that compared to the French children we knew, our daughters were still fussy, picky eaters. But I was so proud of the progress we'd made. I felt as if we weren't getting enough recognition for how much the kids had improved.

Once again, my husband smoothed things over. "The kids are just at the first phase," he said mildly. "Learning different tastes is like learning the alphabet. When they've learned this, they'll be able to go on and learn to like French dishes, just like learning to read."

This led to endless alphabet games at the table. "A is for apple, B is for beets" was my favorite. In response, our grinning children would chant: "And C is for *chocolate*!" This seemed to sum up the French approach: food was serious fun.

It took me a couple of days (okay, a couple of weeks) to get over my mother-in-law's comments. But I realized my husband was right. It was time to launch the second phase of The Plan. Now that they'd learned to eat a variety of foods, we could begin seriously applying the rest of the French Food Rules. This would be the true test of whether my kids could eat like the French.

7

Four Square Meals a Day

Why French Kids Don't Snack

J'ai faim!
Mange ton poing,
Et garde l'autre pour demain.
Et si tu n'en a pas assez,
Mange un de tes pieds
Et garde l'autre pour danser!

I'm hungry!
Then eat your fist.
If you're still hungry, you can eat your wrist.
Then if you still want to eat,
You can nibble one of your feet
And keep the other for tomorrow's treat!

—Traditional French nursery rhyme

By early March, we had reached a turning point. We had met my New Year's resolution goal: the girls were eating ten new things: spinach, beet salad, ratatouille (thanks to our friend Laurence in Provence), salad with vinaigrette (thanks to Sandrine), vichyssoise (potato-leek soup), red peppers (even raw), broccoli (a real victory), tomatoes (ditto), tapenade (mostly Claire, who had developed a fiendish love of olives), and quiche (with a liberal dose of ratatouille in it, so maybe that didn't quite count). At the gentle prompting of her papi, Sophie had even eaten a mussel.

Even Philippe and I had gotten in on the act: we both had an aversion to cauliflower, and to the girls' delight, it had been making a regular appearance on our parental plates—although liberally doused with a creamy béchamel sauce—for the past month. The first few times, Claire and Sophie giggled uncontrollably at the exaggerated faces Philippe and I made when confronted with cauliflower. "Taste it! Taste it!" they would happily urge. Our gradual love affair with cauliflower was only half-pretend and made the process of encouraging the girls to eat new foods that much easier.

We had made real progress, and I felt proud. But something kept nagging at me: snacks. My children were *tasting* quite a few new things and even eating some of them in fairly reasonable quantities. But they were still snacking quite a bit, and the volume of food they were eating at snacktime rivaled (or surpassed) what they ate at meals.

But snacking didn't seem to be an issue for the French parents we knew. In fact, none of the French children we met ever seemed to be snacking. They didn't snack at the park. I never saw them snacking in their cars. I never saw a single French child rummaging in cupboards or the fridge. This was as true for the French children living in our little village as it was for the girls' big-city cousins in Paris and Lyon.

"So when do kids snack?" I eventually asked my mother-in-law.

"They don't snack, of course," she replied. Her surprised look was a sign that I'd asked, yet again, one of those dumb foreigner questions.

Deflated, I dropped the subject. But I kept thinking about her answer. No snacking? Really? At home in North America, any time spent with kids meant time spent feeding them snacks. I did a little research and found out that Sophie and Claire were typical: North American kids snack, on average, three times per day (in addition to their three meals per day). And I was amazed to learn that one out of every five American kids eats up to six snacks per day.

My mother-in-law was right, though. French kids don't snack. I knew this from watching the families around us in the village. Their children ate four square meals per day, on a set schedule: breakfast in the morning, lunch at around 12:30, the *goûter* at around 4:30 P.M., and dinner between 7:00 and 8:00 P.M. That was it. Virginie confirmed my impressions. She even sent me France's official food guide, which emphatically recommends no snacking. It doesn't seem as if this advice is really necessary, anyway. For most French parents and children, this eating schedule is an ingrained, unquestioned habit. And it's not that they are constantly struggling to avoid a secret raid on the pantry. Rather, eating at other times of day simply would rarely occur to them. Just in case anyone strays, snack food ads on French TV carry a large white banner (like the warnings on cigarette packages) bluntly stating: "For your health, avoid snacking in between meals."

Why are French kids raised this way? Partly because French kids (like kids anywhere) are adults in training. And French adults, for the most part, don't snack—at least not in public. They don't walk down the street munching on muffins or sipping coffee. They don't keep snack foods in their purses or pockets (or at least they're not supposed to). When snacks are eaten regularly, and publicly, this is sufficiently out of the ordinary as to merit public comment. I remembered one anecdote about a well-known French politician: even before he made international headlines, Dominique Strauss-Kahn (former minister of finance, and then director of the International Monetary Fund in Washington) was slightly infamous for regularly indulging in a *tartelette*—a sort of miniature pie—for his late-afternoon treat. Hearing this from Véronique (who had written a book about DSK, as he is known to the French), I thought it best to keep some of the more questionable sides of my food past—like the "nibbling diet" I had tried, and actually kind of liked—to myself.

Still, I couldn't quite believe that French adults didn't snack. "But what about all of those cafés in Paris?" I asked Véronique on the phone one afternoon.

"It's true that Parisians love to go out to the café, to wander the city," she told me. (She used the word *flâner,* which roughly translates as "strolling slowly, aimlessly, while enjoying whatever there is to look at"). "But watch the people sitting in cafés, and after a while you'll realize something: most of the people eating outside of mealtimes are tourists. The French customers might be having an espresso, but that's usually it." I was astounded by this and later asked Virginie to confirm what Véronique had said.

"Most French people don't snack every day, and about half don't snack at all," she told me. "And if they do snack, most eat only one snack in the late afternoon, because they will be having an unusually late dinner—maybe starting only at 9:00 P.M. or later."

Even the words that they used to describe snacking were revealing. Virginie talked about an *en cas* (which translates as "just in case," implying a once-in-a-while deviation from your ordinary routine) and *grignotage* (from *grignoter,* which means to nibble or gnaw). The implication is that it is both unusual, and somehow deplorable, to snack. In fact, Virginie explained, it was only when researchers started doing food diaries a few years earlier that the French realized that adults snacked at all. This news of a "snacking epidemic" caused something of a scandal in France, with politicians and experts bemoaning the decline of healthy eating. She sent me some newspaper clippings, and I had to laugh when I read the catastrophic headlines. I found it hard to imagine what they would say about the fact that 98 percent of American adults snack every day, and nearly half of American adults snack three times per day. And I doubted that Americans were eating what French people ate at snacktime: fruit and tea or coffee topped the list, followed by yogurt, and bread and butter.

So the reason that French kids don't snack is simple: they are just like their parents. And the no-snacking rule has some clear advantages for their parents. Their kids' car seats and strollers are not covered in crumbs (fresh white baguette, one of our family favorites, is also one of the world's best crumb-making devices) or sticky juice residue (an excellent adhesive for crumbs). Their purses are not secret storehouses of goodies that send their kids into whining low blood sugar–inspired tantrums (and that leak disastrously onto keys, brushes, and credit cards). One astonishing observation that I made in our first few weeks in France just about sums it up: strollers made in France don't have cup-holders and neither (at least traditionally) do French cars.

This means that snacking is one of the many things to which unwritten food rules apply in France. No snacks are served at school—with the rare exception of three- and four-year-old kindergarteners in some schools (and pressure is mounting in France to ban this somewhat controversial practice altogether). And no French parent expects food to be made available at any event outside the home, except a birthday party (which will be scheduled to coincide with the timing of the traditional afternoon *goûter*). In fact, offering a snack to a child at the "wrong" time is definitely a major food faux pas. I had been reminded of this the week before when we were visiting my mother-in-law's house. We'd been there longer than expected, and I was rushing to leave at 6:00 P.M. when I stopped to offer a snack to Sophie, as I knew she was feeling desperately hungry (mostly because I was feeling the same way).

"It's nearly dinnertime," my mother-in-law protested. "You'll spoil her appetite!" And before my unbelieving eyes, she removed the cookies from Sophie's hands, holding firm despite the wailing protests that followed. Sophie would simply have to wait to eat. Tight-lipped, I gave in, and hauled Sophie to the car. "You're right! Of course she'll have to wait" was all I said to Janine. And wait she did, but not for long; as soon as the car was out of the driveway, I slipped her a baguette in the backseat. "*Grignote* all you like!" I told her, feeling defiant.

This incident was one of many. Since we had arrived, snacking had gradually become a major source of tension in our family. When we moved to France, our family snacking habits were definitely more North American than French. Our daughters had been breast-fed on demand. As they grew older and got more demanding, one of the things they demanded most often was food. And, generally, we gave it to them, pretty much whenever they wanted. In order to respond to the frequent requests for food, I stashed snacks in every possible location: the car, the stroller, the purse, the diaper bag.

This seemed normal because most of the people we knew did the same thing. Back in Vancouver, the little kids we knew grazed constantly. They snacked at school and after school. They snacked at after-school events, sports practices, at the park, and at almost any gathering lasting for more than about fifteen minutes. They snacked in their strollers and cars. The key turning in the ignition generated a Pavlovian response in my kids: "I want something to *eat*." Snacking is so widespread—and so ingrained in North American parenting routines—that I had just taken it for granted. I brought snacks with us everywhere we went (or they were brought to us by devoted armies of volunteer moms who had more flair for baking than I have ever demonstrated).

So I didn't feel as if our family was unusual. And I was resistant to changing our habits. *Kids have little tummies,* so my thinking went. *They need to eat regularly, every couple of hours or so, or they'll get too hungry.*

"Hmmm," my husband responded, when I told him this theory, after I'd had a bristling disagreement with his mother about feeding snacks to the kids.

"Is that how you grew up?" he gently asked. "It's certainly not how I grew up."

He had a good point. I didn't remember a lot of snacking growing up. We certainly didn't snack in the car (music on the eight-track player, not food, was our major distraction). Curious, I went to do some more research. What I found confirmed my memories: our kids snack more than we did when we were their age. When I was growing up in the 1970s, most kids ate one snack per day. And one-quarter of kids didn't snack at all.

Thinking about my own family history, this made sense. My grandparents had been through the Depression and two world wars, so frugality and homemade meals were their norm. This was how they raised my parents. When I was young, we rarely went out to restaurants (even though fast food was readily available then), because it was not how my parents had been raised. And I spent my afternoons playing with the neighbor kids outside, not being ferried in the car from one lesson to the next. We would come home from school, change clothes, and head out to play until dinnertime—without stopping to snack.

I didn't grow up snacking. *But that doesn't mean snacking is bad,* I argued. And argued. (Persistence, as my husband likes to point out, is one of those good qualities that I sometimes don't know how to rein in.)

But my husband is persistent too. He quietly asked Virginie to send him some research, which he started discreetly leaving on the kitchen table. Once I started reading, I couldn't stop. As it turns out, snacking isn't so harmless. One reason is that kids' snack food is (surprise!) not particularly healthy. Sugary desserts are the number-one favorite snack food, followed by salty snacks and sweetened beverages (like soft drinks and sports drinks). Our kids are drinking less milk and eating less fresh fruit than we did when we were their age. Basically, just like adults, they are filling up on "fake food" at snacktime and consuming more calories, but fewer nutrients, as a result. In one article I read, worried nutritionists characterized this as a dangerous trend toward "constant eating." Thinking about all of this made me wonder about the rates of overweight kids in France. Few people in the village seemed overweight—and not a single one of Sophie's classmates. The statistics I read confirmed what I was seeing: 20 percent of kids in the United States are obese, but only 3 percent in France.

Still, I worried that giving up snacking would be a bad thing. To counter my husband's research, I found other studies, which showed that snacking could improve mood, memory, and blood sugar levels.

"Not snacking makes kids stressed," I said, triumphantly, pointing to printouts of some of the studies I'd found.

"I think," Philippe said mildly, "that not snacking makes *you* stressed." It was true that my kids got upset, restless, whiny, and jittery when they didn't snack. But it was also true that I got upset, restless, whiny, and jittery when they didn't snack. I decided to try my next argument.

"Not snacking will mean that Sophie won't do as well in school. Snacking stabilizes blood sugar levels. She *needs* to snack, or else she won't be able to concentrate." I finished, ominously, with "You know what *I'm* like when I get low blood sugar. Cutting out snacks will just mean more family fights and more bad behavior."

"She's doing fine so far this year," Philippe retorted, "and she hasn't been allowed to snack at school at all." This was true. I was actually not so secretly proud of how well Sophie had learned French, adapted to the classroom, and risen to the challenge of an eight-hour school day at such a young age. But I had one more argument up my sleeve.

"Moving to France has been really stressful for the girls. Snacks are reassuring for them. The girls need their bedtime snacks—it's a routine that has stayed the same while so much around them has changed. And they like their morning snacks on the weekends; it's something they look forward to. Let's just go easy on them," I pleaded.

"I think," Philippe replied firmly, "that we would fight less about snacks if we limited them to once a day, only at the *goûter,* just like all the other French kids. Right now, the kids know that snacks are open to negotiation. They have morning snacks, afternoon snacks, and bedtime snacks. And they want more. So they ask to snack all the time. And they persist even when we say no. That's what is creating the stress around snacking."

I wondered whether his mother had been coaching him, but I also had to admit that he might be right. Despite my commitment to French Food Rule #2, I was still using snack food as a substitute for discipline. This made things easier in the short term: I didn't have to teach my daughters the patience they needed to wait in line at the bank or the grocery store because snacks would achieve the same result, without stress. But there was a drawback: once I'd set up the expectation that they'd get a snack at the checkout, the habit was hard to break. And my girls expected snacks in lots of places, at lots of different times. So they ended up snacking randomly, often impulsively, and sometimes pretty much continuously throughout the day. The kids' demands for snacks tended to intensify in the late afternoon and peak right before dinnertime. If I gave in, they usually filled up on cookies, bread and butter, or baguette. I'd spend quality time with my B.B. Kook, only to have them pick at the tasty, healthy things I was serving at dinner. I could see the advantages of reducing or banning snacks. But I feared the whining, crying, and tantrums that would result.

True, the French kids around us weren't throwing tantrums over missed snacks. In fact, they didn't even seem to miss them. They loved their *goûter*, but since they'd never seen people around them eating in between meals, it basically didn't occur to them to ask.

Still, I didn't quite believe that *our* kids could behave like this. So my in-laws waged a quiet campaign. My mother-in-law casually brought up the subject of snacks. And so did Philippe's cousins. And my sister-in-law. All of this made me defensive, even as I had to admit that what they were saying made a lot of sense. Looking back, I now realize that I was feeling homesick and defensive about being a foreigner. Snacking had become one of my primary sources of comfort. And, resentful of the villagers' apparent lack of interest in befriending me, I wanted to hold on to snacking as a childish assertion of my identity.

The turning point happened the night before Easter. A friend of ours back home was diagnosed with type 2 diabetes. And one of Sophie's best friends in Vancouver lost a molar to cavities; when her parents took her to the dentist, they discovered a mouth full of rotten teeth and a gum infection. She would have to have a major operation to remove her molars and install implants as placeholders until her adult teeth came in. When my husband read me the email about Sophie's friend, I was up late at night, sorting bunnies, chicks, and eggs to be hidden in the garden, and writing clues for the elaborate treasure hunt I'd planned to go with them. After he'd finished, I took a long, hard look at the piles of candy and chocolate. Philippe sensed his advantage.

"What about that idea of doing a family food diary?" he asked. He'd been pestering me for days with the suggestion. "It wouldn't hurt, and it would give us a sense of what the kids are eating. And what *we're* eating."

This time, I relented. "Okay, but only for one week," I argued, "and only after the Easter candy is finished."

"Okay," he insisted, "but we have to include *everything* we eat, and *how much* the girls are eating of each thing."

Smugly, I agreed, thinking of all of the wonderful things I was now preparing for the girls. As a result of our variety blitz, dishes that had been rejected before—spinach, peppers, leeks, tomatoes, lettuce, and all kinds of fish—were now on the menu every week. *The diary will prove him wrong,* I thought.

But I was the one who was proved wrong. Philippe was right: the food diary really showed what the girls were (and weren't eating). The quality of their snacks wasn't great: they were mostly eating white bread and sweets (like jam, honey, chocolate, cookies). And they were filling up on snacks—an after-school snack, a bedtime snack, and (on weekends) a midmorning snack. By volume (at least according to my guesstimates, because I refused to weigh the food as Philippe had originally suggested), the girls were eating more at snacktime than they were at dinner. I realized that this might be the reason that they were only picking at most of the vegetable dishes I so carefully prepared and offered at dinnertime. This "sampling" style of eating, a behavior that I'd encouraged in order to get them to try more variety, was at its worst when they had a snack within one hour of dinnertime.

The family food diary exercise made me realize that *serving* a variety of foods wasn't enough. It wasn't just about *what* we offered the kids. We also had to think about *when* and *how* we offered food to the kids. From this perspective, the French schedule started to seem more and more reasonable. If they didn't have a midmorning snack, they'd be hungry at lunchtime. If they had only one afternoon snack, they'd be hungrier at dinner. And—although this was going to be the hardest of all—if we didn't let them have a bedtime snack, they'd be more inclined to actually eat a proper dinner. All too often, the kids picked at their plates at dinnertime, but ate cereal or bread and butter with great relish as their bedtime snack. Philippe was right: snacking was allowing our kids to fill up on poor-quality food. Maybe, I admitted, he was also right about their behavior. Maybe our kids would be just as well behaved (or better) if they weren't allowed to snack randomly.

I mentioned the food diary to our friend Céline, who had spent years living in Vancouver. Apart from Philippe, she was one of the French people I knew who really understood North American culture. Now that she was back in France, I wondered what she would have to say about snacking.

"When I first arrived in Vancouver, it seemed *so* rude!" she exclaimed, when I got her on the phone. "First of all, someone is eating alone, in front of you, and not sharing. And they're often standing up or walking around. The French feel uncomfortable seeing someone eating if they're not sitting down. And I couldn't believe how messy it was!"

It's true: snacking *is* messy. Crumbs get scattered, coffee gets spilled, fingers get oily, and clothing gets stained. For the fastidious French, this is disconcerting. Their children are, as a rule, much tidier than North Americans'. Even in our tiny village, the children came to school dressed in outfits that looked more like "Sunday best" than the rough-and-tumble clothing kids wear back home. Their clothes—just like those of the adults—were carefully ironed. (When I first visited Philippe's family, I was astounded by the fact that his mother ironed all of the family's clothing, *including* their jeans, T-shirts, and underwear. And French women of my generation were similar. My total lack of interest in ironing was, in turn, one of the warning signs for Philippe's family that I was an unsuitable spouse. I eventually, though grudgingly, took to ironing our clothes—although I drew the line at underwear. In turn, my commitment to ironing was seen as a reassuring sign by his family.)

And another thing Céline said intrigued me. "Americans have no self-control!" she kept repeating. This, again, reflects French views: people should show self-restraint when it comes to eating. This means that treats are rare, should be eaten only occasionally, and should be savored. Moreover, it means that food should be eaten only at mealtimes, and only at the table. In breaking all the French food rules, Americans were guilty of demonstrating a lack of self-control. For all of these reasons, the American approach to snacking seems both slightly bizarre and vaguely repellent to the French—particularly the constant sucking and slurping of drinks. I had already realized all of this, of course (and if I hadn't, there had been enough sideways looks from strangers on the street to make it abundantly clear).

Céline's comments really hit home. In spite of myself, I started to see the logic of the French approach—snacking might work for kids, but was a bad habit to take into adult life. I took my list of food rules down from the fridge and added our new snacking rule:

French Food Rule #7:
Limit snacks, ideally one per day (two maximum),
and not within one hour of meals.

Understanding this rule requires some explanation. Feeding children in France often feels like taking a train in Switzerland: it's always on schedule. In their daily routine, French children, like their parents, eat at the correctly scheduled time. (For special days and restaurant outings, this rule may be set aside, which is perhaps why some Americans have the impression that the French are so relaxed about eating times.) Just as important, French children do not eat at nonscheduled times. But scheduling meals does not mean (and is not viewed as) deprivation. The French *anticipate* eating. They have mastered the art of making delicious food of all kinds, and they themselves regularly indulge in it. The same is true with the *goûter,* which is associated with many cozy rituals (sort of like the traditional British afternoon tea). Milk and fresh fruit are often offered, but foods that Americans would recognize as snacks are usually the focus. *Tartines* (fresh baguette with butter and a sweet topping such as jam, honey, or chocolate spread) were the mainstay in my husband's house when he was growing up. They are still his ultimate comfort food. After a couple of thick slices of fresh baguette with creamed honey, it is hard to feel deprived, even if it's the only snack you'll get all day.

We'll just have to have really delicious snacks, I thought. Suddenly, this didn't seem like such a bad idea after all.

I proudly pointed out the new rule to Philippe when he wandered into the kitchen later that day. Thoughtful, he studied it for a while.

"That's good," he said. "But not good enough. We have to change their minds about feeling like they *need* to snack all of the time. It's not that we are *preventing* them from snacking impulsively. They have to learn new habits so that they don't *want* to snack." With that, he picked up a marker, and added a line:

In between meals, it's okay to feel hungry.
At meals, eat until you're satisfied rather than full.

This is likely to seem the cruelest rule to non-French readers. It certainly seemed cruel to me. Not feeding your children when they're hungry? Really? My first impulse was to cross out this rule and cancel the snack-scheduling experiment. But I decided to hear him out.

"Of course I don't believe that children should *be* hungry," he started. "And nobody else in France does either! I'm saying it's okay to *feel* hungry," he added. "That way, kids get used to the feeling of an empty stomach, which is normal and healthy."

This is why French parents don't mind if their children *feel* hungry before meals. They believe that it is better to wait longer, and to eat a larger, healthier meal at regular intervals. The French even have proverb that expresses their attitude to hunger: "*Bon repas doit commencer par la faim.*" This proverb (literally, a good meal must start with hunger) means something like "hunger is the best seasoning." Philippe's comment reminded me of one of my mother-in-law's sayings: "The stomach is a muscle. And just like any other muscle, it should be allowed to rest. It shouldn't constantly be asked to work." According to her philosophy, eating too frequently could cause excess gastric acid to be secreted, which could in turn irritate the stomach. I hadn't bothered to check whether this bit of folk wisdom had any scientific proof, but she firmly believed in it.

"And besides," my husband concluded triumphantly, "French kids don't really feel that hungry because they eat so well at mealtimes!"

This was true. I had noticed this very curious effect myself. When we spent time with his family and ate the meals they did, I felt satisfied for hours. And even when I could sense that my stomach was empty again, I felt so replenished that I really wasn't hungry. This wasn't because we were stuffing ourselves. The portions were usually smaller than what I grew up with, and I never felt that groaning feeling of painful fullness that I'd sometimes had after visiting our favorite all-you-can-eat buffet in Vancouver.

Back home, I had usually eaten one snack in the midmorning and a second snack at some point in the afternoon. I had gradually stopped doing that after we moved. This wasn't deliberate; it was just that I no longer felt hungry in between meals. Part of the reason, I realized after a few months, was that the food was so good that I really needed less. Like the little handmade chocolates that we bought at the local *chocolatier,* which came in amazing flavors (like Earl Grey tea, or rose flower, or lavender) and were so densely delicious that just one was often enough to leave me feeling satisfied.

Only later did I find out that this feeling—of satisfaction, of being replenished—has a scientific basis. The traditional French diet, as it turns out, has a higher proportion of "high satiety" foods than the conventional American diet. These foods are basically ones that make you feel full with fewer calories. A lot of research has been done on satiety, but the basic message is that some foods make us feel more full than others: whole grains, beans, lentils, oats, lean meats, fish, leafy greens, and high water/fiber content vegetables and fruits. As this list suggests, these foods are usually protein- and fiber-rich. They fill you up for longer, delaying the time at which you next feel hungry, particularly when eaten with an appropriate (read: small) amount of high-fat foods (which stimulate the production of hormonal "satiety signals" and therefore make us feel satisfied longer). This, of course, is exactly the mix of foods that French children are fed in the school *cantine:* protein, vegetables, and just a little bit of fat in their cheese or dessert. As a result of eating this way, they feel satisfied for longer.

Contrast this with North America. When American children feel hungry, parental desperation tends to set in immediately. Children are given something—anything—to stave off hunger. If asked, many American parents would prefer to give something unhealthy to their kids rather than make them wait. If French children are hungry, on the other hand, they are simply promised that they'll be able to eat well at the next meal. And this training starts, in some cases, from birth. I saw this firsthand with my husband's friend Margot. We phoned her in the hospital to congratulate her when baby Thomas was two days old. We could hear his bellowing through the phone as clearly as if he were sitting next to us.

"Poor thing," I said, "it sounds as if he's crying a lot."

"Yes," said Margot, resigned, "he *is* crying a lot. And we are still two hours away from his next feeding." I was shocked into silence. At the same age, Sophie and Claire were breast-fed on demand. That meant feeding, in some cases, every hour or two, particularly when they "cluster fed" in the evenings. If I'd had a parenting motto, it would have been: a hungry baby is an unhappy baby. And the easiest way to make the baby happy was, of course, to feed her. But that is clearly not how Margot approached things. Not knowing what to say, I feebly congratulated her and quickly hung up the phone, feeling shocked at her treatment of her baby, which seemed unbelievably cruel to me. But our French family and friends didn't see it that way. From their perspective, training the baby in a healthy food schedule starts at birth. And the earlier kids learn that parents, not children, decide when it is time to eat, the easier it is for everyone. So a routine is imposed right from the start. I saw this up close when my sister-in-law and I had our second children only three months apart. We were both breast-feeding for the first few months. But whereas Anouk was fed at strict three-hour intervals (not a minute too early!), Claire ate on demand—which meant pretty much all the time. As mothers, we regarded each other with mutual incomprehension. I'm sure she was thinking (as I was): *How can she do that?*

But Véronique's children were now happy and healthy (as was Thomas). In fact, most of the kids around us were happy and healthy. This, more than anything, was what made me willing to try snacking the French way. *If they can do it,* I thought, *why can't we?* Plus, it was getting to the point where I was embarrassed to let my in-laws sit in our crumb-filled car. So, by late March, Philippe and I decided to initiate the next phase of The Plan. To maintain my enthusiasm (just in case I was tempted to backslide), I decided to remind myself of the benefits of scheduling meals and limiting snacks. With Philippe's help, I drew up a list:

- *No more negotiating.* I wouldn't have to negotiate and argue about whether or not it was snacktime.

- *No emotional eating.* It would be easier to follow some of the other French Food Rules—like the rule about not using food as a pacifier or a distraction. This would help my kids avoid developing emotional attachments to eating— they wouldn't learn to use food as a way to kill time or fill the void.

- *Less mental stress:* I wouldn't have to be calculating what they ate or when they ate or worrying about whether they'd be hungry enough to eat at mealtime.

- *Time saved:* I wouldn't be constantly checking and replenishing our snack stores in multiple locations (bag, stroller, car). The routine would simplify my life.

- *Money saved:* Our grocery bills would drop, as we substituted fresh food for prepackaged, processed foods.

- *Better nutrition.* Less snacking meant more "real food."

- *Less temptation for me to snack.* Nibbling on whatever the kids were eating had become a habit, and I often finished their leftover snacks. If they weren't snacking, I'd be much less likely to snack as well.

This was, after I'd finished writing it up, a pretty impressive list. I realized, though, that these benefits would take a while to sink in. We would go through a transition period until the kids settled into their new routine. Their stomachs would adjust: they'd start eating more at mealtimes and not feeling hungry at other times. But it would take a while—and I didn't know how long.

To ease the transition, I decided, I'd have to get the kids involved.

I pulled out the cookbooks that Virginie had lent us. Each of them had special sections dedicated to snacks. Letting the kids plan the menu for the *goûter* for the week might soften the blow of no longer snacking on demand. And three weeks was probably about the right length of time to "transition" into our new routine.

I waited for a rainy day when Marie was over for a play date, as I knew she was a more adventurous eater than either Sophie or Claire.

"We're going to decide on some fun snack menus," I gaily announced, hoping I sounded convincing.

"Each of you gets to plan the snack menu for a whole week. Won't that be fun?" I continued, hoping that the social-marketing skills I'd learned would come through.

"Marie, why don't you go first? Extra points for really *unusual* snacks!" I encouraged them.

Taping three pieces of paper to the kitchen table, I divided each into seven rows, labeled with days of the week. The older girls happily paged through the books, and "wrote out" their menus (which were more or less decipherable), decorating the pages with elaborate five-year-old flourishes. Claire happily scribbled alongside them. We had only three rules: you can't eat the same thing for *goûter* more than once per week; vegetables and fruits have to alternate with "sweet treats"; and chocolate can feature on the menu only once per week. Eventually, I hoped to move to the point where only fruit and vegetables were eaten for snacks. But I knew we couldn't get there right away.

The results of our snack-menu planning, proudly taped on the kitchen walls, were presented to Philippe later that evening. The kids each took turns explaining their choices. My strategy appeared to have worked.

Some fairly quirky choices by Marie, like *nectar de pomme aux épices* (spicy apple nectar), reappeared on Sophie's menu. For sweet treats, the girls chose baked apples and crêpes (one of the first French dishes I'd mastered—but only because I could buy the crêpes ready-made at the local market). For the vegetable dishes, the girls made some great choices, like cucumbers and yogurt dip. And I was pleasantly surprised by their "favorite" choices: carrots, cherry tomatoes, even avocados with vinaigrette. Sophie had a newfound love for my homemade vinaigrette dressing, a mix of olive oil, vinegar, and mustard to which I had judiciously started adding a bit of maple syrup from the precious bottle I'd brought with me from home.

At the same time the children were planning snacks, I was planning our dinners. I knew I'd have to make sure that they were eating well at mealtimes so they wouldn't feel too hungry on our new schedule. So I picked a favorite, tried-and-true dish to serve as the entrée for every meal. With a bit of help, the girls drew up lovely cartoon menus, which they proudly stuck on the fridge. And I pulled out some of the books I'd gotten months before, with just the right messages, for bedtime reading.

But there was one thing I was still worried about: banning the bedtime snack. This had been one of *my* family rituals when I was growing up. I still had a bedtime snack myself almost every night (usually toast with lots of butter, maybe with a banana). Philippe had even adopted the habit, much to the distress of his parents. Snacking in the kitchen at 9:30 or 10:00 P.M., with the kids in bed and the house quiet, had become one of our favorite moments of the day. It was often our most relaxed moment together as a couple. So I could sympathize with how the kids would feel.

Finally, I decided that the best plan was to change our whole evening routine. We'd eat a big snack at 4:30, after school. Then the kids could probably last until 7:00 or 7:30 P.M., when we'd eat dinner. Right after that, we'd start our bedtime routine. Philippe's parents had always advised me to give the children a bath before dinner: after eating, the kids (already in pajamas) would immediately start getting ready for bed. Up until now, as we had been sticking to our North American routine of "early dinner–bath–bed," the kids had eaten earlier, so this hadn't worked for us. But the French "bath–later dinner–bed" approach, I thought, would enable us to avoid the bedtime snack *and* get them to bed earlier. Enticed by the prospect of more "couple time" in the evenings, I decided this was the way to go.

Philippe couldn't resist a smirk when I told him about this twist to The Plan that evening.

"Sounds like a great idea! How did you ever come up with that?"

he gently teased. (I did mention that he's pretty good about not saying "I told you so." But he's not perfect.)

"Remember," he said, getting serious for a minute, "if we're not firm, it won't work. So I'll only help you with this if you promise to stick to it."

"Only if you promise to cook at least half of the meals," I responded. It seemed like a good moment to leverage for all it was worth.

Our bargain struck, we started The Plan on a Monday morning. Amazingly, it went off without a hitch. After our food fights throughout the fall and our struggles with getting the kids to eat a greater variety of foods, I was expecting months of battles. But, this time, the kids felt more in charge, and truly excited and happy about the menus they had planned. They filled up at mealtime, adored their *goûter*, and seemed to understand our explanations that they should eat well because they wouldn't be eating again until the next scheduled time. It helped that crêpes (Claire's choice) and avocado with vinaigrette (Sophie's choice) were on the *goûter* menu: the girls felt satisfied, and easily waited until dinner at 7:00 P.M. We had some of their favorite new dishes: spinach puree as a soup to start; *quiche à la ratatouille*; and baked apples. Starting our bedtime routine right after dinner worked like a charm. Happily thinking of the "couple time" we were going to get, Philippe and I were both in unusually good moods, which helped everything go a little faster. The kids were tucked into bed just before 8:00 P.M.—an unusual luxury for us.

The rest of the week unfolded the same way. I could barely believe it. Sophie could hold off snacking in the car, it turned out, if a really great snack was waiting at home. And Claire followed her sister's lead although she did complain a bit about not snacking in the stroller. However, our friend Céline had primed me to distract her with stickers and sticker books, which are a preschool favorite of French parents: good for manual dexterity, and no mess to clean up.

The stickers were just one of the new activities I started to think about now that I could no longer use food as a distraction. I started deliberately spending more time outside with the kids (when it wasn't raining, which it still did far too often for my liking). Forced to think of new things to keep us busy rather than eating, I thought of some great activities, like treasure hunts in the house, and word games like hangman (for Sophie, who was just starting to learn to read). The kids spent more time building forts and playing hide-and-seek.

And—even though I am almost completely devoid of any artistic or decorating abilities—I actually started doing arts and crafts with them. I had always viewed crafts as messy and irritating, and usually ended up offering a snack rather than going through all the extra work of setting up for an "art project," as Sophie called it. But now, when Sophie asked, I made the extra effort. Actually, Philippe made most of the extra effort, as he turned out to be much more skilled than I was at this sort of thing. So *he* ended up doing lots of arts and crafts with them, which had the added benefit of allowing them to spend more time with him. (And I was diplomatically silent on some of the activities that were, in my opinion, of limited educational value, like the several-hundred-piece Big City Hospital Lego set that Philippe bought "for the girls" and that they politely watched him assemble.)

Three weeks into our new phase of The Plan, things seemed to be going almost too well. The girls weren't requesting snacks very often any more. They had seemed to settle into their new routine. We didn't even have to continue making up new snack menus, we decided. On weekends, they'd flip through the cookbooks and pick a couple of new things, but they were mostly happy (as was I) with the things that they were already eating for snack.

Most surprising of all, they didn't seem to miss the bedtime snack. I missed it, though. I missed those moments of quiet complicity we had at the table late at night when I nibbled alongside the girls—who were sleepy enough to be well behaved. We'd dim the lights, and a magical calm would pervade the kitchen. And I missed the second bedtime snack I was used to having later with Philippe after the girls were asleep. But Philippe and I found other things to do together. Jo, who was more than happy to support our transition to French eating routines, would often come over to babysit on the weekend after the girls had been put to bed. Philippe and I started going out to movies—although they were only shown once a week, in the local village hall that doubled as the community center, theater, marriage reception room, and indoor gym. We went out for drinks with Eric and Sandrine and met a few other couples. It was amazing how much Philippe cheered up after an evening outing; we hadn't been on "date nights" since Claire was born.

Banishing snacks, it turns out, was easier and happier than I had expected—at least for Philippe and me. But I still wondered how the girls really felt about giving up snacks. Were *they* happy with the new routine? I had my answer (and knew we'd really turned a corner as a family) when I overheard the girls talking to each other late one afternoon.

"I'm hungry," whined Claire.

"Me too," echoed Sophie. "But don't worry!" she continued brightly. "That means you'll really appreciate your dinner. It's in two hours. Let's go check what's on the menu."

And they did just that.

8

Slow Food Nation

It's Not Only *What* You Eat, It's Also *How* You Eat

Ah! vous dirai-je, Maman,
Ce qui cause mon tourment.
Papa veut que je raisonne,
Comme une grande personne.
Moi, je dis que les bonbons
Valent mieux que la raison.

Maman! I need to tell you
Something makes me feel so blue.
Papa wants me to reason
As if I was a big person.
Me, I say that my candy
Is worth more than rationality.

—This eighteenth-century French song, still one of the most popular songs for French children, is the original source of the melody for "Twinkle, Twinkle, Little Star."

By the end of April, nine months after our arrival in France, our family food experiment was well under way. The girls were eating more new things than I would ever have imagined possible. Our meals were on a good schedule (the French four square meals a day). Food was no longer a bribe or a reward or a distraction. Instead, it was a source of pleasure and family closeness. And "eating French" had turned out to be less time-consuming than I thought; the simple recipes I was using didn't actually take that much time to prepare. True, backsliding happened once in a while. At the end of a long workday, I'd sometimes just cook a pot of pasta. The girls sometimes still whined and fidgeted at the table. And although we were eating a more varied set of menu items, I'd fallen into a bit of a rut; new things weren't being introduced at the same rate as they had been earlier in the year. But overall we'd made progress; our family mealtimes, though far from perfect, were a lot more fun.

However, I had to confess that I still didn't look forward to spending time in the kitchen. I'd usually leave cooking to the last minute, then rush around throwing things together. I thought of this as part of my personality: I walk and talk quickly and am often impatient when things move slowly. In fact, I felt perversely proud of my brisk eating habits. *Why waste time eating when you could be doing something else?* So I would often eat quickly and get up from the table and wash the dishes even before everyone else was finished. Philippe despaired of the fact that I couldn't shelve my multitasking tendencies. He wanted to relax at mealtimes, like any Frenchman would. But when he protested, I resisted.

"It's normal for me to eat this quickly!" I shot back at my husband one evening after he had chided me for jumping up too soon from the table. (To be precise, he had ordered me, in an exasperated tone, and in front of our wide-eyed children, to "sit down and stay put!")

"I'm busy! We don't have the luxury of a thirty-five-hour week back home. I don't have the time to sit for hours at the table. I like working hard!" I triumphantly concluded, and then couldn't resist adding, "And harder than the French!"

This was a strategic error. Within a day, Philippe had the statistics to prove me wrong. He had asked Véronique to double-check them, and then he printed them out and cheerily posted them on our now-crowded fridge (Note to self: Try to look on the bright side of having a Parisian economic journalist as a sister-in-law).

	Working Mothers (Full-time) in France versus the US	
	Percent of mothers who work (full-time)	Average length of workday (full-time)
France	66%	8 hours
US	70%	7 hours

As Philippe pointed out, both French and American mothers work (and hold full-time jobs) at about the same rates. And, he eagerly added, the average length of the workday is actually *shorter* in the United States. To top it all off, he smilingly noted that labor productivity per hour in France was just as high as in the United States.

His point was clear: it's not because the French work shorter hours that they have more time to spend preparing meals and eating. They're busy, harried, working hard, and often running late—just like North American parents. But the big difference is that French parents *choose* to spend more time shopping, preparing meals, and eating—in spite of having the highest number of children per family of almost any wealthy country.

For Philippe, as for most French people, food can only be properly enjoyed if it is eaten slowly: the French love to savor their food and find it genuinely relaxing—even meditative—to take their time eating. But this was a message I didn't really want to hear. After nearly nine months in France, I was deeply restless. I had moved our family to France in order to slow down, but I found that I wasn't well suited to the "tranquil life." Instead, I found myself enjoying the surprisingly fast aspects of French life. French trains run at several hundred miles per hour and are an amazingly efficient way of getting around. People speak quickly; I soon learned to add the word "*lentement*" (slowly) when asking people "Could you please repeat that?" The owner of the tiny café in our village took great pride in the speed with which the little espresso-style coffees would be served (putting to shame the pace at most Starbucks I've visited). The French even walk quickly; the first time I visited Paris, I was amazed at how the tiny Parisian women would outpace me, seemingly serene as they trotted past. Their chic, efficient walking style made me feel lumbering, large, and ungraceful—that is, until I ditched my bulky sneakers (which no self-respecting Frenchwoman would wear on city streets) for a wonderful pair of ballerina flats, which were as comfortable as slippers and could make even my feet seem small and elegant.

But the glacial pace of life in the village remained, for me, maddeningly slow. I spent too much time waiting in long lines at the market, the bakery, the post office, and the bank. There seemed to be endless paperwork every time we interacted with France's famed bureaucracy. (To sign Sophie up for swimming lessons required three forms filled out in triplicate, a visit to the doctor for a medical certificate, two signed photos of the child, one signed photo of each of the parents, and a birth certificate.)

The slowest part of French daily life (and the hardest for me to handle) was mealtime. It wasn't the amount of time spent cooking (the French spend, on average, forty-eight minutes per day cooking, while Americans spend just thirty, the least amount of time of any developed country). Rather, it was the amount of time spent *eating* (or, more accurately, sitting at the table) that I found hard to cope with.

Back home, I was used to eating lunch at my desk in five or ten minutes. I'd wolf down my breakfast if I had time, while rushing to get the kids ready for school. Dinner was similar—I'd try to gobble something down while the children were eating. We might spend fifteen minutes at the table—during most of which I'd be jumping up and down getting things the kids needed, wiping up spills, or managing sibling rivalry. Over the course of a day (including my treasured bedtime snack), I would spend, on average, fifty minutes eating. I'm a typical North American, it turns out. We spend just over one hour per day eating.

In contrast, the French spend more than two hours per day eating: fifteen minutes eating breakfast, just under an hour for lunch, and just over an hour for dinner. And this doesn't include shopping, food preparation, or cleaning up. This length of time is very consistent; French people almost never wolf down their food or eat on the run. And they expect their children to behave the same way. After all, eating is social; more precisely, it is a social *exchange,* in which the most important conversations of the day take place (both at work and at home). So it's no surprise that the French like to take their time.

If this was difficult for my kids, it was just as difficult for me. When we moved to France, *I* found it hard enough to sit at the table for an hour. Meals with our extended family were even longer: they might start at 12:30, but not finish until 2:30 or 3:00 P.M., or even later if guests were visiting (the family record was an Easter lunch that started at noon but didn't finish until the last guest wobbled out the door at close to 7:00 P.M.). Christmas dinner started at 8:00 or 8:30 and finished well past midnight. Each of these meals felt like a marathon, as I fidgeted in my chair and surreptitiously checked the time. Volunteering for errands in the kitchen whenever I could didn't win approval either; I was expected to sit still, just like everyone else.

Bit by bit, however, these long family meals began to grow on me. In part, I learned the art of "slow food" through watching my husband enjoy himself. It's difficult for a foreigner to appreciate how much the French delight in these moments at the table. Even though he had left France as a young man, my husband still missed—even craved—these moments of true relaxation (*détente*) that arise during a long, delicious meal with good friends.

Their nonstop jokes certainly helped make longer mealtimes bearable, and some of the funniest ones were regularly recounted—like the first time Philippe's friends visited our home for a meal—one of the first I had ever made for French *invités*. Everything went smoothly until the cheese course, when Olivier cut the first wedge of a local organic Camembert I had served, proudly proclaiming its virtues. In the midst of recounting yet another joke, he distractedly brought the cheese up to his mouth—and was stopped, just in time, by his wife, who wordlessly pointed to the white maggots wiggling and writhing in the little morsel he'd been about to consume. When questioned by my horrified mother-in-law afterward, it turned out that I hadn't realized that cheese had to be well covered and kept away from flies—particularly in the summer—to avoid Mother Nature taking its course. But no one took offense (certainly not Olivier), and the episode became just one more story to be retold at future gatherings when the cheese arrived on the table. "Is it organic, Karen?" someone would often ask smilingly before taking the first bite.

These meals taught me that pleasure (*le plaisir*) is the most important goal for the French when they're seated around the table. The French children I met seemed to know this intuitively. This was confirmed when I looked up surveys of French children's eating habits. In the biggest one to date, the following statement got the highest "agreement" out of kids:

The most important thing is to enjoy your food.

As the researchers concluded: "Pleasure was a crucial dimension of nutrition, emphasized by both parents and children." Here, French kids' attitudes echo those of their parents, just like those of kids anywhere. In international surveys, North Americans associate food most with health and least with pleasure. The French are at the opposite extreme: they are the most pleasure-oriented and the least health-oriented about food. And pleasurable eating, for the French, means slowing down. You just can't get much pleasure out of a meal if you're in a rush. This is so important that it qualifies as another French Food Rule:

French Food Rule #8:

Take your time, for both cooking and eating.
Slow food is happy food.

This rule is seemingly straightforward. But it is profound in its implications because it means that the *how* and *why* of eating, for the French, is very different than it is for North Americans. Nutrition isn't the primary goal of eating. Fueling yourself (and feeling full) isn't the primary goal of eating. Personal health is not the goal, nor is weight loss.

Rather, *enjoyment* is the goal of eating. You can't enjoy yourself if you are wolfing down your food, or worrying about your weight, counting calories, keeping score of micronutrient consumption, or rushing from one place to another in the car. Variety is a happy side effect of this approach (because new foods are interesting and thus make the French happy), but it is not the primary goal. The goal is to derive pleasure from food—*all* food. Eating well doesn't arise from guilt, and eating isn't an anxious exercise.

For the French, the enjoyment of eating arises because they slow down, savor their food, and find deep meaning in sharing it with other people. The midday meal, for example, is a quasi-sacred event during the day. Whatever they are doing—no matter how stressful, busy, or demanding—the French deliberately pause, savor tasty food, and share the moment with friends, family, or colleagues. It's as if the entire nation takes a big, collective sigh of relief before plunging back into the rat race.

So when we moved back to France, it is no surprise that my husband was in his element. He came alive at mealtime—full of jokes and smiles. After a big meal with friends, he was energized. It literally felt as if his batteries were recharged. This seemed a little ironic, given that the pace of the meals seemed positively lethargic to me. It even seemed contradictory; after all, the French were so fast at doing so many other things.

I asked Virginie, in the hope that she would solve the mystery for me. "We hurry up our lives, in order to slow down at mealtimes," she told me. "Slowing down means that you eat less and enjoy your food more." I wasn't quite convinced until she showed me a scientific study in which two researchers (one French, one American) weighed servings of identical meals at McDonald's restaurants in Paris and Philadelphia. The serving sizes were wildly different: a medium-size serving of fries at McDonald's in Philadelphia was 72 percent bigger than at McDonald's in Paris. The researchers also timed people's meals: twenty-two minutes in Paris versus fourteen minutes in Philadelphia.

After spending endless hours at the table with Philippe's family, I knew what the French were doing: chewing slowly, appreciating the food, deliberately "taking a pause," and in many cases chatting and joking nonstop (few French customers at McDonald's ate alone). They were eating mindfully (which has the notable advantage of allowing the body's signals of fullness to kick in before you've finished eating). This is the irony of the French "slow food" approach: the French take longer to eat less. The practical advantage, Virginie explained to me, is that it helps children (and adults) be more sensitive to their feelings of hunger and fullness. This is based on a sense of *équilibre* (balance), which is, in turn, associated with the principle of moderation: pleasure through self-restraint, based on an appreciation of quality (rather than quantity). My mother-in-law's approach to desserts summed it up: "A little portion is all I need. Otherwise, I won't enjoy it as much."

Even the words used to talk about eating are revealing. Instead of saying "I'm full," French people will say "*Je n'ai plus faim*" (literally, I'm not hungry anymore). Parents will encourage kids to "*manger à sa faim*" (eat until they are satisfied). They don't ask "Are you full?" but rather "Are you satisfied?" or "Have you had enough?"

Finally, I understood why our friend Virginie felt that American food habits are infantile. What she was really saying was that we haven't learned an adult approach to how to eat. The most important adult eating skill is the ability to listen to your body's signals, to know when your hunger has been satisfied, and to be satisfied with reasonable portions. The lyrics of "Ah, vous dirai-je, Maman" (which I'd sung for years before asking myself what they meant) sum it up: growing up and adopting a reasonable, rational, responsible approach to life means abandoning childish tastes and behaviors.

Perhaps this is why "fast food" hasn't really taken off in France to the same extent as in the United States. When we first arrived, I assumed it didn't really exist at all because there wasn't a single fast-food or takeout restaurant in our village. But then Sandrine pointed out the little french fry stand tucked away behind the marina. And, she told me, all of the bigger towns in France had fast-food restaurants—including McDonald's. True enough: there was a McDonald's off the highway in the nearest big town, and the parking lot often looked full as we drove by.

Curious about how much fast food the French ate, I asked Véronique to look up some statistics. As it turns out, Americans spend nearly half of their food budgets away from home. In France, only 20 percent of the food budget is spent on food outside the home, and much of this is for the high-quality meals that children (and their parents) get at the school (or office) *cantine*. And any food that isn't prepared the proper, traditional way is called *"la mal bouffe"* (bad grub, a deliberately vulgar term). The distinction drawn by the French is absolutely clear: only "real" food is called *nourriture* (or *aliments*). The rest is somehow suspect. In particular, the French don't *want* their food to be fast (on the assumption that food prepared quickly must have been carelessly prepared and will be of lower quality). One popular, home-grown French version of fast food captures this difference: the frozen food giant Picard (whose outlets in central Paris outnumber the metro stations). Parisians might shop at Picard, but when they do they buy meals like *cuisses de grenouilles* (frog's legs) and *pavés d'autruche grillés* (yes, a grilled ostrich dish). Even "fast" food could be "slow."

My daughters certainly heard this point of view from their grandparents. The first time we drove past the McDonald's on the highway was a cross-cultural lesson for all of us. We'd been out visiting Philippe's cousin Christine, who ran an art gallery on the other side of the bay. It was late and getting dark, and we were all tired and hungry.

"Yum!" said Sophie. "I want to stop at McDonald's!"

"Their food tastes terrible," replied Janine.

"But it won't take long," insisted Sophie.

"And that's *why* the food tastes terrible!" responded Jo, with an air of absolute finality.

"We'll make you much better French fries, from scratch, at home," added Mamie—and that's exactly what she did.

Needless to say, we didn't go to McDonald's, and my in-laws would never even think of bringing the children there. But some of the teenagers in the village thought otherwise. Our babysitter, Camille, was a frequent visitor.

"Why do you like McDonald's?" I asked her one afternoon, out of curiosity. "There are so many good French restaurants you could go to."

"Well, my parents don't like me going, but it's cheap, and I like it," she replied. "There are no rules. Sort of like the United States, right?"

Describing a visit to McDonald's as an act of teenage rebellion made me smile. But in a funny way it captured the idea of freedom that many French people associate with the United States. French youth—my husband among them—have been rebelling since the late 1960s against the rules that govern French society, and fast food is just one more means of doing so. Philippe still remembers one ad from his college days, when McDonald's had just arrived in the rather remote corner of Brittany where he was studying. A child's voice recites a long list of table manners ("Don't play with your food," "Don't eat with your fingers," "Don't make noise at the table," "Don't put your elbows on the table") as images of people eating in a McDonald's—while breaking each rule—scroll across the screen. He remembers being fascinated by the bright colors, hard plastics, strangely friendly staff, and instant food. "It felt," he recalls, "like a child had designed the restaurant, sort of like a playroom, but with adult-size furniture."

Some of our friends worried about the attraction that fast food had for young French people (which Hugo referred to disdainfully as "McDonaldization" and Virginie called "vagabond feeding"). A documentary that Sandrine brought me to see—*Nos enfants nous accuseront* (Our Children Will Accuse Us)—summed up French fears: a combination of agro-industry, agricultural pollution, junk food, fast food, and globalization that threatened to undermine people's health, French culture, and even the French landscape. By the end of the movie, we were both crying.

One of the people featured in the film was José Bové, a French farmer who was arrested for dismantling a McDonald's in his hometown of Millau in southern France. By the time we moved to France, Bové was a national hero and an elected deputy to the European Parliament. But his McDonald's antics were what the French remembered (and adored) him for. Together with other protestors, he had managed to disassemble much of the building, tile by tile and bolt by bolt, and cart the pieces away to be deposited on the lawn of the local town hall before being stopped by police. Bruno Rebelle, head of Greenpeace

France, summed up the outpouring of national support: "You see, in the United States, food is fuel. Here, it's a love story."

But the problem was that food wasn't a love story for me (at least not at first). The real issue, I had begun to realize, was how I prioritized (or, rather, didn't prioritize) the time necessary for making, and enjoying, good food. I resented spending time in the kitchen but would happily spend hours every week ferrying Sophie to music lessons and insisting (no matter how much she protested) that she practice. I had to confess to myself that, deep down, my children's success was more important to me than teaching them to eat well. I came to this realization one day as we walked home from Marie's house after another lovely long dinner: roast chicken from the local farm, some new spring *mâche* (lamb's lettuce) with a homemade vinaigrette, finishing up with an apple pie in the *tarte tatin* style that I loved (but still hadn't figured out how to make). The girls happily ate everything on offer after playing in the garden for hours. Marie's home was full of games and laughter—with none of the pressure (math games! spelling! music lessons!) that I'd already introduced at home. Life would soon be pressure-filled enough, Eric and Sandrine felt, given that the French school system is one of the most demanding in the world.

My resistance to "slow food," already weakened, abruptly melted away at the beginning of May due to a near tragedy. Philippe had just returned from a work trip to Mexico. I'd been nervously awaiting his return, as the swine flu epidemic had just broken out. Mexico was the epicenter, and I was worried that he would be prevented from traveling home. My relief at his return didn't last long, however. Within a day, he had come down with a high fever and a hacking cough. He spent the next day in bed, exhausted, his cough worsening. By that evening, his fever had soared.

I had just put the girls to bed and was in the kitchen doing dishes when I heard him stumbling down the stairs. By the time I got to him, he was standing at the dining room table, breathing rapidly and shaking so hard that I thought he would fall down. In full seizure, his arms literally jerked up and down, his body jolted back and forth, and his teeth and lips chattered uncontrollably.

My husband is going to die, I remember thinking. Somehow I made my way over to the telephone. My mother-in-law had posted the most important emergency numbers on the phone when we moved in. I breathed a little thank you, and dialed the number for the nearest hospital—nearly three-quarters of an hour away. By now, my heart was beating so quickly that I found it hard to think straight. I could barely think of what to say to the operator.

"My husband has a fever, he's having a seizure, and I think he needs to go to hospital," I managed to croak out. There was an agonizing moment of silence.

"We don't send ambulances that far out," came the reply. "You'll have to bring him in yourself." Stunned, I didn't know what to say. I remember politely thanking the operator and slowly putting the phone down. Philippe, still standing behind me, had gone deathly pale. He was shaking as badly as before. I felt paralyzed. I was alone with the girls. *Should I wake them up and drive the four of us to the hospital? What if Philippe had swine flu? What if they got it? What if I got it? Who would take care of them?* I quickly called my mother-in-law. She promised to come right over, but she was at a friend's house, more than half an hour away. I hung up, wondering how I would get Philippe down to the car. If he collapsed, I didn't know if I could carry him. A minute later, Janine called me back.

"Call Véronique! She's out at the restaurant around the corner, with Inès!" I had forgotten that my sister-in-law was visiting for the weekend. She and Benoît were out for the evening with her best friend, Inès. This being France, Inès was also my husband's former girlfriend—in fact, she has been his very first serious girlfriend. She was also a doctor.

Inès was there in less than five minutes. She took one look at Philippe and whisked him into her car. By the time I got to the hospital, he was being examined by a bevy of worried-looking personnel wearing white protective suits. It was only after several agonizing hours in the waiting room that we heard the good news: it probably wasn't swine flu. And Philippe would probably be fine. They kept him in the hospital under observation, just in case. And I drove home after the longest night of my life.

Philippe's dad brought him home late the following morning. We put him straight to bed, where he fell immediately asleep. By evening, we still hadn't heard a thing. Véronique—who had just dropped in to say good-bye—went upstairs to check.

"He's fine," she said, as she came back down the stairs. But she didn't look very happy. After a moment's hesitation, she continued, "You really upset Inès, and us, last night. You should definitely send her flowers, or chocolates. Better, send both."

Slightly shocked, I rushed to apologize. "I'm so sorry," I told her. "I know that it must have been awkward for Inès to help us out. You know, being Philippe's old girlfriend."

"*Non, non!*" said Véronique, looking surprised. "Nobody cares about that." It was my turn to look surprised. "It was because you *ruined our dinner,*" she explained impatiently. "Inès had just ordered her food, but she didn't even get to finish her *entrée*. We ate the rest of the meal alone. It was delicious, but you ruined it for everyone."

I was stunned. My husband had been at death's door, and all Véronique could worry about was her stomach? And she had stayed to eat at the restaurant while we were rushing to the hospital!? Philippe explained to me later that Inès and Véronique didn't often get to see each other, much less eat out together, and that this was a new restaurant with a *menu gastronomique*. He would have done the same had he been in their place, he assured me. This shocked me even more. However, all of a sudden, I felt that life was too short for arguing. I would just have to accept that some aspects of the French approach to food would probably remain forever mysterious.

The swine flu false alarm did have one lasting effect: it dissolved my resistance to Philippe's desire to start a family "slow food" experiment. While still recovering, he extracted a promise from me: when he got better (and, thankfully, he got better quickly), we'd tackle slow food, together. So, in mid-May, we embarked on the next phase of The Plan: our own, in-house Slow Food Experiment. Or, as we rechristened it, our Slower Food Experiment: I still wasn't quite sure that I could commit to slow food, but I agreed that I could try going *somewhat* more slowly.

Slow food also meant, I decided, getting away from the explicit emphasis on enforcing rules. French food culture was primarily about enjoying things (enabled by a well-honed set of routines). We needed to create a new ambiance at the dinner table in which the children would simply absorb the rules. With a little hesitation, I removed all of the accumulated pieces of paper on our fridge: the lists of rules, tips, The Plan, and the dog-eared pages of our food diary. The fridge looked clean and tidy now that the clutter was gone. It inspired us, in fact, to do a general house cleaning. We threw the windows open, scrubbed off the accumulated winter mold, aired out cupboards, and tidied things away. Even the car got a makeover, with new covers on the seats and new mats on the floor.

With a clean house and lovely weather outside (almost as gloriously sunny as it had been the summer before), I started to relax. May is a month with many holidays in France, and these are often cleverly scheduled on Tuesdays and Thursdays, so that people can slot in a day off work on Monday or Friday and have a four-day long weekend. Most of our friends went away for little family trips. Everyone around us, it seemed, was slowing down. Why not join them?

To commemorate the launch of our Slower Food Experiment, Philippe and I agreed to select two mottos. Philippe's choice was *Manger Bien et Juste* (Eat Well and Right), a saying by the French playwright Molière. My choice was (as is usual with us) a little less elegant: *Slow Food Is Good Food*. But the two mottos paired up nicely. Philippe wrote them down in his lovely cursive script (which is still drilled into French children at an early age), and our pieces of paper (decorated by the girls) snuggled side by side on the fridge.

Next, inspired by my brother-in-law (who is an aficionado of French music), I put together some dinner music: our Slow/Happy Mix, as we christened it. Until now, I had never really paid attention to French music. I was vaguely familiar with household names like Jacques Brel and Edith Piaf, and traditional French *chansons*; some of these made it onto the playlist, along with some *parlé-chanté* (the French "spoken-sung" singing style made famous by singers like Serge Gainsbourg). But, with a bit of exploration, a new world opened up to me: whimsical, wonderful music by Yann Tiersen (composer for one of my favorite movies of all time, *Amélie*), dreamy

Francis Cabrel, Manu Chao (fun post-punk folk-pop), and sassy yet serene acoustic French singers like Rose, Camille, Zaz, and Charlotte Gainsbourg (daughter of Serge).

I got into the habit of putting on our Slow/Happy playlist while I was cooking, and everyone would slowly unwind. Unexpectedly, listening to music was a perfect distraction while the kids were waiting for dinner. Soon, the girls were asking for *la musique* when they got home from school and would dance in and out of the kitchen as I cooked. Even Philippe got in on the act. *"La musique adoucit les moeurs"* (music soothes the savage breast), he would say, grinning, swaying into the kitchen and swinging me around.

Our Slow/Happy songs generally put everyone in a positive frame of mind for our "mindful dinners." Interestingly, I couldn't find anything in French libraries about mindful eating. When I asked in libraries or bookstores about *manger en pleine conscience* (the best translation that Philippe and I could think of), the response was usually a blank look and a classic Gallic shrug (although one person eventually directed me to books about vegetarianism, wrongly assuming that I was talking about ethical eating). Like so many other French food rules, the habit of eating mindfully was so deeply engrained, and so widely practiced, that no one had even invented a term to describe it. So there was no French "Mindful Eating Guide" I could turn to.

Instead I resorted to reading American, vaguely Buddhist-influenced books, such as Susan Albers's *Eating Mindfully* (which a friend had mailed from home after hearing about our experiment). In here, I found some of the ideas I'd already stumbled upon myself (like the importance of *how* and *why* we eat, as well as *what* we eat). But these books were not really that helpful, as they focused mostly on adults with eating disorders or people struggling with weight issues. I also read books by French doctors (like Jean-Michel and Myriam Cohen's *Bien manger en famille*) and psychologists (like Natalie Rigal's *Winning the Food Fight*).

Unexpectedly, though, I came across something that really interested me in *The Simple Living Guide* (authored by Janet Luhrs, former editor of *Simple Living* newsletter), which my godmother had given to me as a "bon voyage" present when we started our year in

France. The *Guide* talks quite a bit about "sensual eating," which I would have dismissed as self-indulgent foodie rhetoric before moving to France. But now I was more open-minded. In fact, I read, underlined, and reread the following passage:

"Cooking can be an act of love and delight, or it can be yet another exercise in racing through life on automatic pilot—never stopping for a moment to notice, feel, or taste. Cooking performed as an act of love brings us renewed energy and vigor."

This, I realized, was amazingly similar to the "taste training" in French schools that I had learned about from Sophie's teacher. But I hadn't thought about the fact that this approach could apply to adults as well as children, and to cooking as well as eating. Given that the kitchen was usually the place where I was most tense, this was quite a revelation.

"Cooking," the *Guide* goes on to say, "is like an embrace."

This is the kind of statement that would have made me run from the room prior to moving to France. But now it brought to mind something I'd read by Natalie Rigal: food education for children should not be about nutrition (although of course this is important information for adults), but should be primarily sensual and sensory because this is how kids learn best. Embracing the act of eating, children learn to listen to their body's signals (such as the "I'm full" feeling) and grow to appreciate the act of savoring food.

All of this gave me enough information to cobble something together for our Slower Food Experiment. Our goal of mindful eating, I decided, was to get our kids to pay attention to their food *and* their bodies. But it had to be easy, so we'd only "Slow Food" one type of food or dish per meal. For this particular item, we'd all try to eat mindfully: slowly and appreciatively, using all of our senses to really savor the food.

Now, how to explain this to the girls? I decided to keep it super simple, and told them: *If you eat your food more slowly, it lasts longer and tastes better.* And instead of long lists of complex words that the adult-focused books used (like "aware," "compassionate," or "sensual"), we'd use just one word: *déguster.* The girls had already heard this word many times from their grandparents, as it tends to get used a lot when French people speak about food. Like many French words concerning food, *déguster* is difficult to translate. It often gets translated simply as "taste" (as in "let's taste the food"). But French people usually use the word "*goûter*" to refer to the physical act of tasting something. The word "*déguster*" actually means to eat something slowly and carefully, to savor, and to appreciate (but not to revel in food, for which the French use the term "*se régaler*"). In the culinary world, the word "*dégustation*" is used to refer to a formal event at which food tasting is conducted with almost surgical precision (like a *dégustation de vin*). But ordinary French people also use the word at home, most often when they are telling their children to slow down when they're eating.

"*Il faut déguster!*" my mother-in-law would often say, which means "Slow down and appreciate your food!" Often this was said with a slightly reproving or exasperated tone—because the kids had been gobbling their food. Most of the time, however, gobbling food was not a problem with our kids, who usually picked at everything except dessert. Sophie, in particular, was a painfully slow eater, serving herself tiny morsels on the tip of her fork, and taking forever to chew. Telling her to speed up only seemed to slow her down even more. But when served a piece of chocolate, she was transformed into a champion speed-eater: she'd literally snatch it from her plate, stuff it in her mouth, chomp the absolute minimum number of times, and swallow. And smile.

Chocolate, I decided, was probably a good place to start. Going back to my motto, I reasoned that if we picked something yummy, the girls would associate slow food with good food. Plus, it would be more likely to capture their attention if it was something they savored. Then the girls would be attentive enough to talk about the food; this was important because a key part of mindful eating is being observant. We'd ask the girls to talk about the smell, the appearance, and the texture of the food they were eating.

So, on our first day of our Slower Food Experiment, I made homemade *mousse au chocolat*. Contrary to what you might think, this is one of the easiest French desserts to make, as it has only four ingredients and doesn't require any baking. I admit that it took me a while to get comfortable making mousse, given my North American concern (paranoia, from the French perspective) about raw eggs. But my concerns started to seem a little silly given all of the raw, unpasteurized things that French people consumed. Mamie made mousse all the time for the grandchildren. And the kids loved watching me make it; they would hover around to lick the bowls (which they were allowed to do only on the condition that they *never* do this in front of my in-laws).

After we got home from school one rainy Monday afternoon, with Rose and Zaz playing in the background and the girls eating their *goûter* at the table, I started melting the chocolate. Usually, given that I was always in a hurry, I'd put it in a pot and start separating the eggs, dashing back and forth from dealing with the eggs to stirring the chocolate. But this, I decided, was not a Slow Food approach (plus it usually resulted in sticky, dry chocolate—which ended up producing crumbly chunks, resulting in oddly crunchy mousse). So, instead, I just stood in front of the stove and stirred, inhaling the slowly unfurling odors. I had never noticed before that the smell deepened, and got rounder, as the chocolate melted.

With the chocolate nicely melted (and having stirred in just one spoonful of *crème fraîche*, so that it wouldn't stick or get hard), I left it to cool. I took my time separating the eggs (and, for once, didn't break any shells into the bowl—another reason my mousse was usually crunchy). And I remembered to add a pinch of salt before I started beating the whites (something I often forgot in my rush) to help keep them firm.

As the girls hovered eagerly, I (slowly!) mixed the chocolate with the yolks and (gently!) folded the mixture into the whites, noting that the mousse looked more fluffy and firm than usual. Heartened, I spooned the mixture into little *ramequins*—small ceramic (or glass) bowls that the French frequently use to prepare and serve food. This is another French food innovation that is both beautiful to look at and clever (automatic portion control!). With the girls happily licking the beaters, I popped the *ramequins* into the fridge to set during the couple of hours before dinnertime.

Then I checked my timer. Out of curiosity, I had decided to time our Slower Food episodes to see how much we were really slowing down. The timer surprised me—thirteen minutes! Usually a mousse took me at least ten minutes to make (in part because I wasted so much time fishing tiny pieces of eggshell out of the bowl). I had added only three extra minutes, but the experience had been totally transformed.

A similar magic was at work at dinner when I pulled the mousse out of the fridge. It was the only time I got up during the entire meal. Usually, I got up and down about ten times to fetch things I'd forgotten, but this time I had prepared the table as if we were going on a long car ride on the highway—I put out everything we would possibly need and only called the girls when I was completely ready. It was remarkable what a calming effect this had, as I was no longer jumping up and down to grab forgotten utensils, bibs, napkins, paper towels, salt, butter, water, or whatever else we needed. I even set out a candle and dimmed the lights. It had a hypnotic effect on the girls, who spoke in hushed tones throughout the entire meal.

"Now, girls, *on va déguster*," I said, reminding myself to speak cheerfully. "What does that mean?" I prompted them.

"*Mangez leeentement, Maman!*" they replied, almost in unison. For a second, I had one of those inspiring moments of parenthood when the children seem angelic, and you can delude yourself about the extent of your parenting skill.

My reverie was predictably interrupted. "Claire got *more* than I did!" Sophie whined, her face crumpling. I looked, and it was true. Claire's *ramequin* was *slightly* fuller on one side than Sophie's (another advantage of *ramequins* is that they enable precisely equitable servings—no more sibling disputes about who got a bigger piece). A little extra dollop of mousse solved the problem, and we began eating.

Or, rather, we began our *dégustation*. After a false start, in which they dug in for their usual huge bites, Sophie and Claire delighted in taking the tiniest possible morsels with their spoons and ever-so-slowly bringing them to their mouths. It even became somewhat of a game: *Who could finish last?* Sophie, competitive as ever, tried to trick her sister into eating faster, but Claire was following her papa's lead.

Eating slowly allowed us enough time to actually talk about the mousse. What did it feel like when you put it in your mouth? How long did it take to dissolve if you held it on your tongue? Was it slightly bitter? Salty? Sweet? Was it less crunchy than usual? Why? Was the mousse less fluffy at the bottom of the bowl? Why? How does it feel when it travels down to your tummy? Sophie had lots of observations to offer, and even Claire had something interesting to say: *Papa, it tickles my tummy!*

"*Oh, la grosse gourmande!*" my husband replied teasingly. I had recently figured out what this word meant: someone who is enjoying, savoring, delighting in their food (perhaps slightly to excess, so when it is used to refer to children, it has a warning yet indulgent undertone). *Glouton* (literally, a glutton), on the other hand, was someone who loves to eat, even overeat, and not necessarily good food. And a *gastronome* is someone who likes—and is educated about—the right way to eat food well (Molière's "*Manger juste et bien*").

Another lightbulb went on. I finally realized why the French were so insistent that ordinary people could be *gastronomes*: these are simply people who *appreciate* food. The best translation I could come up with was "fan" (like a sports fan). From the French point of view, everyone could (and should) be passionate about food, just like Americans with football, Canadians with hockey, or the British with soccer. Eating is France's national passion, just like sports back home—except that everyone gets to play.

Philippe laughed when I told him about this idea later that evening. "Don't get too intellectual," he warned. "It's just food!" We were sitting in the salon, enjoying a *tisane* (French herb tea) after putting the kids to bed. It had taken a little longer than usual, as an unexpected side effect of our *dégustation* was that the girls had been smeared with chocolate—especially Claire, who had gotten a second, unanticipated post-dinner bath. But we had still all enjoyed the dinner—especially Philippe.

Until now, meals with our children had been one of the low points of his day. Coming home tired from work to a house with hungry children whining at the table almost invariably gave him a headache. Now I understood why: he expected the family meal to be a moment to relax and unwind, but instead it was stressful and unfulfilling. And I had been making it worse by rushing around the kitchen, expressing my tension (and, if I'm being honest, my resentment) by slamming cupboards, dropping things, burning pots, jumping up and down, and rushing everyone through the meal. Usually, he retreated to his computer after the meals, in silence. Tonight was one of the first happy evenings we had spent together in what felt like weeks.

My choice to slow down had been focused on the kids, but it had also made Philippe happier. Tonight he'd been relaxed enough to want to chat. I was glad because the months since we had moved to France had been tense. More than once, I wished that we—that *I*—had never decided to move. Maybe, I thought, meals were an unexpected way to start enjoying each other's company again. While we finished doing the dishes in companionable silence, I picked up a marker and made one change to my motto:

Slow food is ~~good~~ happy food.

9

The Best of Both Worlds

Quand on est tout petit
On peut cueillir des radis,
Des oignons, des échalotes,
Des salades et des carottes.
À cinq ans, on se hisse
À la hauteur des cassis,
des groseilles écarlates,
des framboises et des tomates.
Quand on devient un homme,
On récolte des pommes,
Des prunes et des mirabelles,
Les bras levés vers le ciel.

When we are very little
We can harvest radishes,
Onions and shallots,
Lettuce and carrots.
At five years old, we can barely reach
As tall as blackcurrants,
And scarlet redcurrants,
Raspberries and tomatoes.
When we are grown,
We harvest apples,
Plums and prunes,
Our arms raised to the sky.

—*Radis et mirabelles* (traditional French children's song)

June had come, and summer had arrived early. We headed to the beach almost every day after school and slowly forgot about the wet, miserable winter. Often, Jo would come over to babysit after we had put the girls to bed, and Philippe and I would head down to the ocean. The sky was light until nearly midnight, and we'd walk past other strolling couples, up and down the wide seawall that lined the oceanfront. Many of the villagers would turn out—the fisherman from the market, the local pharmacist, Sophie's teacher. Parents we knew from school would be there, and we would often run across our friends—Eric and Sandrine, Céline, Yves. We'd stop to chat and banter, usually about nothing much at all. These slow-paced, intimate evenings were some of my favorite moments in France.

I felt more and more settled. But I was still reminded, in countless little ways, that I was definitely not French. The most memorable incident of all started innocently enough, on one of our weekly visits to the farm. As I was leaving with Sandrine, Hubert stopped to tell us about an upcoming holiday: the National Day of Agriculture and Biodiversity (one of France's many official "National Days," which happen so often that I gave up keeping track).

"Why not organize something at the school?" he asked shyly.

"We could donate food from our farm, and from other local farms, and have the kids learn about what is in season at the moment," offered Joseph. "The strawberries are just ripening!" he added, his eyes sparkling. It was as close to bubbly as I'd ever seen them.

I thought this was a great idea. Sophie's class had been working hard on their little garden so the kids would have some fresh vegetables to share. They'd feel proud to host an event. And, if I was being honest, I would too. Used to volunteering at home, I had felt vaguely shunned at school. My offers of help had not been accepted. I hadn't been invited to accompany the class on field trips—not even once. Maybe this would break the ice?

A week later, I was in front of the school on the appointed day with wicker baskets stuffed full of strawberries, fresh homemade bread, homemade jam, and little jars of *crème fraîche* (a dairy product that is best described as a cross between sour cream and clotted cream). I smiled at the waiting parents and grandparents and began setting out the food on a little folding table covered with a newly purchased Provence-style tablecloth (olives and lavender printed on a cheerful yellow backdrop). On a large tray, I carefully arranged some of the produce from the children's schoolyard garden: tender garlic shoots, chives, baby lettuce, and tiny green beans that had been grown in the classroom (one of Sophie's proudest moments was when she realized that her bean plant was the tallest in the class.)

It was about ten minutes before the bell would ring; just time enough, I decided, to offer an advance tasting. Putting a wicker basket on my arm, I advanced toward the first cluster of parents.

"Would you like to try some strawberries?" I asked.

"No thanks!" came the reply. Not a single person accepted. Slightly surprised, I moved on to the next group of parents.

"Strawberries, anyone?" I asked, a little more timidly this time. Only one person accepted, taking one small strawberry with an apologetic smile. The third group I approached was similar: no takers.

By this time, I was starting to realize that something had gone very wrong. I looked around at the other parents, expecting to see encouraging smiles. But most people were looking away, and those whose eyes I did catch seemed to have frowns on their faces. I had the sinking feeling that I'd broken another one of those unwritten rules.

Still, I felt silly giving up now. Picking out an older, grandmotherly figure from the now sizable crowd of parents, I walked over with my basket.

"Would you like to try a strawberry from the local farm?" I offered.

"*Never* eat between mealtimes!" she snapped, so fiercely that I jumped. Wilting, I retreated back to my table and pretended to putter, organizing and reorganizing the food while tears welled in my eyes.

Luckily, the bell rang and kids started streaming out the doors. *They* didn't seem so resistant to the idea of snacking: the table was soon swarmed with eager kids who happily devoured the berries, cream, jam, and bread, and politely nibbled on the vegetables. But not everyone came to the table: out of the corner of my eye, I saw parents swooping in, grabbing their children by the hand and marching them briskly away, with their protesting offspring casting longing backward glances. I even thought I caught some glares from parents walking by.

This astounded me. That night, still bewildered, I related the incident to my father-in-law.

"Why do you think they were so upset?" I asked.

"Because you didn't ask their permission to feed their children," he replied gently. "And because many of them believe that you shouldn't snack standing up, or eat between meals. You aren't going to make many friends by teaching American manners to French children," he concluded.

I brooded about this incident for quite a while. After almost ten months in France, I was still making blunders. Someone once told me that cross-cultural analysis is even more painful than psychoanalysis. At the time, I didn't understand what she meant. But now I thought I did. When you are living in a different culture, you spend a lot of time second-guessing yourself. Every interaction with people around you is an opportunity for misunderstandings, faux pas, unintended offenses, and general feelings of sticking out like a sore thumb. And this was really starting to get to me.

Unwillingly at first, I admitted to myself that I found it hard to *live* in France, and to be confronted daily with cultural clashes of which I was often on the losing end. I was tired of being different, of being a foreigner. This was a professional as well as a personal issue. I didn't speak or write French well enough, and I didn't have any French qualifications. I had come to realize that this would prevent me from ever finding a job in my field in France. There were no jobs for Philippe either; having gone to university in England, he too had "foreign" qualifications that simply didn't count. How could we make a living if we stayed here?

So I felt worried about our future. I also felt lonely. Philippe's friends didn't live nearby. With the exception of Sandrine and Eric, with whom we had become very close, I hadn't made what I would consider one good friend. And I didn't think this was likely to change.

Not a single person in the village spoke English. My French had gotten much better, but I still didn't feel at ease. The jokes weren't the same. Cultural references—even to people like Oprah—drew blank stares. I was just too different to make close friends (or at least not as quickly as I had expected).

Sure, there were some individual acts of kindness. The village baker confirmed my status as a local when she presented me with an embossed oven mitt on the occasion of the bakery's 150th anniversary (handed to me with a smile after the summer tourists, who were not so favored, had left the premises). We had had a few dinner invitations, and Sophie had been to lots of birthday parties. And I chatted easily with regulars at the market.

But I was beginning to realize that no matter how much time we spent in France, I would never completely fit in, because I'd never *be* French. I'd never be at home. And I also realized what I *would* be: one of the sole immigrants in the village and the only non-Francophone. And France does not treat its immigrants particularly kindly.

Was this a failing on my part, I wondered? I had always thought of myself as someone who was tolerant, who reached out to other cultures. But the more I got to know the French, the more different we seemed. I encountered stark differences in the most intimate areas of life: friendship, child-rearing, romantic relationships. I had spent years fantasizing about the French way of life, but (as Philippe had warned me) the reality of *living* in France was very different.

I was also feeling homesick. I missed things that I hadn't even particularly appreciated before we left. I missed my friends and family. I missed the easy friendliness of strangers. I missed being able to walk with a stroller without bumping along cobblestones or squeezing nervously along narrow streets that had been built before sidewalks were invented. I missed my favorite TV shows. I started fantasizing about my favorite foods, like chewy bagels smothered in cream cheese, topped with lox—none of which was available where we lived. We had even run out of maple syrup.

Finally I admitted it to myself: I desperately wanted to be back in Vancouver. Our move to France had been an interesting experiment, but it was—as far as I was concerned—not a successful one. It was the end of June, and I was ready to go home. The problem was, no one else in the family felt the same way. The girls had even stopped thinking of Vancouver as home. Both of them, in fact, had settled nicely into life in France. Both had good friends. They were speaking French so fluently that a casual stranger wouldn't have known they were half-Canadian. And each had their obligatory *amoureux* (which literally translates as "lover" but, when used with small children means "boyfriend" or "girlfriend"). The way that French parents encouraged these relationships—in which young children platonically played at being amorous—shocked me with I first arrived. It was common to hear adults ask, a bit teasingly, *"C'est qui ton amoureux?"* But, as with so many things, I had adjusted. So when I arrived at day care to find little Hugo embracing Claire, or at school to find Pierre down on his knees, kissing Sophie's feet while she giggled coyly, I didn't bat an eye.

But the ties that were starting to bind my children didn't bind me. I had made up my mind. Or rather, I made up my stomach: I was "feeling with my gut" (*sentir avec mes tripes*). I wanted to go home. In fact, I had *decided* that we were going home. The problem was that Philippe, initially resistant to moving back to France, had slowly come to realize how deeply attached he was to his language, friends, and family. He had even started talking about buying a house in the village. The tables had turned.

I bided my time and broached the subject one evening. We had put the girls to bed early, and Jo had come over to babysit. Philippe and I walked down to the sea and strolled along the beach. The wind had died down as it often did at sunset. The tide was out, and the pale, smooth sand stretched almost a mile in front of us.

"I want to go home. I mean, to Vancouver," I said, surprised at how close I felt to tears. Guilt was an overly simple word for what I was experiencing. To tell the truth, I felt slightly panicked, thinking of how his family and the girls would react.

"I know," Philippe replied, looking down at the sand. He stooped down to pick up another cockleshell to add to Sophie's growing collection.

"I'm sorry," I started, and then stopped. For once, I was at a loss for words. Philippe turned and started walking back to the house. I ran and caught up to him.

"Let's walk down to the water," I suggested.

"No," he said. And kept walking. "You knew that I didn't want to move, and you know that I'm not going to be happy back in Vancouver," he spoke over his shoulder.

Feeling sick to my stomach, I followed him.

"We agreed that it was just for a year," I said to his back.

"The girls *do* like it here," said Philippe. "And you can't just experiment with them like that. You can't just drag them back and forth on a whim."

"It wasn't a whim," I replied. "I *can't* live here the rest of my life. I'll never fit in here. And you know we can't find work. If we're away for more than a year, our jobs won't be waiting when we go back to Vancouver."

Silence. Philippe turned around, and looked moodily down at the sand. There was a long silence. "You know," he said finally. "I've been missing the mountains. And bagels and cream cheese."

We took our time breaking the news to everyone else. Philippe's parents were disappointed, but not really surprised; after all, they had warned us that it would be hard to settle in the village. Pierre, Sophie's *amoureux*, was heartbroken. Sandrine and Eric were excited at the thought of visiting us in Vancouver. News spread quickly in the village. I was surprised (and touched) by the people who stopped by or took a moment at the market to wish us well.

Sophie took it the hardest. Most of her memories of Vancouver had slipped away, and she had settled happily into her new life. She and Marie had constructed that cozy cocoon that young girls create when they make their first "kindred spirit" best friend. It would be a wrenching good-bye.

Claire, on the other hand, took the news calmly. In part, it was because she didn't really realize what was happening; her only obvious reaction was to get excited about the airplane ride. Her cheery mood—that sublime self-containment of a toddler—sustained all of us as we packed. We hadn't accumulated very much during our stay, and we gave most of it away. What was left fit into four suitcases. We had doubled the volume of our possessions in a year.

The weather seemed to sense our mood. We had planned to leave at the end of July, hoping to have a sun-filled farewell with long afternoons at the beach. But it rained—poured—for twenty-seven days that month, setting a new record. The air was cool, and gray clouds hovered low: exactly the weather we'd be living with in Vancouver. It could have been one of the longest, dreariest months of our lives. Instead, we retreated to the kitchen and spent our last few weeks joyously cooking and eating. Papi visited almost every day, bringing treats like local *pâté* (with spicy green peppercorns), *cidre, moules* (which I had now learned to love), and crab. Janine went a step further and moved in for several weeks, baking homemade pies and family favorites like *lapins aux prunes*. And I discovered jam making; despite the weather, the local fruits had started to ripen, and we helped Sandrine and Eric shake a few bushels of *mirabelles* (a kind of prune) from their trees, spending the next two blissful days in their kitchen with gooey pots, long ladles, and jam jars.

The sun reappeared two days before we were scheduled to leave. It was good timing because Philippe's parents were hosting a family meal. This happened once every summer, and was usually a chance for us to see everyone during our annual visits from Vancouver. This time, it was also a chance for everyone to say good-bye. So the preparations were even more elaborate than usual. Two *chapiteaux* (open-air tents) were erected at the back of the house, doubling the size of the dining room. The double French doors were thrown open. Five tables were set up, as we'd be hosting nearly forty people. Janine brought out her linen tablecloths, and the children gathered sprigs of lavender and flowers from the garden for decorations.

The *repas* was scheduled for midday, and people started arriving soon after noon. Cousins with children in tow, aunts and uncles—nearly all of Philippe's extended family turned up. Some of his old friends had driven several hours to be there. And our new friends from the village came too. Serving everyone with champagne and *amuse-bouches* (little toasted crackers with a bewildering array of toppings, brought by Tante Monique) took nearly an hour. We didn't actually sit down to eat until close to two o'clock in the afternoon (which was, of course, exactly as Janine had timed it, knowing her family all too well).

The meal was a celebration of everything Brittany had to offer. Janine had asked the chef at the little local hotel (which had all of ten rooms) to prepare one of his specialties for us: *terrine de poisson*: a light fish mousse draped with "noble algae," the chef told me proudly when I picked it up (I tried to look suitably impressed). We moved on to *coquilles St. Jacques* (king scallops), which came right from our little bay—supplied by my friendly fisherman at the market. Hubert and Joseph brought salad and cheese platters—the little goat cheeses we loved so much came from a farm just up the coast. At half past four in the afternoon, we were still eating dessert: *far breton* (a cakelike flan stuffed with brandy-soaked plums), followed by darkly sweet, nutty *mignardises* made from traditional spelt, buckwheat, and chestnut flours.

Although they can't get enough of good conversation at the table, the French only rarely give speeches or toasts. But Eric summoned up the courage to speak in front of the guests. "Wherever you go, and whether or not you return, you all have a little bit of Brittany in you now," he smiled. And we drank a toast: *"Toujours le vin sent son terroir."* Later, as we all walked down to the beach (a family ritual that I much appreciated after hours at the table), Philippe tried to translate this proverb for me. "A good wine smells and even tastes like its *terroir,* the landscape where it was born. And people are the same: where we come from is always part of who we are. No matter where we go, we'll take a little bit of Brittany with us."

Vancouver has a way of buoying your spirits, even when you're in the worst of moods. As we flew over the downtown, ringed by mountains and the ocean, Philippe perked up, likely imagining himself summiting some icy peak. I perked up too, imagining myself eating a fresh warm sesame bagel slathered with cream cheese. Even Sophie cheered up when we visited with her old friends later that week. They were charmed by her French accent, her polished manners, even her clothes: our rapscallion child had been transformed by her year in France into someone straight out of the pages of *Madeline.*

Claire had a harder time. Her wide-eyed looks made it clear that she was completely baffled by the "new" language spoken around her. At least she had stopped scowling and saying "*Non, Maman!*" when I spoke English to her. Listening intently to the foreign sounds everyone was suddenly making seemed to take up all of her energy, and she became intensely clingy. It seemed as if August was going to be another long month.

Even I had a hard time readjusting. I had been longing for the "convenience" of North American–style shopping. But by the time I drove the girls to the supermarket (through traffic much worse than I remembered), found parking, wandered up and down the endless aisles, waited in line, loaded the groceries into the car, and made it home, I was exhausted. Doing my shopping at the *marché*, I realized with chagrin, took me less time—with the bonus of getting exercise, being outside in the fresh air, and socializing with other people.

Plus, the things we bought at the supermarket didn't seem nearly as fresh as in France. Philippe swore (*putain!*) at the smell of the chicken when we unwrapped it. After a year of farm-fresh produce, I was surprised by the slightly unsavory smell, and the overly smooth, slimy skin, like something that had been wrapped in plastic way too long. Cooked, the meat was tasteless and strangely limp. Even the organic chickens had some of the same whiff about them (plus, they were so expensive). Philippe was so put off that he threatened to turn vegetarian, sparking a search for a new supplier. Eventually, we found a local butcher who brought in chickens from a Mennonite farm (their wings, plucked and primly folded, did look as if they were tucked in a little prayer). I realized that I would miss our village *marché* more than I had thought.

Even more surprising were my reactions to the food habits of people around us. I had never noticed the number of people eating while wandering through the streets. Now I found the sight oddly disconcerting. I was surprised to see the slow trickle of children emerging every lunch hour at one of our neighborhood schools to be handed a McDonald's drive-thru takeout meal by their moms (who were comfortably waiting in their idling cars). At work, I was amazed when a colleague entered the room for a midmorning meeting, opened a bag of chips, dumped them on a piece of paper on the table, and calmly announced: "This is my breakfast. Anyone want some?" Our office lunchroom, where I now reheated my homemade, two-course lunch every day, was deserted; people were hunched over their computers eating sandwiches. *Was this how it was before we left?* I wondered. *And how come I never noticed?*

Sophie faced her own challenges at school. She quickly became aware that she didn't eat like the other children. Much of this had to do with snack foods. At first, I didn't want to send her to school with a snack at all, planning to feed her the afternoon *goûter* as usual. But when I picked her up after her first full day of school, she looked wan and upset. "Maman, I'm *huuungry*!" she sniffled. Puzzled, I opened her lunch box: carrot soup in a thermos, baguette and butter, yogurt, and slices of apple. Almost nothing had been touched.

"Why didn't you eat your lunch?" I asked.

"I didn't have enough time," replied Sophie, bursting into tears.

It was true that we had been a bit surprised by the schedule that the school had sent home. They had allocated all of ten minutes for lunch, from precisely 12 noon to 12:10 P.M. This included time for unpacking and packing up. "But *zat ees rrreedeeculous!*" my husband snapped, when I showed him the schedule (his French accent, which I still find unbearably cute, is more pronounced when he's upset).

"How can she possibly manage to eat her lunch in so short a time?" he went on. "She'll be hungry, and she won't be able to concentrate on her schoolwork!" I had a strange sense of déjà vu.

"She'll just have to eat quickly, like everyone else," I said firmly but (I hoped) calmly.

"Humph!" snorted Philippe. "They're training them to rush while eating, and to eat bad-quality lunches at their desks when they grow up. Now I know where these terrible habits come from," he concluded disdainfully.

I agreed with him, but (just as in France) there was not a lot we could do. I had no choice but to relent on our "no snacking" rule. So I started reluctantly sending Sophie to school with snacks. At first, I only provided raw fruit and vegetables. But as Vancouver's cold, wet winter weather arrived, I began to reconsider. Given how little Sophie ate at lunch, she needed more calories, even if she gobbled them at recess in the rain.

Reluctantly, I started sending crackers, and even cookies (having found a source for the lovely little Petit Lu biscuits that had been a favorite back in France). But Sophie came home with a different list: Fruit by the Foot, Oreos, Gummi bears. My refusal to provide these sorts of processed snacks led to fights and resentment; no matter how much I told her she needed to eat healthily, she just wanted to be like the other kids. The only problem was that some of the other kids ate doughnuts for snacks. In frustration, Philippe sat Sophie down in front of the computer and showed her pictures of children with cavities: rotting stumps that impressed Sophie (and us) with their sheer vileness. But she still pestered me for the snacks that other children had. Frustrated, I realized that by banning certain snacks, I was actually inducing cravings for the very same food in Sophie. This seemed to run counter to what I had learned in France.

It didn't help that some of the snacks I preferred to give her instead *were* different. When Sophie invited two classmates over to our house for one of her first play dates, I proudly offered up a French-style *tarte aux pommes,* served in the classic style, with apples carefully arranged in a spiral on the pastry, drizzled with a little lemon and sugar, absent the filling and pastry topping that North American pies usually have. It was greeted with puzzled looks.

"What is this? Apple pizza?" ventured one girl, with that accusatory caution that North American kids so often display around new foods. After some gentle encouragement, she delicately tasted it with the tip of her tongue. The pie, it soon became apparent, didn't pass muster.

"Can I have some Oreos instead?" Oreos had, in fact, made it into our house. I had finally succumbed to Sophie's badgering and bought a box. With great anticipation, she had tucked two cookies into her lunch bag earlier that week. They came home almost untouched after she decided that they were "too sweet." So we had leftover Oreos to share, which the other girls munched happily before leaving the table to play.

I heaved a sigh of relief that my daughter had passed whatever strange social tests six-year-old girls devise for one another and resolved to keep "normal" snacks in the cupboard for just such purposes. And, because I didn't want Sophie to feel that she was denied foods (and thus develop cravings), I started to be more permissive about snacks. But I also encouraged her to develop preferences for relatively healthier options, like squares of dark chocolate (rather than Oreos) or juice-based "natural" gummy bears. I told her about artificial colors and flavors (so that she'd know why I refused to buy her some snacks). With some grumbling, she consented to my "healthy" choices, and I agreed she could have "sweet treats" twice a week at school: granola bars, natural fruit leather, Petit Lu chocolate cookies.

We even agreed to compromise on fast food. I carefully explained why I wouldn't take our family to McDonald's (the fact that my first job as a teenager was a McDonald's cashier gave me some credibility, which I used for all it was worth). I'm not sure that my explanations of factory farming and "fake food" made much headway with Claire, but they certainly impressed Sophie. Instead, we agreed on an alternative fast food: sushi, which is an easy enough choice in Vancouver, with little mom-and-pop sushi restaurants on nearly every block. And I gave permission for Sophie to accept fast-food restaurant invitations from her friends, following the French principle that "it's okay to have treats once in a while." If her friends' parents took her to McDonald's while on a play date, I simply smiled and practiced my Miss Manners rule of "if you don't have anything nice to say . . ." Usually, I simply (and truthfully) observed: "Sophie must have enjoyed her meal." To Sophie, I merely said: "I liked McDonald's too when I was a child. But it's something that you grow out of."

However, we still hadn't solved the school lunch problem. Sophie continued to come home hungry with half-eaten lunches. I pleaded and scolded, and even made special concessions (like slicing all of the crusts off her sandwiches to make them easier to chew). But it didn't make much of a difference. Sophie had been trained to eat slowly and properly. We had instilled the importance of *dégustation* in her, and now it was coming back to haunt us.

"Why don't you just *gobble* your lunch?" I found myself scolding her one afternoon. I couldn't quite believe this came out of my mouth after all the time spent teaching her how to eat mindfully.

"All of the other kids are so messy! I chew slowly, with my mouth closed!!" Sophie wailed. It was true—a year of harping on her eating behavior had paid off, and she was a lot tidier than she had been (although still sometimes a messy eater by French standards). This sometimes posed problems at school. The worst was the infamous Cupcake Episode, which Sophie still remembers. One day, she spent her carefully saved pennies on a luscious cupcake at the school's only bake sale that term. It was crowned with a thick layer of icing and topped with sprinkles. As she tearfully narrated the story to me later that afternoon, she had slowly savored the cupcake, taking little licks of the icing, until the bell rang—lunch was over. Her teacher, seeing the unfinished cupcake, told Sophie she'd "count her down," but hearing the 5 . . . 4 . . . . 3 . . . made Sophie so nervous that she choked, and dropped her beloved cupcake on the floor. It finished in the garbage, and Sophie mourned the lost treat as only a young child can. But she soon learned to gobble her food if need be (although she regularly told us she missed the *cantine* in France, and still managed to "slow food" her breakfasts and dinners at home).

The lost cupcake wasn't the only example of wasteful eating that we encountered. The school didn't have a cafeteria, but it had organized "hot lunches" three days per week. Children were given the option of pizza on Mondays, Subway sandwiches on Wednesdays, and sushi on Fridays. Drinks and food came in individual packaging, necessary because each child got to choose their own toppings (but they got only one choice, which they had to eat every week for four months). We couldn't believe the sheer volume of waste that was generated, particularly given the contrast with France, where everything had been reusable—napkins, tablecloths, cutlery, plates, cups, even the breadbaskets on the tables. This was a side benefit of the French approach that we hadn't thought of: in addition to requiring children to taste a wide variety of dishes and foods, the French approach to eating was much more environmentally friendly.

As the year went on, Sophie grew increasingly sensitive about our attitudes toward the food at school. But we—and Philippe, in particular—didn't hesitate to let her know what we thought. One afternoon, she came home smiling and waving a permission slip. Her class had raised the most money in the school walk-a-thon, and the reward was . . . a trip to McDonald's. Grumbling, Philippe signed the form, but crossed out the "Happy" in "Happy Meal," scrawling *Happy but not Healthy* across the form in large indignant letters.

Claire, meanwhile, was rediscovering the pleasures of snacking. She tucked into the morning and afternoon snacks (up to three servings!) at her new day care with obvious delight. Soon, she began refusing to eat breakfast, passing up my lovingly prepared oatmeal and fresh fruit because she knew that she could eat the early morning snack that would be waiting upon her arrival at day care. And large snacks were often served at 5:00 P.M., right before we picked her up. Claire would fill up and then toy with her food at dinner. I was frustrated, to say the least. But I realized that I wasn't the only one who felt this way after I tried mentioning snacking to a few other parents. So at our next parents' meeting, we politely proposed a solution: only fresh fruit was to be served at afternoon snack, and no snacking after 4:00 P.M. The day care staff was happy to oblige. A large, attractive basket was placed at the entrance next to the sign-in sheet, and parents were encouraged to bring "fresh fruit to share." Claire proudly brought in strawberries, cantaloupe, and even a watermelon.

Lunch was a more difficult challenge. The staff started cooking one hot lunch for children every month. And parents began returning the favor and making meals for the staff (my favorite contribution is homemade apple-rhubarb crumble). But apart from that one day a month, Claire's lunch often came home unfinished. Health regulations (predicated on a fear of food poisoning) prevented staff at our day care from heating up the food brought from home. Hot food could be sent in a thermos, but it would sit for hours before being served—hardly an appetizing option. We were reduced to cold foods, but our choices were limited as the girls weren't used to eating cold foods at lunchtime. They didn't like sandwiches (Claire still won't eat them). And I didn't want to serve them what the other kids seemed to be getting: juice, crackers, and fruit were popular, but hardly a substantial lunch.

Was I the only parent that felt this way? I started striking up casual conversations with other parents at drop-off and pick-up. But

I did so warily. The topic of family food choices, as I found out, is very sensitive. In a culture that associates food with guilt rather than pleasure and focuses on the consequences rather than the experience of eating, people are very ready to take offense. I didn't want anyone to think that I was passing judgment.

My first allies were moms from places like Iran, Italy, China, Brazil, and Spain. They also had traditional food cultures in which lunch was an important meal. From chatting with them, I realized that I wasn't the only parent who despaired at my kids filling up on snacks, eating little at breakfast and less at lunch. In fact, nearly every parent I spoke to who was not from North America felt the same way. We compared notes and found that our kids were having three snacks a day: morning, afternoon, and at pick-up. And most of our kids' food consumption (at least in terms of calories) happened at snacktime rather than mealtime.

Was this the case for most kids? I wondered. *How could we find out?* I didn't relish the thought of hovering outside the day care, canvassing busy parents as they hurried past. But I didn't want to jump to conclusions before going to the day-care manager and suggesting changes to how the children were fed.

Would it be impossible to serve hot meals to the kids, like the French do? I wondered. Each day care (there were over a dozen side by side) had a fully outfitted kitchen, complete with stove and oven. But it was little used—mostly for reheating staff meals or making light snacks such as muffins. *Would it be possible to start a hot lunch program if enough parents were interested?*

"Why don't you do a survey?" suggested Philippe one evening. "It wouldn't be hard to do. There are even free survey websites on line. And that way you'd have more evidence that other parents actually like your idea."

Daunted, but intrigued, I spent the next few weeks drafting questions and immersing myself in the world of online surveys. One month (and several late-night marathon sessions with SurveyMonkey) later, I had produced my first-ever survey: twenty-one questions about what children ate, what parents fed them, and their interest in a hot lunch program. One Friday night shortly after midnight, I blearily clicked the "send" button on my email, sending the invitation to complete the survey out to the parents. *How many people will even bother to respond?* I wondered grumpily, as I got ready for bed, knowing that Claire would likely be up before 6:00 A.M.

I was more than pleasantly surprised when, two weeks later, a grand total of 126 families had completed the survey. The survey had gone viral, circulating through the day-care network. And the answers to my questions were often long, thoughtful, and fascinating. Parents had been invited to respond with three actual menus for what they put in their children's lunch. Pasta was hands-down the overall winner in the menus posted by parents, ranging from the straightforward "Pasta and fruit" to the more adventurous "Pasta, spinach nuggets, kiwi, yogurt." Sandwiches and crackers were close runners-up. Although a few exotic menus stood out (my favorite was "bean/avocado quesadillas, applesauce, red peppers, grapes"), and a few attested to parental culinary devotion ("steamed organic chicken, steamed organic carrots, steamed organic beans, boiled new potatoes, 10%MFG yogurt mixed with organic blueberry puree"), most lunch menus were short and to the point, with none of the elaborate, playful, tempting titles of French dishes at the *cantine*.

I also asked parents their feelings about their kids' lunches and their interest in having a hot lunch program. Reading through the answers, what came through most clearly was parents' fatigue and frustration.

> "Having a prepared hot lunch would be great, especially since our daughter doesn't eat sandwiches (she's two). It would significantly cut down on prep time in the morning and I wouldn't have to worry about food spoiling."

> "I would do anything in order to stop sending these lunch boxes every day . . ."

> "I DON'T HAVE TO TOSS IN BED WORRYING ABOUT WHAT TO PREPARE THE NEXT MORNING."

"I always wish my son could live in Beijing where many quality day cares provide nutritious, tasty food for kids."

When asked about the potential benefits of a hot lunch program, many parents' responses suggested that they had intuitively grasped the food rules that I had seen at work in France:

"I have observed that my child is more willing to try new foods when other children are eating the same thing. She eats things at day care that she would refuse at home!"

"I grew up in Europe and part of the day-care experience was learning to eat with other people and to eat what other people had prepared for us (i.e., we learned to wait for the food to be served, how to say 'No, thank you' instead of 'I don't like that')."

"I come from a country where sharing the food is an essential part of socialization. Each kid eating his/her own meal without sharing disturbs me. It can create jealousy. Mothers also have to face questions like: 'John's mother is nicer than you, she gives cookies and sweet fancy yogurt while you only give bread and plain yogurt,' so that the 'war' against sugar and junk found is really hard to fight!"

"I believe that it is good to learn at that age that a proper meal is something cooked and enjoyed, not a bunch of cold snacks eaten with no pleasure."

And most parents, it seemed, were willing to pay for the hot lunches (one of the issues I had been worried about). One of the questions asked them to calculate how much they were spending on their children's lunches (most people guessed about $3), and the next question asked them how much they would be willing to pay (75 percent of parents were willing to pay $3 per lunch or more). According to the rough calculations I had done, this would be a feasible amount to serve wholesome and nutritious lunches *if* the lunches were mandatory (with few kids, the cost would be too high).

This was the problem. Although three out of every four parents thought that a hot lunch was a good idea, support dropped to just under half if the proposed program was mandatory.

> *"Young children can be picky eaters, so 'one meal for all' can be a hit and miss for some children. And what about food allergies and cultural/ethnic restrictions? I don't think only one option at lunch is sufficient for all children, and some may go hungry."*

> *"We want family food, not institutional food, for our child."*

> *"I would be very resentful if I were compelled to pay for poor-quality, non-organic food with uncontrolled ingredients."*

> *"I am worried about ending up with pizzas and bad-quality macaroni and cheese every day."*

> *"I want to be in control of my child's food."*

Reading this, I started to get discouraged. And I got even more discouraged when I read the responses to the question about what foods parents would *not* let their children eat. Candy, pork, beef, lamb, eggs, chocolate, nuts, ice cream, strawberries, shellfish, meat, pizza, hot dogs, white sugar, peanut butter, cakes, trans fats, any fat, non-organic food, juice, GMOs, tomatoes, MSG, dairy products, and soy were just a few of the things on the very long list of foods that parents would refuse to serve to their children (although one family—but only one—simply responded: "WE EAT EVERYTHING").

It was difficult to see how nutritionally complete, varied menus could be served if people's individual preferences were to be totally respected. The parents I surveyed were apparently as picky as their children. And some people's preferences were diametrically opposed, including ardent pro- and anti-vegetarians, protein fanatics and carb lovers, parents ardently convinced of the importance of hot food, and others who served only cold food to their children at lunchtime. The reality of attempting to serve shared, healthy meals to children in a multicultural environment suddenly hit home.

This is impossible, I thought, my heart sinking. *Parents don't believe that children can learn to eat new things. They want convenience, and they're worried about their children going hungry: they are focused on how much they eat, rather than what they eat. Plus, families have such conflicting food preferences that there is no way to provide satisfying, nutritionally sensible menus for everyone.*

The concept underlying a hot lunch program—the idea that someone other than the parents would control eating and organize the feeding of new foods to their children—seemed to push many parents out of their comfort zones. Preserving individual choice (even if the choice was to eat poor-quality foods with limited variety) seemed, for most parents, to be more important than teaching children to learn to love new foods. I was reminded of the conversation I'd had months before with Philippe's friends. *How can I convince people here that a French approach might work?* I wondered. *In France, I saw the evidence with my own eyes. But here, people have such a hard time believing that there is another way.*

After weeks of thinking about it, I still didn't have an answer. But given that I had put in nearly a month of work, I decided to bring my results to the day-care management anyway. I asked if I could brief the person overseeing the entire day-care network, was given an appointment, and two weeks later dutifully showed up clutching copies of the thirty-two-page report I had prepared, which analyzed the survey results in detail.

Along with a couple of co-workers, the day-care manager and her boss heard me out patiently. I explained that a majority of parents were supportive of a hot lunch program, and I outlined the benefits: less work for parents and better nutrition and food habits for children. Despite the large number of foods on the "do not serve" list that parents had provided, I had managed to come up with a sample set of menus that would, I thought, please everyone, drawing on some of Sophie's school menus in France. A little shyly, I shared some sample dishes (while wryly acknowledging that a year ago I hadn't believed that my children would eat many of these dishes): lentil-apricot soup, apple compote, avocado salad, and green pea risotto.

Silence filled the room as everyone looked through the list. Finally, one staff member put his head up, looked me in the eye, and matter-of-factly said:

"Kids only eat pasta and fishy crackers anyway. Why would you want to cook them all this stuff? It would only get thrown out!"

"But I know that most kids can eat lots of different foods. I've seen it with my own eyes, in France," I said, stung. "At our day care, one of the staff prepared hot meals for the children every day, and they all learned to eat lots of things—like beets!" I added, a bit weakly. I hadn't planned for this kind of challenge; taken by surprise, I couldn't think of very good arguments.

"Um, and the French have food rules for their children. They really work!" I continued, a little more enthusiastically. "Most French kids eat everything, and like it!"

But before I could continue, someone cut in.

"Our staff has advanced training in early childhood education. They are professionals. Cooking is not part of their job description, nor should it be. They are educators, not cooks."

"But isn't teaching children how to eat healthily, a variety of things, a balanced diet, isn't that part of educating them?" I feebly offered. Judging by the looks on their faces, I hadn't convinced anyone.

"It's not in their job description, and it shouldn't be," I was told, politely but firmly.

"Um, we just came back from a year in France, and the day-care workers and teachers there believe that it *is* part of their job description. It's even in the school curriculum," I offered hesitantly. I didn't want to offend anyone, but I really did hope that they might be inspired by the French example.

"That wouldn't work here," was the response. "We're too different."

After that, I didn't have much else to say. The meeting ended quickly, and I left the building in a slight state of disbelief. Even though 75 percent of parents—nearly one hundred families—had supported the idea of a hot lunch, my suggestion had been flatly turned down. I felt a little silly. I was an accidental food activist, and a failed one at that. Who did I think I was, trying to change the world?

Still, I was convinced of the value of the lessons we had learned in France. I had seen with my own eyes that the French approach worked. We couldn't go back to the way we were before. We'd have to figure out how to instill a genuine food culture in our children, even in North America. And parents' beliefs about what foods children could like (hopefully not just pasta and fishy crackers) were the starting point. In thinking about this, I realized there was another rule that I had picked up in France without even being aware of it.

French Food Rule #9:

Eat mostly real, homemade food, and save treats for special occasions.
(Hint: Anything processed is not "real" food.)

This rule, I decided, was key to feeding children well in North America. First, parents had to serve (and eat) real food rather than processed food. Second, they could allow treats but make sure that "real food" was the majority of what their children were consuming. Now, this rule is not an explicit French Food Rule, because so much of what French people eat is, by default, "real food." But, I realized, we needed to have something like this in Vancouver in order to maintain the healthy relationship with food that we had established. And this rule summed up a key aspect of the French approach: that the quality of what kids eat is key to healthy eating. This was a corrective to the bias toward processed foods in North American food culture.

Part of this healthy relationship with food arises in France because of something called *terroir,* a word related to the French word for land (*la terre*). *Terroir* refers to a close relationship between people, their land and climate, and their food. So *terroir* might mean drinking apple cider and eating oysters in Brittany, eating Roquefort or drinking rosé in southern France, or eating moose meat and maple syrup in Canada. French people have strong affinities for local foods—there are many cheeses, for example, that are hard to find outside their home *terroir*. And the French have distinct eating habits in different regions: the *galettes* made from "black flour" (buckwheat) that we ate almost every week weren't found in markets outside of Brittany. Even at the big supermarket where I shopped in France, everything from wine to dairy products was labeled with an *appellation d'origine contrôlée* (AOC)—a "label of origin" letting consumers know where their products came from. My favorite supermarket butter, for example, had hand-dried salt from the French town of Guérande. Jo's favorite steak came from Camargue—a swampy region in southern France renowned for its beef. Janine's favorite lamb was from the *prés salés* (literally, salty meadows) in the bay surrounding Mont Saint Michel, where sheep grazed on grass delicately flavored by tidal waters. Even vegetables could receive the label "AOC," like the *coco de Paimpol* (a savory white bean) that came from a small town west of where we lived, but that was renowned (and sold) all over France. These "labeled" products filled the shelves of the big-box supermarket and weren't much more expensive than "unlabeled" ones.

Food, in fact, is big business in France: as Véronique explained to me, agro-industry is the largest industrial sector (even bigger than the car industry) and the second-largest employer in the country. France has the largest agro-industrial sector in Europe (nearly one-fifth of Europe's total production) and is the world's fourth-largest exporter of agricultural and processed food products (despite being ranked twenty-first in terms of population size). What amazed me was the fact that this highly developed agro-industry coexists with an extensive network of local farmers who live and work on the land in a way that enables local connections between growers and consumers. The French have never forgotten what North Americans are now trying to relearn through school and community gardens or "locavore" initiatives like the 100-Mile Diet. And so their tastes are more demanding, as any visit to a local French market will quickly reveal; the French simply won't buy produce that doesn't taste farm-fresh. The French food system has adapted accordingly. This is another apparent paradox of the French food system: they have a highly modern, efficient food system *and* they get the food they want—tasty, fresh, local.

Learning to know local *terroir*, I decided, was one of the better countermarketing strategies that I could develop with my children. Just before we left, the book *The 100-Mile Diet* had sparked a huge debate about the benefits (and downsides) of eating locally. Reading it, I discovered things I never knew about the region around Vancouver (who knew that we could grow wheat in a rain forest climate?).

Inspired, I sought out local farmer's markets—which (I was embarrassed to admit) we had never visited. We soon became regulars. And I found a little *chocolaterie* (the deliciously named Cocoa Nymph) in our neighborhood, making handmade chocolates—sometimes flavored with local foods in season (like rhubarb, blackberry, or even sorrel). They were expensive, but (just as in France) so rich and delicious that one little chocolate was enough. These became some of our favorite treats for the girls (and for Philippe and me too). For things we couldn't find at the markets, we joined a food coop that was dedicated to distributing local produce to city dwellers. Wednesdays, when the big boxes full of "vegetable surprises" (as Sophie termed them) would be dropped off at our house, quickly became my favorite day of the week.

We also decided to try to introduce the girls to local food through family outings: "close encounters with *terroir*" rather than a trip to the mall on the weekends. We took the girls on "berry walks," amazed at the feast of food along Vancouver's back alleys and woods. August produced a bumper crop of blackberries, which we ate in salads, on top of cereal, even crushed on top of bread as a kind of instant jam. We had missed salmonberry season, but discovered huckleberries (which Claire insisted on calling "blue-bellies," in a strange hybrid of the English "blueberry" and its French translation *bleuet*).

Inspired by our success with berries, we went to watch salmon spawn. Their fierce flopping impressed the girls as much as the watchful eagles and the gorging bears, so assured of a plentiful harvest that they would take only a few bites from each fish before casually flinging the remains into the forest. Inspired, we made our way down to the docks early one Saturday morning, and came home with enough sockeye salmon to fill half of our newly acquired chest freezer. The other half I filled with local fruits—blueberries, plums, and peaches— to last the winter. The money we saved covered the cost of the freezer in the first month.

I even planted a little garden the following spring: raspberries, strawberries, spinach and lettuce, tomatoes, and (daringly) grapes. Given our rather dark, dank, north-facing backyard, my husband scoffed (*none of this will ever ripen!*). But the sight of the girls nurturing "their" plants with their watering cans and their excitement over our (admittedly rather meager) harvest gradually changed his mind. Our "summer salad" snacks—fresh spinach, lettuce, strawberries, and raspberries plucked and eaten right in the garden—have become a family favorite. And, although it took a while, we even eat our own grapes (small, sour, hard grapes the size of big blueberries, but still all ours).

We aren't eating exactly like the French do in France. But then, we don't want to. The essence of the French approach is this: find a balance between the foods available where you are living, your *terroir* and traditional cooking skills, and a schedule that lends itself to mindful cooking and eating. We had found, at least for the moment, that harmonious balance (*juste équilibre*) that is the core principle of French food culture.

10

The Most Important Food Rule of All

Voici mon petit jardin!
(Here is my little garden!)
Adult holds child's hand, palm up

J'y ai semé des graines
(Here I sowed my seeds)
Taps index finger in child's palm

Je les recouvre de terre noire
(I cover them with soil)
Closes child's hand

Voici la bonne et douce pluie!
(Here is the gentle rain!)
Gently taps child's hand with fingers

Le soleil brille dans le ciel!
(The sun shines in the sky!)
Makes a large, sweeping gesture

Et voici une, deux, trois,
(And here are one, two, three,)
Unfolds child's fingers one by one

quatre, cinq petites fleurs!
(four, five little flowers!)

—Traditional French nursery rhyme

So, what have been the results of our ongoing experiment with French food education?

Sophie is now seven, and Claire is nearly four. Tonight's dinner was sole, quinoa, and steamed broccoli, followed by *mousse au chocolat*. They ate it all, happily. The girls now eat a whole host of things they wouldn't touch a few years ago, from grapefruit to granola, tofu to tomatoes. Sophie will even eat cauliflower (although we're still working on Claire). The other day, a neighbor brought over a handful of sweet pea pods from her garden. Claire's face lit up when she tasted them. "They taste as good as chocolate!" she said wonderingly. (No, I am not making this up.)

My daughters have remained more open-minded about food than I had ever expected, given where we were before we moved to France. In fact, we've passed the ultimate hurdle: I'm no longer anxious about bringing our girls to a restaurant with their French relatives.

This has attracted some interest from friends of ours, like the parents of three-year-old Theo, who were worried by his refusal to eat vegetables. After a conversation about the French approach, they tried cutting out his late-afternoon snack, and serving a small bowl of carrot soup as the first course at dinner, which resulted in . . . Theo loving carrot soup. He's now on to spinach soup. *Eureka!*

As for our family, we're managing to observe most of the food rules, most of the time. The most important rule of all is the one about eating together—every day, at least once a day. In the midst of our hectic schedules, our family meal is a haven. We tell stories about our respective days, talk about the future, ask each other questions, wonder out loud. Eating together has allowed us to have conversations we might never otherwise have had. It has helped us to be a happier family.

Most of what we eat is real food. Preparing it takes more time. But I have my personal shortcuts: frozen homemade soups, and the quick versions of French dishes that I learned in France. To my great satisfaction, I can now whip up a delicious quiche in less than five minutes. This is our family's version of "fast food." As this suggests, I still haven't completely managed the "slow food" thing. I still sometimes succumb to the urge to cook as quickly as I can. But I am eating more slowly. I can usually sit through an entire meal (although my husband still sometimes needs to remind me to sit still). I've even found a new favorite restaurant: just down the street is a tiny hole-in-the-wall oasis called the Dharma Kitchen, which "serves the food of mindfulness" (a motto that would have had me steering well clear before our year in France, but that now has me hooked).

Our family has also, more or less, succeeded in removing emotional attachments from food. I no longer use food as a toy, a pacifier, a bribe, a punishment, or a reward (although I admit, from time to time, to using it as a distraction. But only if I really, really need to). We rarely get into power struggles about food with our children. Eating healthily has become part of our routine, just like brushing our teeth. Like the French parents I met, I try to be nonchalant but cheerful about the food I serve my children. I don't hover. I don't prepare special meals. I never substitute. I still coax, but I give it only a few tries. If either Sophie or Claire refuses to eat, I simply remove the food without too much fuss. But I rarely have to do this anymore.

We have also settled into a routine of four square meals per day. Sophie and Claire have accepted that they have to wait for dinner even if they feel a little hungry. And they are usually calm about waiting because they know dinner will be satisfying when it is time to eat. I admire how patient they have become. There is, however, one (big) exception. Because we've found it impossible (and, from a child's point of view, highly unfair) to prevent the girls from snacking at school and day care, we still let them snack like other children during the week. But we don't snack outside of mealtimes on the weekends. In fact, the kids don't ask, except for the inevitable Halloween, Easter, and Christmas candy frenzy. I'm not happy about it, but I tell them that they will eventually outgrow it (and I think they believe me).

What do they snack on? Despite our periodic lessons in *terroir*, the girls have remained predictably focused on the prepackaged, tasty treats that North American society serves up. So we have struck a balancing act. Mostly they go to school with fruits and vegetables for snacks, but once in a while I pop some chocolate-covered Petit Lu cookies into their lunch bags. We've restricted fast food to "days that start with F," but once in a while we have girls-only pizza pajama parties (Philippe, who can cope with only so much girl power, gets a night off). This seems to satisfy everyone; although I keep processed snacks on hand for play dates, the girls are equally happy with buttered bread and pieces of fruit for their afternoon *goûter*.

I admit that our progress hasn't been entirely straightforward. Claire has recently decided she's not interested in lettuce (after eating it happily in the past). I'm hoping that this will pass quickly (like her inexplicable refusal, for an entire month last winter, to eat oatmeal, which she now "loves" again). Sophie still absolutely refuses to eat most cheese (although she now eats grilled cheese sandwiches). And she still sometimes whines when something not to her liking appears on her plate (although she doesn't leave the table anymore). And Philippe and I still often overreact to her whining—but less than we used to. I am sometimes so busy that I fall back into a cooking rut and tend to serve the same dishes more frequently than I would like. So we're not learning "new" tastes at the same rate as we were in France. But the need to do so isn't as great because the girls' willingness to eat things has increased so much.

So we're not eating perfectly. But my time in France taught me to be wary of magic bullets or perfect diets. In fact, the French taught me that food rules can occasionally be suspended. The French love food, but their approach to food education is positive and upbeat because it starts from the "pleasure principle." They don't obsess about calories, and they don't punish their children (or themselves) for liking "bad" food. They're not (with rare exceptions) health nuts. In fact, they believe that it is normal—and even secretly satisfying—to bend or even break the rules once in a while. So they allow their children to do the same. This is so important, particularly in our North American culture of food extremism, that I've named this the Tenth (and Golden) French Food Rule:

French Food Rule #10 (The Golden Rule):
Eating is joyful, not stressful.
Treat the food rules as habits or routines rather than strict regulations;
it's fine to relax them once in a while.

Simply put, this rule means that the French seek to avoid excesses in eating. Excessive control of food and obsession with healthy eating are to be avoided, just as much as indulgent or unrestrained eating of poor-quality food. Both, in fact, are examples of an obsession with food that the French think is unhealthy. Rather, the principles of moderation and balance (*équilibre*) guide the French. This is even true for their own food rules: you have to be moderate in following the rules, not overzealous and strict.

This is the balance we've struck now that we're back in Vancouver. But it is a balance that is admittedly difficult to maintain. In France, schools and governments actively help to create the conditions in which parents can teach their children to eat well. This includes helping children develop good eating habits through positive reinforcement (like the lessons provided during Tasting Week), as well as selective regulations on the production, marketing, and sale of food. The French have created a modern and efficient food system, aligned with an education system, that helps families make good food choices. This isn't the case where we now live.

So it's hard for families to change. However, I'm determined to try. I have started a quiet campaign to have "real" food hot lunches served at Sophie's school, although I have no idea whether or when I'll be successful. But I'm hopeful, because what I saw in France made me realize that *how* our children eat is largely influenced by what and how we *believe* they can eat. And so changing our own attitudes and beliefs can go a long way to helping our families eat better.

What do we believe about kids' food? Many North American parents believe that kids don't like vegetables. We assume that kids don't like spicy foods, flavorful foods, colorful foods, textured foods, strange-looking foods, or new foods. Basically, we believe that kids don't like real food. And we also take it for granted that what kids do like is restricted to an extremely short list, topped by things like pasta, chips, and crackers.

But what if we were to believe the opposite? French parents believe that their children will grow up to eat like they do: to enjoy tasting new foods, to choose a balanced diet, to eat their vegetables uncomplainingly, and to enjoy food—all food—in moderation. French parents and teachers encourage children every step of the way, believing that their children will turn out to be healthy eaters. The French government and schools support parents and teachers with an appropriate curriculum and regulations, in addition to the lessons kids learn from eating healthy school lunches. But the French also know that a true food education starts in the home. And it begins with the belief in your children's innate capacity to eat well and your capacity to teach them to do so.

Alors, bonne chance et bon appétit!

FRENCH FOOD RULES

Rule #1

Parents: <u>You</u> are in charge of FOOD EDUCATION!

2. Avoid emotional eating — ↙ so hard ...

  (NO) food rewards, bribes, etc.

3. Parents ~~plan~~ schedule meals & menus

KIDS EAT WHAT ADULTS EAT!

<u>No</u> short-order cooking!

4. Eat family meals together → no distractions

5. **EAT YOUR VEGGIES**   key: Think "variety"

(6.) | You don't have to **LIKE** it but you **DO** have to **TASTE** it | ↰ Say @ EVERY meal!

7. **NO SNACKING!!** 💡

It's OK to feel hungry between meals!

8. **SLOW FOOD** is ~~good~~ happy food

as in — Eat slow!

9. eat mostly **REAL FOOD**

treats → special occasions – OK

#10
Remember: eating is joyful — **RELAX!**

Tips and Tricks, Rules and Routines for Happy, Healthy Eaters

This section summarizes the French Food Rules together with practical tips to help you foster healthy eating habits in your children, just as the French do: through a combination of rituals and rules, culinary flair and common sense.

Why are food rules useful? First, they simplify life. They create boundaries so that you reduce impulsivity and don't have to rely so much on willpower or imposing parental authority. Second, they create structure because respecting the rules often requires creating routines. This provides children with a sense of security, and if they feel more secure, they are more likely to eat well. Third, these rules provide guidance on regulating your eating habits and on healthy food choices—which is so important, given the fact that North Americans are confronted with an overabundance of relatively cheap, hypermarketed, often unhealthy food. And, last but not least, rules minimize negotiating and arguing with your children (and, if you're like me, with your spouse).

When we were in France, we tried to apply the food rules as French families do. But when we moved back to North America, this wasn't possible. Because our children eat a relatively small, hurried lunch at school, for example, we had to allow more snacking during the day. So we adapted our rules to combine the best of both cultures. French food culture—with its codified common sense and time-tested traditions—is a great basis for family food routines. Their combination of rules and routines with good taste (and their balance of self-restraint and pleasure) is something I want my children to grow up with. But I have shaped these rules to fit North American sensibilities, which prioritize flexibility and respect for individual differences.

So these food rules are not hard and fast. They're more like goals, or habits. And I'm certainly not suggesting that every family should follow the same rules, which might not always be appropriate or even possible. No two families (and indeed no two children) are alike. Rather, my hope is that reading about these rules, and our stories, will trigger insights and intuitions about what might work best for your family.

You can innovate with these rules as much as you like in order to adapt them to your needs. Here's an example from our family. When we returned to Vancouver, our daughters started craving fast food. Our older daughter did everything children do to get their way: pleaded, begged, moped, stamped her feet. So we put a House Rule in place: Our family only eats fast food on days that start with "F." And in our case, fast food means the little sushi restaurant down the street (admittedly easy in our city, where every second restaurant is a mom-and-pop-style sushi place). This doesn't mean that other fast food, such as pizza, is totally forbidden, but rather that it is a once-in-a-while treat.

French Food Rule #1:
Parents: You are in charge of your children's food education.

How should parents handle feeding their children? Research suggests that *authoritative* (rather than authoritarian) feeding has positive results. For example, kids who have authoritative parents are more likely to eat more vegetables and to have a healthier weight. In contrast, children whose parents are overly controlling tend to be *less* eager to taste new foods and *less* able to effectively regulate their own eating habits.

I had a hard time getting my head around this food rule at first and instead veered between being authoritarian and indulgent. Often my children totally controlled the feeding situation, and in order to deal with this I overreacted and became overly controlling myself. Then I felt guilty, started to indulge them, and the cycle started all over again. But after watching the French in action, I realized that there is another way: I could be authoritative, rather than indulgent or controlling. ("Think of it like being a tabby cat mom rather than a tiger mom," my husband suggested, "and you'll have it just about right. You'll cuddle up and purr if all is going well, but won't hesitate to [gently] show your claws if someone is out of line.")

So what is authoritative parenting? An authoritative parent is kind but firm. An authoritative parent sets clear limits for children's behaviors, within which they respond to children's needs. And an authoritative parent sets clear goals—and then helps children reach them. The goal of authoritative parenting is the development of healthy eating habits in your children: helping them learn to prefer healthy food choices, to eat appropriate portion sizes, to be responsive to their own hunger cues (and feelings of fullness) to determine how much they eat. The goal is to educate children to be self-confident eaters who eat a wide variety of foods, who are comfortable trying new things, and who know how to balance self-restraint with pleasure. In other words, the goal is not to control what they eat, but to teach them *how* to eat well. French parents do this with flair, and I've seen their children grow to develop a healthy love of food—all food.

Rule #1 Tips for Authoritative Family Food Lessons

- Healthy eating is about *how, when,* and *why* you eat, as much as it is about *what* you eat.

- Create House Rules about food, and stick to them. For example, kids always have permission to reach for a piece of fruit but have to ask permission for anything else.

- Give your children simple choices about vegetables (eggplant or spinach this evening?), but don't let them plan your menus or ask them to make all of the choices. Fear of new foods is heightened when children are confronted with choice. And young children don't usually know enough about nutrition to consistently create appropriately balanced meals.

- Be firm rather than hesitant when serving meals. Rather than "Are you going to come eat now?" try saying "It's time to eat now." Rather than "Will you try this?" try a warm but firm statement like: "Here's the delicious dish that I prepared for us."

- Kids do as we do, rather than as we say. Model positive eating behaviors. If parents eat well, chances are that children will too.

French Food Rule #2:

Avoid emotional eating.
*Food is **not** a pacifier, a distraction, a toy, a bribe,*
a reward, or a substitute for discipline.

French kids, like their parents, rarely eat for what psychologists and nutritionists term "non-nutritive" reasons. In other words, they are not emotional eaters. This is in part because French adults aren't either. Although they love to provide tasty treats for their children, they don't tend to do so in response to children's emotional needs. They wouldn't offer a candy to an upset child, or a whiny child, or a bored child.

Here, as in many things, modern science has verified the wisdom of the French approach. Scientists have found (surprise!) that using specific food as a reward for good behavior increases children's preferences for those foods; and because unhealthy foods are often used as a reward, children are being taught to prefer them. Why not give an apple, rather than a candy, to reward a child? Even better, do as the French do—don't use rewards at all.

Many of the other rules listed here (like scheduling meals, eating a variety of foods, and teaching children to be open to new foods) will also help avoid emotional eating. Think of other ways to soothe or reward your children, and they will, in turn, learn how to regulate their own emotions without the use of food.

Rule #2 Tips for Avoiding Emotional Eating

- Teach your children to seek out good foods (rather than avoiding "bad" foods). The difference is subtle but important.

- Teach your children that while food is a source of pleasure, eating should not be emotionally driven. For example, don't give a child candy as a reward or as solace for hurting themselves. If you feel you need to comfort your kids with food, offer an easily accepted fruit (like an apple) or vegetable.

- Encourage children to focus on food as a source of sensory pleasure. The French do this through describing food (which is a form of food education that involves all of the senses). Teach children to use words to describe food. Rather than saying "it's good" or "it's bad," ask them to describe the sensations. "It's dry." "It's spicy." "It's soft (or hard)." Ask them, "How does it feel on your tongue?" "How does it feel when you swallow it?" (Note: Sensory education [how food tastes, feels, smells, looks, and sounds] works best with young children. Save nutritional education for older children.)

- Try "logical consequences" rather than punishments. "First we eat our vegetables, then we eat dessert." Note that framing dessert as a reward ("Eat your vegetables, or you won't get dessert") may encourage children to devalue or even dislike vegetables. Instead, French parents establish a logical sequence for meals, which creates an easy routine of "first this, then that."

- Most American parenting books focus on food *supply,* emphasizing nutrients and energy to support growth and development. French parents focus on *demand.* Their goal is to teach children how to enjoy healthy food, so that they ask for it themselves when they're older. If they associate food with rewards or punishments, they're less likely to do so.

French Food Rule #3:
Parents schedule meals and menus.
Kids eat what adults eat: no substitutes and no short-order cooking.

French kids are just like their parents: they love to celebrate food, but at the same time they are expected to follow a schedule and show self-restraint regarding what, when, and how much they eat (especially treats). This applies even to the littlest of kids. The majority of French children eat no more and no fewer than three meals per day, with the largest meal (up to 40 percent of daily caloric intake) being eaten at lunch. Most people eat at the same time of day, all over the country: 7:30 for breakfast; 12:30 for lunch; 7:30 for dinner. They don't skip meals because food is a priority—often *the* priority of the day. This is especially true for lunch, but it is also true for other meals: 90 percent of the French but only 50 percent of Americans eat breakfast seven days a week.

This rule about scheduling meals may be hard for North Americans to accept. Scheduling meals sounds authoritarian. It sounds overly strict. It sounds, to be frank, kind of mean. What could be crueler than denying food to a hungry child? But the point is that French children don't usually feel that hungry between mealtimes because they eat so well *at* mealtimes. And some scientific research does show that children will regulate food intake at meals accordingly, depending on what they are fed, and when mealtimes are scheduled.

In my experience, French kids' stomachs have been trained to expect food at certain times; in between, they have been trained to happily sit and wait. Yes, I am saying that French children eat less often but also feel hungry less often. If it seems contradictory, remember that French kids don't really get that hungry because they eat reasonably sized portions at regular times with a balanced menu at each meal. And they eat high-satiety foods, so they feel satisfied for a long time.

One final point: Scheduling meals does not mean that there is a "one size fits all" approach to eating. Rather, implementing this rule means thinking about what schedule best suits your family, given your goals. Maybe your goal is to have your children eat more of the healthy food you serve at dinnertime rather than filling up on snack food. Or maybe your goal is to stop your children's demands (and your concessions) for fast-food "treats." Or maybe (like us, at the moment) your goal is to make sure everyone eats a good breakfast rather than a midmorning snack. If a schedule will help you to meet your goals, then use one.

Rule #3 Tips on Meal Scheduling and Choice

- Decide on a set time for at least one sit-down family meal per day (like dinner). Set the table (this is a good chore to assign!), and keep mealtime as structured as possible.

- Make sure there is always one thing on the table your child likes. Other than this, kids eat what adults eat. This means no substitutes. It also means an end to being a short-order cook. Yes, this does mean that your children may leave the table hungry now and then (but they won't starve). The French believe that they'll simply eat more at their next meal.

- Take a look at your schedule, including kids' extracurricular activities. Is your busy lifestyle preventing you from eating proper meals? Being able to manage one's schedule in order to make sufficient time for healthy eating is an important skill to teach your children.

- Offer choice within appropriate boundaries. For older children, set up weekly menus like a "food contract." Or offer menu options for the week. Once decided, the menu is fixed.

- Don't force children to finish everything on their plates. Serve smaller portions and allow them to ask for more if they want. Children who retain a sense of control over eating are healthier eaters as adults.

French Food Rule #4:
Food is social.
Eat family meals together at the table, with no distractions.

The French believe that eating is innately social. The family meal is a daily ritual that cements the bonds of French families. Now, the fact that food is social doesn't only mean that you need to eat together. It also means interacting, learning, and sharing ideas. Family meals are moments during which French children learn about the world (through hearing the stories their parents tell) and where they learn important social skills (how to argue without offending someone, how to ask good questions, how to wait your turn to speak). This is why conversation is so important at French meals.

Eating together also means that food choices are not solely a matter of individual preference. Specifically, parents expect that children will learn to be comfortable with eating a variety of foods. This is crucial, French parents believe, for instilling a healthy relationship with food in young children (starting with babies). Expressing individual food preferences is bad manners in France. So, from an early age, French children sit down with their parents to eat, and everyone eats the same thing, which has an important effect on kids' tastes. This is partly true because most French adults tend to eat healthy meals, with "real" (rather than processed) food. It is also true because children are more likely to try a new food if an adult tries it first.

Now, eating together doesn't mean eating *anything* together. If we want children to learn to like and eat healthy foods, they need repeated, positive, and early experiences with those foods, as well as lots of chances to watch others consuming those foods. Kids do as we do, rather than as we say. So model healthy eating and positive food attitudes yourself.

Rule #4 Tips on Eating Together

- Eating is more than an essential physical act. It should also be a shared social event, in which children experience a sense of pleasure, discovery, and well-being.

- No TV, radio, phones, or other electronic devices: mealtime is family time.

- Meals are moments during which children get your undivided attention. How much misbehavior at the table is simply attention-seeking?

- Conversation can capture your children's attention, keep them at the table, and put them in a positive frame of mind for eating. As soon as my children sit down, I sit with them and start talking.

- Create rituals. One of our favorites is asking each person in turn to tell a story about his or her day.

- Ask grandparents (or other elders) to get involved. They often have the time and skills and are only too willing to share.

- Older children who like to eat well have a magical influence on my children. Invite them to dinner, and see if positive peer pressure works!

- Prime the pump: include a little something that your children like with the meal.

French Food Rule #5:
Eat vegetables of all colors of the rainbow.
Don't eat the same main dish more than once per week.

Kids all over the world—and the French are no exception—naturally prefer sweet or salty, calorie-rich foods. The problem today is that our culture supplies a glut of these foods, and our eating habits and parenting routines aren't designed to cope. So adults need to guide children in developing healthy eating routines in and outside the home.

This is where variety comes in. We all know that eating a variety of whole foods is important. But how do you get your kids to do so? The French answer is: nutritional literacy. Children, in their view, should learn the basics that set them up for life: how to read, how to do basic math, and how to eat. So teaching children to like eating a variety of foods, and to be open to trying new foods, is one of the most important parenting tasks. And early childhood is the critical phase for learning to eat well, especially before the age of two, when children are more likely to be open to trying new things. (Don't worry if you're starting later: I started when my children were five and two, and the French approach has still worked for us. But if you're starting earlier, so much the better.)

French parents believe that children's tastes are very adaptable; taste is acquired rather than innate, and can be learned (and taught). Adults' job is to help children grow out of juvenile tastes and to help them develop their tastes to mature. From the French point of view, neophobia is a stage of development through which children should move fairly quickly. If you cater to children's limited food preferences, the French believe, children get "stuck" developmentally. This is where Rule #5 comes in.

Rule #5 Tips on Eating a Variety of Healthy Foods

- Make variety fun! Try "taste training" with your children. Encourage them to move beyond judging food by its color or appearance—and use their other senses to assess foods. The "stuff sack" is one game played in French schools: place a "mystery food" in a bag, and allow children to feel it, then guess what it is. The results will often surprise adults as well as kids. Or try taste-testing blindfolded. Adults participate too!

- Create your own Family Food Rule for variety: We won't eat the same thing more than _____ every _____. For example, we try not to eat the same dish more than once per week.

- Build variety on top of what kids already like. If they enjoy one type of cheese, try others. If they like pasta, serve it tossed with broccoli one day, spinach leaves the next.

- North America's multiethnic melting pot makes a wonderful variety of cuisine easily available to us (which isn't always the case in France). Why not try a new type of cuisine as a family? Mildly spiced Indian food, Chinese food, and Thai food are usual kid favorites.

- Introduce variations on your children's favorite dishes. Try pasta with olive oil one time, canola oil the next, and butter the next. Or try store-bought grated cheese, then grate your own Parmesan with your child. Sprinkle a bit of parsley on cooked carrots one night, and a bit of dill the next. The options are endless, and all of them help teach your children that variety is okay.

- Don't disguise or hide variety: make "healthy" foods obvious and appealing. Try making little "happy face" plates (I often do this with two tomatoes for eyes, half a grape for a nose, an apple slice for the mouth, grated carrots for the hair) to serve at the start of a meal.

- What do you do if your child resists variety on the plate (e.g. if he or she is fussy about multiple foods, or about foods touching)? Encourage your child, gently, to grow out of this habit. Try combining two ingredients they like. Or let them do it themselves, using this method: at a moment when your child is calm and ready to eat (hungry, but not too hungry), place two complementary foods in two separate bowls in front of them (e.g. yogurt and jam, or pasta and cheese). Give them a third, empty bowl, and encourage them to mix the ingredients themselves. You might want to model the same mixing exercise yourself with your own bowls and see if they follow your lead.

French Food Rule #6:

For picky eaters: You don't have to like *it, but you do have to* taste *it.*
For fussy eaters: You don't have to like *it, but you do have to* eat *it.*

A lot of parenting advice in North America sets up a division of labor between parents and kids. According to this view, parents decide when to eat and what is served; kids decide whether and how much to eat. The French view on this would be mildly skeptical. Their view (and one that is backed up by scientific research) is that children need to be firmly encouraged to try new things. Most children have to taste (rather than simply see) new foods to begin liking them. Research shows that it will take them up to a dozen or more tastes before they consent to eat something new. This is normal: don't rush to make assumptions about your child's food preferences after only a few tries. Many parents often give up after only a few attempts. And don't be surprised if children "like" something one day but then refuse it the next. It's all part of the learning process.

Rule #6 Tips for Trying New Foods

The goal is for your children to be curious and comfortable with trying new foods, and to be able to politely decline eating them. Staying calm around new foods is a skill they should be learning, as well as the ability to experiment with tasting and eventually eating them.

- Start early. Many babies and toddlers are very open to new tastes. Take advantage of this, before neophobia (fear of new foods) sets in at age two or three.

- Children shouldn't be forced to eat (or, even worse, to clean their plates) but simply to taste the things that are served.

- "Taste this, you'll like it" works better than "Eat this, it's good for you."

- If your children don't like something, encourage them to believe that they eventually will. "Oh, you don't like it?" I'll say to my children. "That's okay. You just haven't tasted it enough times yet. You'll like it when you grow up."

- Don't serve the new food in isolation. Serve it as part of an enjoyable meal. Make sure there is at least one thing that your child likes on the table.

- When encouraging children to try new foods, serve small portions of new things. This may work better than larger portions.

- Don't offer new foods unless you are in a sufficiently relaxed mood, and sufficiently attentive and available, to make the experience pleasant for both you and your child.

- Try simple textures. We often introduce new foods in purees or soups, even for our older daughter. Children get used to the taste and can then move on to the "real" texture of the food.

- Some children truly have more sensitive taste buds. Be patient with your child's progress; it may take over a dozen tastes before a child will eat something new.

- Try an indirect, low-pressure way of offering a new food. Place a little plate with a small portion of the new food on the table, near but not directly in front of your child. Taste a piece or two, with clear enjoyment. Then leave it. Chances are, your child will pick up a piece and try it. If not, remove anything your child has not eaten after a short while, without a fuss. Above all, don't substitute with anything else.

- When trying to introduce a new food to toddlers, don't present new foods in too many different ways. Finding the right balance between novelty and familiarity will reassure your toddler. For example, if you have successfully introduced a new food, serve it the same way once or twice more. But then try serving it a different way, so that you don't get "stuck" with only one rigid recipe.

French Food Rule #7:
Limit snacks, ideally one per day (two maximum),
and not within one hour of meals.
In between meals, it's okay to feel hungry.
At meals, eat until you're satisfied rather than full.

One of the food rules that the French are most fervent about is the "no snacking" rule. The official French Food Guide advice is that adults should eat three times per day, period. And children should eat four times per day, period. This is how North American children used to eat in the 1970s, when most of today's parents were born. Today, in contrast, American kids eat nearly three snacks per day, and one in five children eats up to six snacks per day.

Now, there is no scientific consensus on how often you should eat per day. Some experts advise three meals per day. Some advise more. Scientists still debate whether it is better to graze (several small meals throughout the day) or eat "three square meals per day." And there is no consensus about the timing of meals and the distribution of calories across those meals (Is it better to have a big lunch? A big dinner?). Basically, science doesn't provide definitive answers on snacking. The French compromise is to schedule three meals and one big snack per day. This gives kids the benefits of snacking while minimizing the potentially negative effects. These benefits are psychological as well as physical: if parents allow kids to eat whenever they want, French parents believe, they fail to learn self-control, and risk filling up on unhealthy foods.

The French are also cautious about grazing. Unscheduled, any-time-you-like grazing only works for people who have a keen sense of their own feelings of hunger and fullness. Helping your children to develop this sense probably means minimizing their snacks—both in volume and in the amounts consumed. The "no unscheduled snacking" rule also helps teach your kids to avoid eating for emotional reasons (like boredom). Plus, your children will eat better at mealtimes because they will have better appetites. And remember, scheduling snacks is not about deprivation, but rather about moderation.

Kids tend to self-regulate the total calories they eat over the course of a day. So if they don't eat a lot at breakfast, they'll have a bigger midmorning snack. Or if they eat lots at after-school snack, they won't have a big dinner. The goal of scheduling (or reducing) snacks is to have most food consumption happen at mealtimes—when the foods are likely to be healthier.

Rule #7 Tips on Snacking

- Teach your children the difference between feeling *satisfied* and feeling *full*. Encourage them to stop eating when comfortably full (but not stuffed). Most young children have a natural "fullness feeling" to which they are sensitive, so don't push them to override and suppress this.

- To encourage children to tune into their body, ask them: "Tell me when you are feeling half full? Nearly full?" Encourage them to stop at that point, pause for a minute or two, and then ask whether they'd like more.

- Think of snacks like mini-meals: they should be mostly made of healthy, unprocessed foods, just like at (say) dinnertime. Snack only at the table.

- Create a snacking rule that suits your family: for example, children never have to ask to reach for a piece of fruit, but they do have to ask permission for anything else.

- If your child doesn't eat much at one meal, advance the timing of the next meal rather than giving an extra snack.

- Water, for the French, is like a food group. Drink water at snacktime. Teach your children to distinguish between feelings of thirst and feelings of hunger.

- Keep a family food diary for a week, and track what your children are eating, and how much. Take a look at the results. Should you rebalance snacks and meals? Should you eat more of some foods, and a little less of others?

French Food Rule #8:
Take your time, for both cooking and eating.
Slow food is happy food.

French parents train their children to be "mindful eaters." This is basic psychology for the French, who teach kids to learn how to link the "feed me" messages from our stomachs with the decision-making "controls" in our heads, so that kids (like adults) only eat until they are satisfied (not necessarily full).

French kids are also taught all of the commonsense things we know (but often forget): eat slowly; pay attention to what you are eating (which means don't do anything else, like watch TV, drive, or read); serve smaller portions. Even if they don't learn these things at home, they learn them at school, where these rules are applied every day in the *cantine*. These, I realized, were the things I really needed to teach my children.

American kids, in contrast, get used to super-sized portions at an early age. They live in a culture of overeating, of food as fuel, of eating-on-the-go, which creates a vicious cycle in which impulsive eating of calorie-rich but unsatisfying foods propels people into further eating in order to satisfy their cravings. And ever-increasing serving sizes in restaurants and bigger containers at the supermarket also encourage us to overeat. The result, as nutritionists warn, is that children's "physiological basis for eating is becoming deregulated" in many countries.

An easy way to correct this is to eat more slowly. That way, your brain has time to catch up with your stomach. As soon as my children sit down at the table, I sit down with them and start a conversation or a story. This captures their attention (so they are more likely to want to stay sitting at the table) and usually puts them in a better mood (so they are more open to eating). Plus, it relaxes me too—which is really important after a long day at work. After having children, dinnertime used to be the highest-stress part of my day; now, my new goal is to make it a moment of relaxation. (I admit we don't always achieve this goal, but it's one worth having!)

Rule #8 Tips on Creating a Happy, Relaxed, Eating Atmosphere

- Children are naturally slow eaters. Slow down your eating to their pace, just as you slow down your walking pace.

- Encourage (and model) food choices based on maintaining good health and pleasure, rather than focusing on fears of being overweight. Being positive about food will have better results in the long run.

- Praise those who eat well rather than punishing those who don't.

- Don't create a negative emotional setting (pressure, demands to hurry, criticism, tension).

- Make the table festive. Use an "every day" tablecloth, and get the kids to help decorate it. Use your imagination!

- Don't be anxious: don't hover, don't worry, don't get irritated, remain calm. (I have a hard time with this one.) Relax and enjoy and your kids will too.

French Food Rule #9:

Eat mostly real, homemade food, and save treats for special occasions. (Hint: Anything processed is not "real" food.)

Ellyn Satter, one of America's best-known writers about children and food, argues that parents should help their children become "competent eaters." This is another way of thinking about the French Food Rules: they develop competence. But the French also emphasize the importance of pleasure (not unrestrained pleasure, not gluttony, but rather simple, sensual enjoyment) and balance, both nutritional and psychological. Eating too much, or too little, is a sign that something is out of balance. Gaining too much pleasure from food, or too little, is also a sign that something is out of balance. Eating only "super-healthy" food, or only junk food, is also a sign of imbalance.

By practicing moderation, and by following routines and rules that they know will help them eat a nutritious, balanced diet, the French are free to focus on enjoying themselves. Note that this does *not* mean that the French deprive themselves of treats. On the contrary, they believe that allowing moderate consumption of treats helps everyone (not just children) develop a healthy, balanced attitude toward food.

Rule #9 Tips on Eating "Real Food"

- Only eat fast food on days starting with F. (For a while, my husband succeeded with this variation: "Only eat fast food on days starting with Z." But that only worked until Sophie learned how to spell the days of the week in both languages.)

- Fill your kids up with real food before they are served treats. For example, serve fresh fruit after the main course and before sweetened desserts.

- Try just a dot of butter, rather than ketchup, on vegetables. Fat is an essential nutrient (everyone needs it in small quantities), and the French believe that butter (in moderation) is best! Plus, kids have fun watching it melt!

- Limit junk, fast, and "fake" foods to a once-per-week treat.

- The average French household spends one-quarter of its food budget (excluding desserts) on vegetables. What would your weekly menus look like if you did that?

- If your children like a food that you consider unhealthy, don't try to talk them out of liking it. Instead, tell them: "That's for kids. You'll grow out of liking that as you grow up."

French Food Rule #10:
Eating is joyful, not stressful.
Treat the food rules as habits or routines rather than strict regulations;
it's fine to relax them once in a while.

A "food rule" sounds a bit ominous to North American ears. It implies exerting control over someone (or something). But the French don't view it that way. They view rules as the basis for good habits and routines. The goal of "food rules" is not to police children's eating. Rather, the goal is to help your children acquire healthy food beliefs and eating habits for themselves.

In fact, some research has shown that overly controlling ("authoritarian") parenting styles can backfire. Forcing children to clean their plate, for example, can disrupt children's own internal cues and responsiveness to feelings of hunger and fullness—literally teaching them how to overeat. Forcing them to eat their vegetables may actually increase dislike of those vegetables and reduce their willingness to accept new foods; studies have shown that children of strictly controlling parents actually eat fewer vegetables and more high-fat foods. And strictly serving only healthy, low-fat foods can create preferences for high-fat foods. Studies of adolescent girls, in particular, suggest that parental pressure is associated with the emergence of unhealthy eating behaviors—precisely the results that worried parents *don't* want.

A simple way to check whether you're on the right track or not is to ask yourself whether what you're doing will create long-term anxiety for your children. French parents believe that healthy eating habits can be achieved without anxiety. Food is a source of pleasure rather than worry. This comes as a surprise to many Americans. For us, eating is often anxiety-ridden: after all, eating can make you sick or make you healthy. So we tend to focus on nutrition and vitamins, and take a quasi-medical view of food. For the French, eating is about enjoyment: food is one of life's shared pleasures. They don't count calories (certainly not for their children), but rather have an intuitive sense of a balanced, reasonable diet.

Yes, this seems contradictory (and somehow unfair). We worry more, and we eat less well. The French worry less, and eat much better. But if you remember the "food is fun" principle, it all makes sense. This philosophy also applies to the food rules: don't worry if they get bent or broken once in a while. Think of them as routines that your family usually (but perhaps not always) follows, and you'll be on the right track, because nobody is perfect, *n'est-ce pas*?

French Recipes for Kids
Fast, Simple, Healthy, and Tasty

The simplicity of these recipes may surprise you. Most French families don't eat Cordon Bleu cooking every night and don't spend hours slaving over the stove. Ordinary French families make dishes that are tasty and healthy while still being simple to make, which I very much appreciate as a full-time working mom with no help at home. So these recipes are quick and easy, with an average of four main ingredients per dish.

There is another advantage to simple recipes: they awaken children's interest in food without overpowering their taste buds. So when making meals for their children, French families don't overseason. They typically use just a small number of seasonings, like butter, fresh herbs, and lemon juice. The natural tastes of foods are the focus. In fact, this is one of the central principles of French cuisine: the preservation of natural flavors and textures.

There is also a practical reason for this simplicity: because most children eat their largest meal of the day at school, and a majority of French mothers work outside the home and have relatively little time to cook in the evenings, they choose recipes that are quick to prepare and that are light rather than heavy. The classic sauces that made French cuisine famous, for example, are rather rich and time-intensive, so they aren't suitable for everyday evening meals. In its use of fresh ingredients, and its simplicity, French family cooking is closer to *nouvelle cuisine* than the heavy, sauce-rich *haute cuisine* for which French chefs gained a global reputation in the past.

The French are also minimalist when it comes to equipment. You won't need any fancy utensils or machines. Steaming is the cooking method of choice for vegetables, either with a pressure-cooker (*cocotte-minute*) or a simple steamer that is placed inside an ordinary pot. A handheld blender ("wand") to puree soups and vegetables is convenient, but a countertop blender will work just as well. I still swear by the BabyCook, which steams and blends in one unit. Every French family we knew had one.

Since so much emphasis is on the taste of the foods themselves, seeking out high-quality, fresh ingredients is worth your while. According to the Harvard Center for Health and the Global Environment, foods that have been locally grown tend to have higher nutritional value. Local producers also tend to select varieties for taste rather than for production value or durability for transport. This is why the French continue to seek out local markets for their vegetables, fruits, and even meats.

A comment about butter is necessary, given that it appears in many of the recipes in this book. Those so inclined should feel free to substitute vegetable oils. But my personal preference is still to use butter. The French have never really believed that butter is bad for you. In fact, it's relatively rare to find French families who eat margarine, as they tend to reject the artificial taste and are wary of anything that has been overly processed. The French have always believed what nutritional science has now confirmed: a small amount of fat is nutritionally essential even for adults and is critical for the proper development of growing children. However, as with any fat-rich foods, the French are judicious in their use of butter. So use it sparingly, and enjoy!

Similarly, salt is optional in all of the recipes. Traditional nutrition advice for young babies emphasizes the dangers of habituating them to too much salt too early. So I never salt my baby purees or vegetable soups. For older children and adults, I find that a small dab of salted butter on top works wonders—the salt is noticeably tasty, but I've used a minimal quantity. This, in fact, is my general philosophy for children's food. If I salt it at all, I sprinkle the smallest bit of salt on the dish when it is already served, just before eating. You'll be using less salt, for better taste results. I use fine sea salt, as it dissolves more slowly and has a rounder, fuller taste.

Finally, a word about presentation. The French know that *how* food looks influences our desire to eat it. Small portions are usually more attractive to children; I find that it is better to serve a small amount and allow a child to ask for a second helping than to serve a large amount that is off-putting. Try using small ramekins or small bowls to encourage reluctant kids. If you don't have these, try using other small containers—like egg cups or custard cups (small Pyrex dishes)—in which vegetables, dips, and purees can be individually served; some children find that this makes eating more fun. And remember to serve something your children like at most meals, which will tend to reassure them and make them more willing to try new things. Most important, try to enjoy eating yourself; in eating, as in so many things, our children often do as we do, rather than as we say.

Bon appétit!

List of Recipes

Sophie's Spinach Surprise

Preparation: 2 minutes
Cooking: 3 minutes
Servings: 6 to 8 "baby jar"–size servings, or four
  children's servings

We devised this simple recipe in order to encourage our daughters to get used to eating green-colored food. Both of them still love this dish, even though they both eventually graduated to other green vegetables.

This dish is mild and incredibly smooth and is an easy way to introduce your children to green vegetables. The zucchini provides a light, almost fluffy, melt-in-your-mouth texture, so that the spinach tastes airy and almost sweet. If you think the dish is still bitter (although I never do), add a tiny bit of honey before serving (or reduce the proportion of spinach to zucchini).

Serve in a small bowl; I find that a little goes a long way with this puree. Top it with tiny dabs of butter in the form of a happy face; your children will love to watch them melt.

1 medium-to-large zucchini, peeled and chopped (2 cups)
1 cup water
2 or 3 big handfuls of baby spinach leaves (about 1 cup,
  tightly packed)
Optional: 1 teaspoon butter and, if the spinach is slightly
  bitter, a small spoonful of honey

1. Place the zucchini in the bottom of a pot with 1 cup of water (not too much!). Bring to a boil over high heat, lower the heat, and simmer until the zucchini becomes transparent, about 2 minutes. Immediately add the spinach leaves, letting them wilt for a minute or so. Don't overcook the spinach! Drain the vegetables, saving the cooking water.

2. Remove the pot from the heat and blend until perfectly smooth, using as much cooking water as necessary to achieve the desired consistency.

Tip: This dish freezes wonderfully well and reheats quickly. But you may want to add a little water when reheating, as it tends to thicken slightly after being frozen.

Baby's Vichyssoise (White Leek Soup)

Preparation: 5 minutes
Cooking: 7–8 minutes
Servings: 4 "baby jar"–size servings, or two children's servings

Leeks are traditionally introduced to French children at a young age. Mild yet savory, young white leek tips (the only kind you should use for this soup) are more digestible than their older, greener versions. For older children, increase the amount of potato and decrease the amount of pear, creating a potato-leek soup that is similar in spirit to the classic French vichyssoise.

This soup has become comfort food for us, and we often serve it on cold winter evenings. In the summer, it can be eaten at room temperature or even chilled.

1 small potato, peeled and diced small (about ½ cup)
2 small (or 1 large) leeks, washed carefully, peeled, and sliced
    (use white stems only) (about 1 cup)
1 pear, peeled, cored, and chopped
1 teaspoon honey or maple syrup
Optional: pinch of fine sea salt

1. Steam (if you have a pressure-cooker) or simmer the potato and leek in water to cover (about 1½ cups) until tender (6 to 7 minutes), adding the pear in the last 2 to 3 minutes. Drain, saving the cooking water (you'll need between ¾ and 1 cup).

2. Blend the vegetables with honey (or maple syrup), adding cooking water until the desired consistency is achieved.

Note: For younger babies, you can eliminate the potato. They will love the pear-leek combination all by itself (it has the consistency of applesauce).

Tip: Too much potato will overpower this soup, making it bland. Big chunks of potato may lead to a "gluey" mixture, so chop finely and don't overcook.

Claire's Beet Puree

Preparation: 5 minutes
Cooking: 10 minutes
Servings: 8 "baby jar"–size servings, or 4 children's servings

This recipe gently introduces your baby to beets, which are a favorite vegetable of French kids. The first time we encountered beet puree was at Claire's day care, where it was served perched on top of puff pastry (and where one of my first French food faux pas was to mistake it for a sophisticated adult hors d'oeuvre). Beet puree became a favorite item on the day-care menu, although it was usually served warm in little bowls. I also began serving this at home, and it became one of our family's favorite dishes.

As French children grow older, they graduate to eating cooked beets, which are regularly served at home and in schools, eaten in small chunks as part of a cold salad, topped with chopped parsley and a classic homemade vinaigrette dressing (see page 248).

This recipe has a mild flavor, and babies love the bright pink color. The zucchini lends a light, airy taste. This helps make the beets more palatable and digestible. Over time, you can reduce the proportion of zucchini and increase the proportion of beets. But don't serve this to babies younger than twelve months, as beets (like other root vegetables) can occasionally be high in soil compounds such as nitrates that only older tummies can handle.

1 *medium beet, peeled and diced (about 1 cup)*
2 *medium zucchini, peeled and chopped, seeds intact (about*
   3 cups)
1 *tablespoon butter*

1. Place the beets in a small pot with water to cover and simmer over medium heat until tender, adding the zucchini in the last 3 or 4 minutes. Simmer until the zucchini is transparent. Drain, and set the cooking water aside. Blend until velvety smooth, adding enough cooking water to obtain the desired texture.

2. Top with a dab of butter and serve warm. The puree freezes well.

Tip: Beet stains are hard to remove, so make sure to have bibs and wipes at the ready!

False Alarm Alert: Beets can turn kids' pee (and even poo) pinky-red, so don't be alarmed. In fact, this effect might encourage some kids!

Lentil Apricot Soup

Preparation: 5 minutes
Cooking: 40 minutes
Servings: 8 to 10 adult servings

Okay, this recipe is not actually French. But it is very much in the French spirit: simple and quick to make, and the perfect combination of two foods that taste heavenly together.

Served as suggested, it makes a lovely puree (for babies twelve months or older). Diluted slightly with water, it is a perfect soup for a winter evening. The nutty taste of the lentils is offset by the darkly sweet flavor of the unsulfured apricots (which are much tastier than the conventional kind, so it is worth splurging). Make sure to blend it a long time—this soup should be so creamy that it is almost frothy.

This soup freezes well and is one of our homemade "fast foods." I freeze it in small portions (yes, I still sometimes use baby ice-cube trays) and then simply pull out what I need and reheat.

> *2 cups dried red lentils*
> *7 to 8 cups water*
> *¾ cup unsulfured apricots, whole (they'll be dark brown rather than orange)*
> *Optional: 1 tablespoon canola or olive oil*

1. Wash and rinse the lentils twice (if not pre-rinsed), or until the water runs clear. Put the lentils in a pot with 7 to 8 cups of water

(don't reuse the lentil rinse water!), depending on how thick you want the soup. Top with the apricots.

2. Bring to a boil over high heat. Reduce the heat to low and simmer for about 40 minutes, or until the lentils and apricots are tender, stirring every few minutes.

3. Blend until frothily smooth. Optional: adding a little canola oil will make the soup slightly richer and creamier (plus, it is a good source of omega-3s).

Tip: Don't put the apricots on the bottom of the pot, and be sure to stir regularly; otherwise the apricots will sink and stick to the bottom of your pot.

Variation: For a slightly more complex, grown-up taste, add chopped onions and paprika. Sauté the onions in a skillet over a low heat in a little vegetable oil. When the onions are golden, add the paprika and stir. Add to the lentil mixture, and proceed with the rest of the recipe.

Endive and Kiwi Salad

Preparation: 5 minutes
Servings: 4 small adult "side salad" servings

French families eat a lot of endive, both raw and cooked, and it is one of the vegetables that many French children seem to like. Chopped finely, endive has the texture of lettuce hearts, but is just slightly tangier. Some children may initially find endive to be a bit bitter until they get used to the taste. So in this recipe, vinaigrette and sweet-tart kiwi are used to offset any bitterness, while providing a little acidity to keep the leaves looking fresh.

This dish makes a lovely summer salad, or "starter" for a meal any time of year, and keeps well in the fridge for a day.

If you don't have kiwi, use any type of fresh fruit that your children like.

4 endive heads, sliced crosswise (the thinner the better), hard
   ends removed
4 tablespoons vinaigrette (see page 248)
Optional: minced fresh chives
2 kiwis, peeled, sliced, and quartered

In a large bowl, combine the endive and vinaigrette. If you like, sprinkle the salad with minced chives. Lay the pieces of kiwi on top.

Tip: Serve the vinaigrette on the side as a dip if this is a new flavor for your family.

Vinaigrette (Classic French Salad Dressing)

Preparation: 2 minutes
*Servings: Makes a little less than 1 cup, to serve a family-size
    salad*

Vinaigrette captures the spirit of French cooking: easy to make,
healthy, inexpensive, and tasty. French children get used to the taste
of vinegar at a very early age (and often use it where North American
children would prefer ketchup). To accommodate palates slightly less
used to acidic dressing, I have modified this recipe just slightly, with
a Canadian twist.

This dressing stores well for at least a week in the fridge.

½ cup extra virgin olive oil (or canola oil)
¼ cup red or white wine vinegar
1½ teaspoons Dijon-style mustard
Optional: 1 tablespoon maple syrup
Optional: 1 tablespoon finely minced shallot,
    scallion, or onion

1. Put the ingredients together in a jar with a lid, close the jar, and
   shake vigorously.

2. Taste before serving, and adjust quantities according to your
   preference (my mother-in-law prefers a more acidic vinaigrette,
   whereas I prefer my slightly sweeter, gentler version).

Tip: Kids love using this as a dip. Before the main evening meal, I serve the vinaigrette in little individual bowls along with crudités (raw vegetables) like carrots and cucumber sticks. This vinaigrette can also be used as a dressing for cooked vegetables (like beets) or grated carrot salad (another French kids' favorite, often served at school lunches).

Crêpes (Savory and Sweet Pancakes)

Preparation: 5 minutes
Standing: 1 hour (optional)
Cooking: 2 minutes per crêpe
Servings: Makes 8 to 10 large crêpes

Brittany is famous for its crêpes (thin pancakes), and *crêperies* can be found all over the region. Stuffed with savories like ham, spinach, or egg, crêpes make a filling meal (think of them as a French version of tortillas). Our children love "crêpes night." The anticipation of the sweet dessert crêpes puts them in a good mood, and I find that they're more willing to try the new fillings in the savory dinner crêpes served first.

Once you get the trick of crêpes, they are fast, easy, and fun to make. The batter is usually foolproof, but the art of cooking the thin crêpes (with the right flick of the wrist at the right time) is something you learn with practice; I'd recommend watching an online video or two first, if this is your first time.

Batter
3 eggs, lightly beaten
2 cups all-purpose flour (presifted if possible)
3 cups milk (whole or 2 percent, but not skim), plus ½ cup water
2 tablespoons melted butter (or vegetable oil)

Optional: 1 pinch salt
Butter or vegetable oil for cooking
For dessert crêpes: 2 tablespoons sugar, 1 teaspoon vanilla
    extract

1. Place the flour in a large bowl, make a well, and add the eggs. Slowly pour in the milk, and then the water, stirring gently but constantly. Don't overmix. The batter should be the consistency of heavy cream (if not, add more milk to thin the mixture). If you can, let the batter sit for at least 1 hour on the counter or, preferably, overnight in the fridge (your crêpes will have a nice smooth texture).

2. In a separate bowl, set aside some of the batter (approximately one-third to one-half) for the dessert crêpes; into this dessert mixture, stir the sugar and vanilla.

Cooking the crêpes

The trick is to cook the crêpe in the right way, so that the
    filling can heat up and the crêpe can be crispy without
    being burnt. Here's the method I use, taught to me by my
    mother-in-law.

1. Preheat a medium nonstick skillet to a medium-high temperature (just hot enough to make a drop of water "sputter"). Melt the butter (or vegetable oil) smoothly over the cooking surface (I use a bit of paper towel to spread it evenly). Pour in the batter (approximately ¼ to ⅓ cup per crêpe, depending on how thick you like them), while moving your wrist in a circular motion so that the batter forms a large circle (covering the entire surface of the frying pan). Do this quickly (as the batter dries almost instantly), using something from which it is easy to pour. The crêpe should be thin, so it will become crispy at the edges when cooked.

2. The crêpe should start turning golden around the edges within 30 to 40 seconds. When browned on the bottom, carefully loosen

and lift the edges with a spatula, and flip. While the second side is browning, place the filling in half of the crêpe, smoothing it out evenly. By the time the underside is done, the filling should be perfectly warm. Fold in half over the filling, and serve immediately by sliding the crêpe onto a plate (or a warming pan placed in the oven).

Suggested savory spinach filling

The traditional filling in Brittany is fairly rich: a slice of ham, one egg (like a sunny-side-up egg, inside the crêpe), and grated cheese. But I like this lighter alternative:

2 cups baby spinach leaves
2 tablespoons butter
Optional: a pinch of salt, a pinch of nutmeg, ½ cup grated hard white cheese

To prepare the spinach filling, gently wash the baby spinach, then place in a small pot (no added water!), and stir over high heat until wilted and tender (a minute or less). Stir in the butter and sprinkle with salt and nutmeg, if desired. Spoon the spinach mixture in a line down the middle of each crêpe, roll it up, and tuck the ends underneath like a wrap. Repeat with the rest of the crêpes. Pop the crêpes into a baking dish. Sprinkle with grated cheese (optional), broil for 2 to 4 minutes, and serve hot.

Note: To save time, you can use the spinach puree listed on page 239 as a filling.

Suggested dessert fillings

Now that you have enjoyed your dinner crêpes, it's time for dessert! The classic filling for dessert crêpes is beurre-sucre: a teaspoon of butter and a sprinkling of sugar. Here are some classic French fillings:

Lemon-honey: A spoonful of honey, a squeeze of lemon juice.

Chocolate: Melt a square of dark chocolate over the crêpe surface.

Berries: Fresh blueberries, raspberries, or blackberries.

Jam: Any kind will do, but we love blackberry jam the best.

Note: If you want to serve everyone at the same time, place crêpes on a plate in the oven to keep warm while you prepare the rest. Repeat until you have the desired number of crêpes (usually one per child or two per adult as a main dish, plus one per person for dessert).

Tip: For some reason known only to the gods of French cooking, the first crêpe is almost always a disaster. Set it aside, add a little butter if you need grease on your cooking surface, and just keep going!

Quick No-Pastry Quiche

Preparation: 5 to 7 minutes
Cooking: 30 to 40 minutes
Servings: 4 to 6 small adult servings

Note: This recipe, designed for busy parents, deliberately leaves out the pastry; the result is just as tasty.

Easy and quick to make, quiche is a classic French recipe that pleases adults and children alike. Quiche is also one of the most versatile recipes in the French household, as it can be eaten hot or cold, for lunch or for dinner, and works well with any combination of vegetables that you can think of. French families often make it in advance, as it lasts well for a couple of days in the fridge (or even for a few hours in the cupboard—my mother-in-law tries to avoid refrigerating her quiche, arguing that it changes the texture). In a pinch, I find that quiche freezes fairly well, although most French people don't do this.

The recipe presented here is the children's version, which uses a higher proportion of milk and a smaller number of eggs than a quiche intended for adults. The resulting dish is fluffier, less dense, and less eggy, and so more likely to please young palates. For older children or adults, reduce the milk by half a cup, and add one more egg (or play with the ratio of eggs and milk until you find the texture that your family prefers).

Most French cooks have their personal twist on this dish. For a while, my favorite recipe was a ratatouille-style quiche, with eggplant and tomatoes. A quick survey of our extended family turned up as many recipes as there were cooks: zucchini, broccoli, carrots—almost any vegetable you can think of. Chopped or grated finely, most vegetables don't even need to be cooked in advance.

8 large eggs
1½ cups milk (or ¾ cup milk and ¾ cup cream)
Salt and pepper, if desired
1 cup flour

Filling suggestions (These are some of our favorites, but feel free to make up your own.):

Quiche lorraine: 1 cup cubed or sliced ham and 1 cup grated
  cheese (Gruyère works best, but Cheddar will also do)
Quiche aux légumes: one small onion, finely diced, ½ cup
  thinly sliced greens (I use spinach or chard, but not kale,
  which is too chewy), ½ cup finely chopped red pepper
Quiche provençale: 1 cup ratatouille (this is a great way to
  use leftovers)

Optional: dried herbs such as parsley or oregano

1. Preheat the oven to 325°F. In a large bowl, beat the eggs; add the milk (or milk and cream) and mix well. Add a pinch of salt and pepper, if desired. Stirring constantly with a fork or whisk (to avoid lumps), add the flour a little at a time. Mix in the cheese, followed by the fillings you are using.

2. Pour the mixture into a greased 9- or 12-inch pie plate and bake for 30 minutes, or until the quiche puffs and starts to brown on top. Cool 5 minutes before serving (the quiche will settle, and you'll be able to cut it more neatly).

Tip: Changing your quiche ingredients is also a great way to introduce new vegetables: the reassuringly familiar look of the dish may entice even the wariest of eaters.

Note: Take care not to overfill your pie plate, as the quiche will puff up as it bakes. I place mine on a baking sheet in the oven, in case of spills. The quiche will deflate after you remove it from the oven: this is normal! Kids like watching this soufflé effect.

Tomates farcies (Stuffed Tomatoes)

Preparation: 10 minutes
Cooking: 20 minutes
Servings: 4 small adult (or older child) servings

This is one of our family's favorite recipes. *Tomates farcies* (stuffed tomatoes) are both filling and fun. The tomatoes are hollowed out and stuffed (in this case, with a savory ground beef mixture), and then baked to perfection. The *farce* peeks out of the tomatoes in a *coquettish* sort of way, and children love lifting up the tomato "hats" to see what lies underneath. Served with something that can absorb the delicious juices (rice and couscous are our favorites), this is a complete and easy tasty meal.

2 tablespoons olive oil
1 small onion, minced
½ pound ground beef
4 large tomatoes
¼ cup bread crumbs
¼ cup grated Parmesan
Optional: 1 minced red or yellow pepper, 2 teaspoons dried
   parsley and/or oregano, salt, pepper

1. Preheat the oven to 375°F.

2. In a large skillet, heat the olive oil over low heat. Add the onion and sauté until golden brown, about 5 minutes. Increase the heat to medium-high, quickly add the ground beef (to "seize" the meat), stir vigorously for 1 minute, and lower the heat to medium-low. Simmer the meat until thoroughly cooked, about 6 to 8 minutes.

3. Meanwhile, prepare the tomatoes: slice off the tops and set them aside, then hollow out the insides of the tomatoes with a small spoon, removing the flesh and pulp to a bowl. (The result will look like little bowls.) Turn the tomatoes upside down on a plate to allow the juices to drain. Chop the tomato insides and add them to the simmering beef mixture. (Optional: add diced red or yellow pepper along with the tomatoes.)

4. Combine the bread crumbs, herbs, and spices in a mixing bowl. (I use a little parsley and oregano, salt and pepper, but my sister-in-law uses paprika. Get creative!)

5. Add the bread-crumb mixture to the meat in the skillet and stir thoroughly. Spoon the resulting mixture (the "*farce*") into the tomato "bowls." Sprinkle with Parmesan. Put the tops back on the tomatoes like little "hats."

6. Place the tomatoes in a baking dish, and bake for 20 to 25 minutes, or until they are deliciously melt-in-your-month (*fondant*). Cool for 5 minutes before serving.

Tip: this dish can easily be prepared in advance and stored in the fridge until ready to bake. If you put the tomatoes straight into the oven from the fridge, you'll need to increase the baking time to 25 or 30 minutes.

Gratin de chou-fleur (Cauliflower Casserole)

Preparation: 10 minutes
Baking: 10 minutes
Servings: 4 adult servings

This dish is tastier than it sounds, I promise!

I have to admit that cauliflower is not one of my favorite vegetables, but I love this dish, in which cauliflower is baked in a classic French béchamel (white) sauce. The classic French *gratin* is usually made with potatoes (and called *gratin dauphinois*), but you can make a gratin with almost any vegetable.

1 cauliflower, chopped in bite-size pieces
4 tablespoons butter
3 tablespoons flour
2 cups milk
½ cup bread crumbs
½ cup grated Parmesan
Optional: salt, pepper, and a pinch of nutmeg or cinnamon

1. Put a pot of water to boil on the stove, preheat your oven to 350°F, and butter a medium casserole dish.

2. Meanwhile, chop the cauliflower into bite-size pieces. Add it to pot when water is at a rolling boil. Reduce the heat slightly and cook for 5 minutes while making the white sauce.

259

3. To make the white sauce, melt the butter in a medium pot over medium heat. Sprinkle in the flour, stir well (until the flour is absorbed), raise the heat to high, and stir for 30 seconds. Add the milk and stir constantly until the mixture has thickened, about 3 to 4 minutes. Stir in salt, pepper, and nutmeg or cinnamon (if desired). Set aside.

4. To make the topping, mix the bread crumbs and Parmesan in a small bowl.

5. To make the gratin, drain the cauliflower (which will be soft but not floppy) and place it in the dish. Pour the white sauce on top, sprinkle with bread-crumb mixture, and bake for 10 minutes, or until the top is golden-brown and crunchy.

Five-Minute Fish *en Papillote*

Preparation: 5 minutes
Cooking: 10 minutes
Servings: 1 adult, 2 children, or 4 toddlers per fillet

Many of the families we got to know in France had two working parents. So I was always amazed when we got dinner invitations and saw what these busy couples (okay, usually the mom) had managed to whip together. Part of the secret is that they had figured out how to streamline their cooking. This fish dish is an excellent example of how a tasty and elegant dish can be prepared quickly.

Cooking *en papillote* means tightly wrapping something (usually fish) in parchment paper and baking it in the oven. The dish steams in its own juices, and the flavors are wonderfully concentrated.

This dish is also fun to serve. *Papillon* is the French word for butterfly, which is a lovely metaphor for the visual effect of this dish. Bring the baking dish to the table, and watch everyone's faces as you unfold the wrapping to release the savory steam.

1 tablespoon olive or canola oil
1 fillet of fish per person: (salmon, sole, and
  halibut are our favorites)
1 medium zucchini (for every 2 fillets), sliced
  thin (but not peeled)
Juice of 1 lemon

½ cup plain yogurt (or mayonnaise or crème fraîche, *if you
    have it)*
½ cup fresh minced chives
Optional: salt and pepper

1. Preheat the oven to 375°F.

2. Choose a baking dish that's just big enough to hold the fish in a
    single layer. On a work surface, spread out a sheet of parchment
    paper or aluminum foil that's twice as big as the dish. Spread
    the oil over half of the sheet and lay the fish on the oil (skin-side
    down, if appropriate).

3. Layer the zucchini slices on top of the fish.

4. Mix the lemon juice, yogurt (or *crème fraîche*), chives (and salt
    and pepper, if desired), and pour the mixture on top of the fish.

5. Fold and close the paper *tightly* so that no steam can escape (I
    usually make two or three folds with the two edges, then tuck the
    ends under). Bake for 10 minutes per inch measured at the thick-
    est part of the fish (no peeking!). You'll know it's done when it
    flakes easily when a fork is inserted gently.

Tip: Kids love helping to prepare this meal: wrapping the fish in its
"cocoon" before it heads into the oven feels festive, like preparing a
lovely present.

Bouillabaisse for Babies (*Soupe de poisson de Madame Georges*)

Preparation: 15 minutes
Cooking: 20 to 30 minutes
Servings: 4–6 small adult servings

The best-known version of France's famous seafood soup—bouillabaisse—comes from Provence, in the south of the country. But Provence also has its own smooth, creamy version of fish soup, which happens to be much more suitable for babies and young children. Traditionally, this soup was made by fishermen's wives. As the boats came in, they would carefully separate the catch. The "noble" fish would be taken to market, and the rest—typically smaller fish of less value—would be cooked at home. My brother-in-law's parents, who live just outside of Aix-en-Provence, make this soup with the fish they catch themselves in the Mediterranean. Madame Georges's recipe is adapted from the oldest French cookbook in continuous print (for well over a century): *La cuisinière provençale*.

2 tablespoons olive oil
2 medium onions
1 garlic clove, crushed
6 large tomatoes, chopped
½ pound boneless white fish (see next page)
2 bay leaves

3 fennel stalks, whole
1 piece of orange peel (unwaxed)
Salt and pepper to taste
1 teaspoon saffron

1. In a large skillet over medium-low heat, sauté the onions in the olive oil. When the onions start to turn golden, after about 3 minutes, add the garlic. Wait one more minute, and then add the tomatoes. Raise heat, and simmer for 2 minutes.

2. Next, add the fish, the bay leaves, the fennel, and the orange peel. Cook at medium-high heat for 5 to 10 minutes, and then add 2 liters of boiling water, as well as (if desired) a dash of salt and pepper. Add saffron, and simmer (close to a rolling boil) for 20 minutes.

3. Remove the bay leaves, fennel, and orange peel. Blend the soup with a hand blender (any remaining bones should be so small as to simply dissolve).

Tip: If serving to very young children, you may wish to slowly pour the soup through a fine sieve before blending (in order to check for bones). Most of the fish meat should have dissolved, and will pass easily through the sieve.

Note: The onion is important for reducing the acidity of the tomatoes; it makes the soup more creamy. Trust me: don't leave it out!

Tip: Purists argue that the soup's distinctive flavor requires fish heads, but I don't use them myself. Traditionally, French families use a mix of white fish and small fish with an intense taste, like sardines. I simply suggest that you use a mix of fish that suits your family's tastes. Ask at your local fish store for whatever is in stock: my local fishmonger often has smoked salmon scraps, as well as bits of sole and other white fish. Ask for pieces without bones, but note that cooking will soften the small bones sufficiently that they will dissolve into the soup.

Zesty Orange Salad

Preparation: 5 minutes
Servings: 4 adult servings (or 8 child-size servings)

This dessert salad is a great way to introduce a new flavor to children. The sweetness of the orange offsets the bitterness of the orange zest. Children will be reassured by the familiar (the pieces of orange) and so hopefully will be more willing to try something new: the thin, almost playful curlicues of sweetened orange rind.

Have your children watch you prepare this dish, and let them sample if they are curious. When serving, remember that eating can sometimes be about encountering new tastes rather than consuming large quantities.

Serve this dish in a quiet moment when you have the time to sit and discuss the ingredients with your child. Questions are usually helpful (and helpfully distracting): How does the orange "zest" taste? Does it taste orange-y at all? How does it taste when you nibble a tiny bit? Place a tiny piece on your tongue? What does it smell like? If your child doesn't want to eat any, that's fine too, but try to encourage them to taste it.

Our daughters graduated from this to eating grapefruit, which they now enjoy as a breakfast "treat." Claire, our younger one, will purse her lips and say: "*Ooohhh, Maman, c'est amer* (it's bitter)!" And then continue eating with delight.

4 seedless oranges
4 tablespoons sugar

1. To make the zest, wash 1 orange, dry it, and use a paring knife to carefully peel the outer layer, taking only the very outside of the rind and avoiding any of the white pith underneath. Slice the zest into very thin strips.

2. Make a *sirop* (syrup) by mixing ½ cup water with the sugar in a small saucepan and cooking it over medium heat just until it bubbles. Add the zest, and cook for 10 minutes, or until the zest is tender and the *sirop* is golden but not brown or caramelized.

3. Peel the remaining oranges, removing the zest and pith so that you have just the fruit itself left. Slice the oranges crosswise and place them in little salad bowls. Pour the zest and *sirop* on top. Serve immediately!

Tip: Because of its sweetness, the French would serve this as a dessert, even though it is called a "salad."

Pain d'épices (Spice Bread)

Preparation: 10 to 15 minutes
Cooking: 50 minutes
Servings: 1 loaf

This "spice bread" (which tastes more like cake) is a French favorite for after-school snacks. Adults eat it too, but for *l'aperitif*, toasted and topped with thin slices of *foie gras*. This sweet treat is so beloved by the French that there is even a museum dedicated solely to the *pain d'épices* in Alsace (northern France). The Breton version has a high proportion of honey (sometimes half of the cake by weight!) and was sold freshly made every week at the honey stall at our local market. The honey also helps to preserve the loaf (which can last for weeks if well wrapped and frozen). Traditionally, *pain d'épices* is made with rye flour and dark buckwheat honey, giving the loaf a rich, nutty taste.

1½ cups all-purpose flour
1½ cups whole wheat flour (or dark rye or buckwheat flour)
2½ teaspoons baking soda
1½ teaspoons ground cinnamon
Optional: ¼ teaspoon nutmeg, ¼ teaspoon ground cloves, 1
    teaspoon anise seeds, ¼ teaspoon ginger
1½ cups honey (use an aromatic, dark honey or use 1 cup
    honey plus ½ cup molasses)

*3 tablespoons salted butter, at room temperature (or use
    unsalted butter, but add a pinch of salt)*
1 tablespoon finely grated orange zest
*1½ cups milk (water with 1 tablespoon vegetable oil can be
    substituted)*

1. Preheat the oven to 325°F. Butter a 9-inch (23cm) loaf pan and
    dust it with flour.

2. In a large bowl, sift together the flour, baking soda, and spices.

3. In a medium pot, gently heat and combine the honey, milk, butter,
    and orange zest. Remove from the heat. Add half the flour mix-
    ture. Stir gently, then add the remaining dry ingredients and stir
    until just combined. Do not overmix.

4. Pour the batter into the loaf pan and bake for 50 to 60 minutes,
    or until a knife inserted into the center comes out clean. The top
    will be dark brown.

5. Cool 10 minutes, then turn the cake onto a cooling rack. Let cool
    completely before slicing.

Tip: This cake is often left to sit several hours before serving: it becomes more tasty and moist, and slices better.

Storage: *Pain d'épices* can be wrapped in plastic and stored for at least
a week, during which time the flavors will meld and it will get denser.
It can also be frozen, and is delicious toasted, topped with savory or
sweet spreads.

Les pommes au four (Spiced Baked Apples)

Preparation: 10 to 15 minutes
Cooking: 25 minutes
Servings: 1 apple per person

This dish is a real time-saver, and one of our favorite wintertime desserts. The first thing I do when I get home from work is preheat the oven and pop the apples inside. By the time the meal is ready to serve, the smell of the apples fills the house, beckoning the children to the table (at least, that's the theory!). Usually, I take advantage of the hot oven to bake something for dinner (see Five Minute Fish *en papillote,* page 261, or *Gratin de chou-fleur,* page 259).

In Brittany, we use sweet and crunchy Dalinette apples. In Vancouver, I tend to use the Fuji or Gala variety (McIntosh, Delicious, and Granny Smith aren't as tasty once cooked).

To avoid drying out the apples, just put a little water in the bottom of the baking dish. I drizzle a little maple syrup over each apple just before serving, but they're just as lovely on their own.

1 apple per person, washed, skin pricked with a fork,
*   stemmed and cored*
1 teaspoon maple syrup per apple (or 1 tablespoon sugar and
*   1 tablespoon butter)*
Optional: ground cinnamon

1. Preheat the oven to 350°F.

2. Place the apples in a baking dish after pricking with a fork. Drizzle maple syrup into the hole in each apple, or do as the French do and use sugar and butter instead. Dust with cinnamon if you like.

3. Bake the apples for about 25 minutes, or until they have reached your desired consistency.

Warning: Be sure to remove the apples from the oven at least 5 minutes before you plan to eat them. They stay piping hot inside, and can burn little tongues. Don't rely on the heat of the outside of the apple to judge whether it's safe to serve; the flesh inside will remain much hotter than the outside surface, which will cool down quite quickly. We cut the apples for our children, and let the pieces cool on plates on the counter before bringing them to the table.

Tip: This recipe can be used to help transition babies to more solid food. Baked long enough, the texture of the apple is as creamy as applesauce. Reduce the baking time, and the consistency gets progressively more solid.

Mamie's Chocolate-Stuffed Baguette

Preparation: 2 minutes
Servings: 4 per baguette

Long before prepackaged snack foods appeared on the shelves, French families were making delicious homemade treats for their children. This one is still a favorite when our children visit their grandmother. They hover around the table as she slices and prepares their treat, savoring the smells of chocolate and fresh bread.

Although it seems decadent, this snack is relatively healthy, especially if you limit the butter on the baguette. Chocolate provides essential elements like copper, magnesium, and iron. Butter provides vitamin D and fat—both essential for children's growth. The bread provides carbohydrates necessary for kids' active lives—but without any preservatives or additives.

3 to 4 squares of dark chocolate (70 percent cocoa or higher)
1 fresh baguette, unsliced, but cut into four equal pieces
Butter

1. Make a relatively shallow slit lengthwise in each piece of baguette (along the side, not the top). Pry the baguette open about halfway (but not completely open!). Slide your buttered knife inside, and butter the bread.

271

2. Split the squares of chocolate into pieces that will fit inside the slit. Stuff the baguette with the rectangles of chocolate placed parallel to the length of the baguette. That way, your child gets some chocolate—but not too much—with every bite.

Mousse au chocolat (Chocolate Mousse)

Preparation: 10 to 15 minutes
Waiting: 2 to 3 hours
Cooking: None
Servings: 6

Mousse (whether lemon, chocolate, or any other kind) is amazingly quick to make. My French relatives need only about 5 minutes, but I've been generous with the time allowance here. The ratio of time spent to pleasure derived is probably the best of any dessert recipe I've encountered.

There are as many recipes for mousse as there are members of the family. Use this recipe as your point of departure. There are lots of little innovations you can try: serve with a bit of whipped cream if you like, or adjust the amount of sugar to suit your taste. But I like the minimalist version served below: dark and delicious.

The French are not, by the way, as fearful of raw eggs as are North Americans. I still can't shake that slight paranoia, so I make sure to buy my eggs from a reliable source to avoid any chance of salmonella poisoning.

½ pound semi-sweet Baker's chocolate
4 teaspoons butter
6 eggs, whites and yolks separated
Zest of half an orange
Pinch of salt

1. Melt the chocolate and butter in a *bain-marie* (double boiler). (Quick alternative: In the microwave, melt the chocolate in a fairly large bowl; I put a tiny bit of milk in the bottom to keep the chocolate from sticking.) *Allow the chocolate to cool!* Otherwise, you risk cooking the eggs. When the chocolate is melted (but not too hot), add in the egg yolks and the orange zest, and stir well.

2. In a standing mixer (or in a large bowl with a whisk or mixer), beat the egg whites until they reach stiff peaks (adding a pinch of salt at the start will help them stiffen).

3. *Gently* fold one-third of the egg whites into the chocolate mixture. Mix gently, then fold in the other half, mixing very gently. Spoon the mousse into little serving dishes and chill for 2 to 3 hours, or until firm. Serve with berries or crisp little cookies on the side.

Tip: Served in a big bowl, this makes a big impression. But it will be tidier and more elegant (and the mousse will likely remain more firm) if prepared and served in little individual bowls (plus, no fighting about who got more!).

Clafoutis (Sweet Cherry Soufflé)

Preparation: 10 minutes
Cooking: 40 to 43 minutes
Servings: 6 generous pieces

Clafoutis is a version of the French flan that is traditionally made with cherries (or other moist fruit such as plums, prunes, raspberries, or blackberries), enveloped by a simple cake batter. The fruit is polka-dotted in the cake, giving it a playful look that children love. Even the name is fun to say: kla-foo-TEE. Traditionally, this dish is cooked with the pits left inside the cherries (purists believe that this intensifies the flavor of the dish). I pit the cherries (or, when I'm in a rush, use small plums instead, which are easier to pit).

Our source for the cherries is an old tree at Philippe's aunt's house. Tante Odette's tree is the most productive I've ever encountered; the branches, weighed down with cherries, hang down almost to the ground. In late June, the extended family is mobilized for cherry picking, cherry jam making, and (of course) cherry eating. *Clafoutis* is my daughters' favorite recipe from this time of year.

2 cups pitted cherries or plums (or other moist fruit)
⅓ cup granulated sugar
½ cup flour
Pinch of salt
3 eggs
1¼ cups milk

1 teaspoon vanilla extract
1 tablespoon confectioners' sugar (or brown sugar—I like
    muscovado)

1. Place the fruit in a bowl with half the granulated sugar, stir well, and set aside.

2. Preheat the oven to 350°F. Grease a 9-inch baking dish.

3. In a large bowl, sift the flour with the salt and remaining sugar. In a medium bowl, beat the eggs and milk to combine. Add the vanilla. Add the egg mixture to the flour mixture and combine well. Spread the fruit evenly in the baking dish and pour the batter on top. The cherries may float to the surface now (or later, during baking).

4. Bake for 40 to 45 minutes, or until the top is firm and golden brown. Cool, then sprinkle with confectioners' sugar. Serve immediately.

Note: Julia Child recommends baking this twice (briefly baking a thin layer in the bottom of the dish, then adding the fruit topped with the remaining batter and baking until done). But the French parents I know use this "express" method, with wonderful results!

Tip: Serve the *clafoutis* in the baking dish, as it is quite "wobbly" and won't transfer well. Fresh out of the oven, the cake is puffed up and golden. It will settle and sag a little bit, but that's exactly what it is supposed to do.

Resources

The North American food movement is enormous and is growing rapidly. These are just a few of my personal favorites.

Books for Parents
Winning the Food Fight (Natalie Rigal)
Food Politics (Marion Nestle)
Food Rules (Michael Pollan)
Just Take a Bite (Lori Ernsperger and Tania Stegen-Hanson)

Books for Kids and Teens
Eating the Alphabet (Lois Ehrlert) (preschoolers)
I Can Eat a Rainbow: A Fun Look at Healthy Foods and Vegetables (Annabel Karmel and Dorling Kindersley) (preschoolers)
Alexander and the Great Food Fight (Linda Hawkins) (5 to 8 years)
Did You Eat Your Vitamins Today? (Ena Sabih) (5 to 8 years)
The Vegetables We Eat (Gail Gibbons) (8 to 12 years)
The Omnivore's Dilemma: The Secrets Behind What You Eat. Young Reader's Edition (Michael Pollan) (teens)
Chew on This: Everything You Don't Want to Know About Fast Food (Eric Schlosser) (teens)

Campaigns and Resources
- Slow Food USA's "Time for Lunch" campaign: slowfoodusa.org
- Chef Jamie Oliver's "Food Revolution": jamieoliver.com
- Great school lunch reform guide from the Centre for Ecoliteracy: ecoliteracy.org.

- Chef Ann Cooper's school "Lunch Box" campaign: chefann.com
- The Farm to School movement gets local farm produce into school lunches: farmtoschool.org
- Great ideas for starting a school garden: schoolgardenwizard.org
- Helpful tips for picky eaters from the USDA: mypyramid.gov/preschoolers
- Find a local farmer's market near you: localharvest.org
- The Centre for Science in the Public Interest is a powerhouse of the food reform movement: www.cspi.org.

Acknowledgments

Paul and Pauline were the first to hear this idea, and enthusiastic supporters right from the start. Andrew Wylie kindly gave the proposal a read, and his words of encouragement took me a very long way. Martha Magor Webb is as much a muse as an agent; together with Chris Bucci and Anne McDermid, she saw more in this project than even I did. Without her, this book would never have seen the light of day. Kate Cassaday at HarperCollins Canada and Cassie Jones at William Morrow, editors extraordinaire, were also ideal readers: incisive, insightful, funny, and warm. I'm grateful to them and the entire team at HarperCollins.

In Canada, friends and family (Philippe, Roberta, John, Kristine, Deborah) devotedly read through drafts and (later) blog posts, listened to my stories, and told many of their own in return. Glen and Catherine inspired us with their real-life "slow food" example close to home. Kathy Wazana, Alexandra Greenhill, Leslie Paris, Paula Rosen, Step Carruthers, and Kia Robertson were enthusiastic early supporters. Sonja shared a love of France, and French nursery rhymes galore. And phenomenal illustrator Sarah Jane Wright provided delightful drawings and much-welcomed encouragement (including testing some of the French Food Rules and recipes with her own family).

In France, unfailingly delicious meals with with Janine and Jo, and the entire Le Billon clan, fuelled many of our conversations. Family and friends (Janine, Jo, Véronique, Benoît, Christelle, Laurent, Didier, Sylvie, Manon, Olivier, Virginie, Eric, Hélène, Rony, Frédérique, Antoine, Manu, and Cécile) were unfailingly gracious and patient with questions, faux pas, and more questions (I admit to learning as much from watching their children as I did from them). And I am still grateful for the dedication of many teachers and caregivers at École André Guigot and the Crèche de Saint-Alban, as well as folks at La Binée Paysanne.

My intellectual debts are many, but I'll single out a few. I've relied heavily on the insights of academic researchers, including Claude Fischler, Natalie Rigal, Paul Rozin, and other researchers at the Institut du Goût in Paris, and the Centre des Sciences du Goût et de l'Alimentation in Dijon. In North America, authors Marion Nestle, Michael Pollan, and Adam Gopnik continue to inspire. Many of the nursery rhymes and *contines*—wonderful windows into French culture—were drawn from Marie-Claire Burley and Lya Tourn's charming illustrated book *Enfantines: Jouer, parler avec le bébé* (L'école des loisirs, 1988).

Last but not least: our daughters (whose names have been changed in this story) were (mostly) enthusiastic eaters, adorable table companions, and insightful commentators on the perils and pitfalls of cross-cultural parenting. And my husband, Philippe—who first toured me throughout his beloved France in his battered Renault 5 car so many years ago—was there from beginning to end. I need say no more, for he already knows.

Notes

Chapter 1: French Kids Eat Everything (and Yours Can Too)

4   *Le plaisir de la:* Brillat-Savarin's *Physiologie de goût* is considered to be a foundational text of modern gastronomy.

7   *France's rate of child obesity:* Yannis Manios and Vassiliki Costarelli, "Childhood Obesity in the WHO European Region," in *Epidemiology of Obesity in Children and Adolescents,* edited by Wolfgang Ahrens, Luis A. Moreno, and Iris Pigeot, Springer Series on Epidemiology and Public Health, Part 1 (New York: Springer Science+Business Media, 2011), 44–68; Wolfgang Ahrens, Luis A. Moreno, and Iris Pigeot, "Childhood Obesity: Prevalence Worldwide—Synthesis, Part I, in *Epidemiology of Obesity,* 219–235; Sandrine Lioret, Mathilde Touvier, Carine Dubuisson, et al., "Trends in Child Overweight Rates and Energy Intake in France from 1999 to 2007: Relationships with Socioeconomic Status," *Obesity* 17, no. 5 (2009): 1092–1100; Benoit Salanave, Sandrine Peneau, Marie-Françoise Rolland-Cachera, et al., "Stabilization of Overweight Prevalence in French Children between 2000 and 2007," *International Journal of Pediatric Obesity* 4, no. 2 (2009): 66–72; Sandrine Lioret, Bernard Maire, Jean-Luc Volatier, et al., "Child Overweight in France and Its Relationship with Physical Activity, Sedentary Behavior and Socioeconomic Status," *European Journal of Clinical Nutrition* 61, no. 4 (2007): 509–516.

7   *And while rates of overweight:* Cynthia Ogden and Margaret Carroll, *Prevalence of Obesity among Children and Adoles-*

cents: United States, Trends 1963–1965 through 2007–2008 (Atlanta: National Center for Health Statistics, Centers for Disease Control, 2011); Benoit Salanave, Sandrine Péneau, Marie Françoise Rolland-Cachera, et al., *Prévalences du surpoids et de l'obésité et déterminants de la sédentarité, chez les enfants de 7 à 9 ans en France en 2007* (Saint-Maurice: Institut de Veille Sanitaire, Université de Paris 13; 2011).

7 *Vitamin pills seemed like a cop-out:* David R. Jacobs and Lyn M. Steffen, "Nutrients, Foods, and Dietary Patterns as Exposures in Research: A Framework for Food Synergy," supplement, *American Journal of Clinical Nutrition* 78, no. 3 (2003): 508S–513S; David R. Jacobs, Myron Gross, and Linda Tapsell, "Food Synergy: An Operational Concept for Understanding Nutrition," *American Journal of Clinical Nutrition* 89, no. 5 (2009): 1543–1548; Mark Messina, Johanna W. Lampe, Diane F. Birt, et al., "Reductionism and the Narrowing Nutrition Perspective: Time for Reevaluation and Emphasis on Food Synergy," *Journal of the American Dietetic Association* 101, no. 12 (2001): 1416–1419.

11 *and they have carefully studied strategies:* Natalie Rigal, "La consommation répétée permet-elle de dépasser la neophobie alimentaire?" *European Review of Applied Psychology* 55, no. 1 (2005): 43–50. See also Bérengère Rubio, Natalie Rigal, Nathalie Boireau-Ducept, et al., "Measuring Willingness to Try New Foods: A Self-Report Questionnaire for French-Speaking Children," *Appetite* 50, no. 2–3 (2008): 408–414.

Chapter 2: Baby Steps and Beet Puree: We Move to France, and Encounter Unidentified Edible Objects

25 *This, in their view:* J. L. Carper, Jennifer O. Fisher, and Lean Lipps Birch, "Young Girls' Emerging Dietary Restraint and Disinhibition Are Related to Parental Control in Child Feeding," *Appetite* 35, no. 2 (2000): 121–129; Sandrine Monnery-Paris, Natalie Rigal, Claire Chabanet, et al., "Parental Practices Perceived by Children Using a French Version of the Kid's Child Feeding Questionnaire" *Appetite* 57, no. 1 (2011): 161–166.

26   *French kids, like their parents:* Adam Drewnowski, Susan Ahl-
      strom Henderson, Amybeth Shore, et al., "Diet Quality and
      Dietary Diversity in France: Implications for the French Para-
      dox," *Journal of the American Dietetic Association* 96, no. 7
      (1996): 663–669; Paul Rozin, Claude Fischler, Sumio Imada,
      et al., "Attitudes to Food and the Role of Food in Life in the
      U.S.A., Japan, Flemish Belgium and France: Possible Implica-
      tions for the Diet–Health Debate," *Appetite* 33, no. 2 (1999):
      163–180; Paul Rozin, Kimberly Kabnick, Erin Pete, et al., "The
      Ecology of Eating: Smaller Portion Sizes in France than in the
      United States Help Explain the French Paradox," *Psychologi-
      cal Science* 14 (2003): 450–454; Dara R. Musher-Eizenman,
      Blandine de Lauzon-Guillain, Shayla Holub, et al., "Child and
      Parent Characteristics Related to Parental Feeding Practices: A
      Cross-Cultural Examination in the US and France," *Appetite* 52
      (2009): 89–95.

Chapter 3: Schooling the Stomach: We Start Learning to "Eat French" (the Hard Way)

36   *They were also inexpensive:* For more information on French
      school lunches, see the Ministère de l'Éducation Nationale
      (www.education.gouv.fr) and the Agence Nationale de Sécurité
      Sanitaire (www.anses.fr).
41   *Since vending machines are banned:* Loi n° 2004–806 du 9 août
      2004, art. 30.
42   *At school, under the influence:* Leann Lipps Birch, "Effects of
      Peer Models' Food Choices and Eating Behaviors on Preschool-
      ers' Food Preferences," *Child Development* 51, no. 2 (1980):
      489–496; Elsa Adessi, Amy Galloway, Elisabette Visalberghi, et
      al., "Specific Social Influences on the Acceptance of Novel Foods
      in 2–5-Year-Old Children," *Appetite* 45, no. 3 (2005): 264–271.
42   *"School is a privileged place":* "L'école est un lieu privilégié
      d'éducation au goût, à la nutrition et à la culture alimentaire."
      www.education.gouv.fr/cid138/la-restauration-au-lycee.html.
      Accessed November 1, 2011.

43   *Entire books on this topic:* Natalie Rigal, a developmental child psychologist, has written *La naissance du goût: comment donner aux enfants le plaisir de manger* (Paris: Agnès Viénot, 2000). See also *Le goût chez les enfants* (Paris: Flammarion, 2000) by French oenologist and "taste philosopher" Jacques Puisais, who created the Institut du Goût in 1976, and initially developed some of the "taste-training" ideas that are now used in French classrooms.

44   *Edging closer:* INPES, *La santé vient en mangeant et en bougeant: Le guide nutrition des enfants et ados pour tous les parents* (Paris: Institut National de Prévention et d'Éducation pour la Santé, 2004).

45   *Schools, she proudly noted:* See the research by the Institut du Goût (Paris) and the Centre des Sciences du Goût et de l'Alimentation (Dijon).

47   *And low-income parents: Early Childhood Education and Care Policy in France* (Paris: Organisation for Economic Cooperation and Development, 2004). Marie-Thérèse Letablier, "Why France Has High Fertility: The Impact of Policies Supporting Parents," *Japanese Journal of Security Policy* 7, no. 2 (2008): 41–56.

47   *The French approach levels the playing field:* Luc Bronner, "La place croissante de l'Islam en banlieu," *Le Monde*, October 4, 2011.

48   *This explanation made Madame's:* Nadine Neulat, "L'éducation nutritionnelle à l'école," *Enfances & Psy* 27 (2005): 96–100.

52   *But 60 percent of Americans:* Claude Fischler and Estelle Masson, eds., *Manger: Français, Européens et Américains face à l'alimentation* (Paris: Odile Jacob, 2008).

Chapter 4: *L'art de la table:* A Meal with Friends, and a Friendly Argument

56   *Children's food is not fuel:* Simone Gerber "L'empreinte de Françoise Dolto sur mon métier de pédiatre,"*Le Coq-héron* 168 (2002): 105–110.

74   *Good taste (and thus good food):* Claude Fischler, *L'homnivore* (Paris: Odile Jacob, 1990).

75   *In France, Hugo explained:* Thierry Mathé, Gabriel Tavoularis,

and Thomas Pilorin, "La gastronomie s'inscrit dans la continuité du modèle alimentaire français," *Cahiers de Recherche*
267 (2009).

Chapter 5: Food Fights: How *Not* to Get Your Kids to Eat Everything

80   *Searching for an explanation:* Trémolières' last and probably
best-known work is the book *Partager le pain* (To Break Bread
Together), published in 1975.

92   *Fischler's work on adults:* Fischler and Masson, eds., *Manger.*

93   *In contrast, only 40 percent:* Data from Child Trends Data
Bank, available at www.childtrends.org.

Chapter 6: The Kohlrabi Experiment: Learning to Love New Foods

107   *A decade ago:* Elena Byrne and Susan Nitzke, "Preschool Chil-
dren's Acceptance of a Novel Vegetable Following Exposure to
Messages in a Storybook," *Journal of Nutrition Education and
Behavior* 34, no. 3 (2002): 211–214.

109   *And this starts early:* Carolyn J. Gerrish and Julie A. Mennella,
"Flavor Variety Enhances Food Acceptance in Formula-Fed Infants," *American Journal of Clinical Nutrition* 73, no. 6 (2001):
1080–1085; Camille Schwartz, Claire Chabanet, Vincent Boggio, et al., "À quelles saveurs les nourrissons sont-ils exposés
dans la première année de vie?" *Archives de Pédiatrie* 17, no.
7 (2010): 1026–1034; Sophie Nicklaus, Vincent Boggio, Claire
Chabanet, et al., "A Prospective Study of Food Variety-Seeking
in Childhood, Adolescence and Early Adult Life," *Appetite* 44,
no. 3 (2005): 288–297.

109   *"Opposition to food can't persist":* Vanessa Saab and William
Memlouk, *Mon bébé refuse de manger: L'aventure alimentaire du
jeune enfant* (Saint-Julien-en-Genevois Cedex: Jouvence, 2008).

110   *And tasting new foods:* Susan A. Sullivan and Leann L. Birch,
"Infant Dietary Experience and Acceptance of Solid Foods,"
Pediatrics 93, no. 2 (1994): 271–277; Camille Schwartz, Claire
Chabanet, Christine Lange, et al., "The Role of Taste in Food
Acceptance at the Beginning of Complementary Feeding," *Phys-
iology and Behavior* 104 no. 4 (2011): 646–652; Andrea Maier,

Claire Chabanet, Benoit Schaal, et al., "Effects of Repeated Exposure on Acceptance of Initially Disliked Vegetables in 7-Month-Old Infants," *Food Quality and Preference* 18 (2007): 1023–1032.

110   *That's not all:* Rigal, *La naissance du goût.*

117   *The French recommendation:* The most recent report by the Institut de Veille Sanitaire (*Situation nutritionelle en France en 2006,* Paris: IVS) uses data gathered under France's national nutrition and health program (Programme National Nutrition Santé).

117   *In contrast, only about 10 percent:* Barbara A. Lorson, Hugo R. Melgar-Quinonez, and Christopher A. Taylor, "Correlates of Fruit and Vegetable Intakes in US Children," *Journal of the American Dietetic Association* 109, no. 3 (2009): 474–478.

117   *And the most common type:* Another interesting point is the difference between French and American food guidelines. The French have nine guidelines for exercise, limiting certain foods, and drinking water (called *MangerBouger* or EatMove); the guidelines specify variety as well as quantity of fruits and vegetables. In contrast, the American food guidelines (see myplate .gov, where a plate has replaced the well-known food pyramid) don't mention exercise, and don't specify how many types of fruits and vegetables to eat—they just specify a target proportion of total foods consumed.

118   *If eating is something:* Daniel Cappon, *Eating, Loving, and Dying: A Psychology of Appetites* (Toronto: University of Toronto Press, 1973).

118   *As the American Academy of Pediatrics:* See the AAP's Healthy Children website: www.healthychildren.org/english/ages-stages /baby/feeding-nutrition/pages/Switching-To-Solid-Foods.aspx. Accessed November 1, 2011.

118   *The book contains some views:* Laura A. Jana and Jennifer Shu, *Food Fights: Winning the Nutritional Challenges of Parenthood Armed with the Insight, Humor, and a Bottle of Ketchup* (Washington, D.C.: American Academy of Pediatrics, 2008).

118   *The French equivalent of the AAP:* Alain Bocquet, Jean-Louis Bressor, André Briend, et al., "Alimentation du nourrisson

et de l'enfant en bas âge," *Archives de Pédiatrie* 10, no. 1 (2003) 76–81. (Feeding of infants and toddlers.) See also C. Turberg-Romain, B. Lelièvre, and M-F Le Huezey, "Conduite alimentaire des nourrissons et jeunes enfants âges de 1 à 36 mois en France: evolution des habitudes des mères," *Archives of Pediatrics* 14 (2007): 1250–1258.

121 *I read these with a growing sense:* Claude Fischler and Matty Chiva, "Food Likes, Dislikes, and Some of Their Correlates in a Sample of French Children and Young Adults," in *Measurement and Determinants of Food Habits and Food Preference,* edited by Joery M. Diehl and Claus Leitzmann. Report of an EC Worshop, Giessen, Germany, 1986, 137–156. C.R.E.A., *L'adolescent et l'alimentation* (Paris: Centre de Recherche sur l'Enfant et l'Adolescent, CFES, 1990).

122 *As I read in another book:* Rigal, *La naissance du goût.*

123 *But I had also learned from my research:* Leann L. Birch, Linda McPhee, B. C. Shoba, et al., "What Kind of Exposure Reduces Children's Food Neophobia? Looking vs. Tasting," *Appetite* 9, no. 3 (1987): 171–178.

128 *But what was fascinating was that kids:* Janette Greenhalgh, Alan J. Dowey, Pauline J. Horne, et al., "Positive and Negative Peer Modeling Effects on Young Children's Consumption of Novel Blue Foods," *Appetite* 52, no. 3 (2009): 646–653.

129 *We ate exactly what they ate:* Leann Lipps Birch, Jennifer Orlet Fisher, Helen Smiciklas-Wright, et al., "Eat as I Do Not as I Say: Parental Influences on Young Girls' Calcium Intakes," *Journal of the Federation of American Societies for Experimental Biology* 13 (1999): A593; Jennifer Orlet Fisher, Diane C. Mitchell, Helen Smiciklas-Wright, et al., "Parental Influences on Young Girls' Fruit and Vegetable, Micronutrient, and Fat Intakes," *Journal of the American Dietetic Association* 102, no. 1 (2002): 58–64.

Chapter 7: Four Square Meals a Day: Why French Kids Don't Snack

134 *Traditional French nursery rhyme:* The English translation is slightly adapted in order to mimic the rhyming structure of the original nursery rhyme.

136 *And I was amazed to learn:* Lisa Jahns, Anna Maria Siega-Riz, and Barry M. Popkin, "The Increasing Prevalence of Snacking Among US Children from 1977 to 1996," *Journal of Pediatrics* 138, no. 4 (2001): 493–498; Carmen Piernas and Barry M. Popkin, "Trends in Snacking among U.S. Children," *Health Affairs* 29, no. 3 (2010): 398–404.

136 *For most French parents and children:* INPES, *La santé vient en mangeant et en bougeant: le guide nutrition des enfants et ados pour tous les parents* (Paris: Institut National de Prevention et d'Éducation pour la Santé, 2004).

137 *I found it hard to imagine:* Carmen Piernas and Barry M. Popkin, "Snacking Increased among U.S. Adults between 1977 and 2006," *Journal of Nutrition* 140, no. 2 (2010): 325–332.

137 *And I doubted that Americans were eating:* France Bellisle, Anne Marie Dalix, L. Mennen, et al., "Contribution of Snacks and Meals in the Diet of French Adults: A Diet-Diary Study," *Physiology and Behavior* 79, no. 2 (2003): 183–189; France Bellisle, Marie Françoise Rolland-Cachera, and the Kellogg Scientific Advisory Committee, "Three Consecutive (1993, 1995, 1997) Surveys of Food Intake, Nutritional Attitudes and Knowledge, and Lifestyle in 1000 French Children, Aged 9–11 Years," *Journal of Human Nutrition and Dietetics* 13, no. 2 (2000): 101–111. See also the reports produced by the Nutrinet study: www.etude-nutrinet-sante.fr.

138 *No snacks are served at school:* AFSSA– Saisine no 2003-SA-0281: *Avis de l'Agence française de sécurité sanitaire des aliments (AfSSA), relatif à la collation matinale à l'école* (2004); Alain Bocquet, Jean-Louis Bresson, André Briend, et al., "La collation de 10 heures en milieu scolaire : un apport alimentaire inadapté et superflu," *Archives de Pédiatrie* 10 (2003): 945–947; H. Thibault, C. Carriere, C. Langevin, et al., "La collation à l'école maternelle: évolution des perceptions et pratiques des enseignants d'Aquitaine entre 2004 et 2008," *Archives de Pédiatrie* 17, no. 11 (November 2010): 1516–1521.

140 *Our kids are drinking less milk:* Rhonda S. Sebastian, Linda

E. Cleveland, and Joseph D. Goldman, "Effect of Snacking Frequency on Adolescents' Dietary Intakes and Meeting National Recommendations," *Journal of Adolescent Health* 42 (2008): 503–511; Y. Claire Wang, Sara N. Bleich, and Steven L. Gortmaker, "Increasing Caloric Contribution from Sugar-Sweetened Beverages and 100% Fruit Juices among U.S. Children and Adolescents, 1988–2004," *Pediatrics* 121, no. 6 (2008): e1604 –e1614.

147   *This is, of course, exactly the mix of foods:* Hector Araya and Jacqueline Hills, "Short-Term Satiety in Preschool Children: A Comparison Between High Protein Meal and a High Complex Carbohydrate Meal," *International Journal of Food Sciences and Nutrition* 51, no. 2 (2000): 119–124. See also Jean-Xavier Guinard and Patrice Brun, "Sensory-Specific Satiety: Comparison of Taste and Texture Effects," *Appetite* 31 (1998): 141–157; S. H. Holt, J. C. Miller, P. Petocz, et al., "A Satiety Index of Common Foods," *European Journal of Clinical Nutrition* 49, no. 9 (1995): 675–690; Susanna H. A. Holt, Jennie C. Brand-Miller, and Paul A. Stitt, "The Effects of Equal-Energy Portions of Different Breads on Blood Glucose Levels, Feelings of Fullness and Subsequent Food Intake," *Journal of the American Dietetic Association* 101, no. 7 (2001): 767–773; C. Marmonier, D. Chapelot, and J. Louis-Sylvestre, "Effects of Macronutrient Content and Energy Density of Snacks Consumed in a Satiety State on the Onset of the Next Meal," *Appetite* 34, no. 2 (2000): 161–168.

147   *As a result of eating this way:* John M. de Castro, France Bellisle, Gerda I. J. Feunekes, et al., "Culture and Meal Patterns: A Comparison of the Food Intake of Free-Living American, Dutch, and French Subjects," *Nutrition Research* 17, no. 5 (1997): 807–829.

Chapter 8: Slow Food Nation: It's Not Only *What* You Eat, It's Also *How* You Eat

156   *This eighteenth-century French song:* The melody was first known as "Ah! vous dirai-je, Maman," and appeared some-

where between 1760 and 1770, in "Les amusements d'une heure et demy [demie]" by M. Bouin. See Robert A. Green, *The Hurdy-Gurdy in Eighteenth-Century France* (Bloomington: Indiana University Press, 1995). Mozart later wrote twelve variations on this theme.

158   *Table: Working Mothers:* Sources for statistics: Institut national de la statistique et des études économiques and US Bureau of Labor Statistics. *Women in the Labor Force: A Databook* (2010 Edition), BLS Report 1026, December 2010.

159   *It wasn't the amount of time spent cooking:* OECD, *Society at a Glance 2011-OECD Social Indicators* (Paris: Organization for Economic Cooperation and Development, 2011).

160   *And this doesn't include shopping: L'enquête sur les comportements et consommations alimentaires en France* (CRÉDOC, CCAF, 2007).

161   *The French are at the opposite extreme:* Rozin et al., "Attitudes to Food and the Role of Food."

162   *The serving sizes were wildly different:* Paul Rozin, Kimberly Kabnick, Erin Pete, et al., "The Ecology of Eating: Smaller Portion Sizes than in France Help Explain the French Paradox," *Psychological Science* 14, no. 2 (2003): 450–454.

163   *Curious about how much fast food:* The precise figure for expenditure on food away from home is 47.5 percent of the food budget, on average (source: USDA Economic Research Service online "Briefing Room" data). See also Shanthy A. Bowman, Steven L. Gortmaker, Cara B. Ebbeling, et al., "Effects of Fast-Food Consumption on Energy Intake and Diet Quality among Children in a National Household Survey," *Pediatrics* 113, no. 1 (2004): 112–118; Lisa Mancino, Jessica E. Todd, Joanne Guthrie, et al., *How Food Away from Home Affects Children's Diet Quality* (US Department of Agriculture, Economic Research Service, 2010); S. A. French, M. Story, D. Neumark-Sztainer, et al., "Fast Food Restaurant Use Among Adolescents: Associations with Nutrient Intake, Food Choices and Behavioral and

Psychosocial Variables," *International Journal of Obesity* 25, no. 12 (2001): 1823–1833.

164 *In France, only 20 percent of the food budget:* INSEE (2011) *Dépenses alimentaires et part de la restauration dans le budget des ménages.* Paris: Institut national de la statistique et des études économiques; Jean-Luc Volatier, *Le repas traditionnel se porte encore bien.* (Paris: CRÉDOC, CAFF; 1999).

165 *French youth—my husband among them:* Rick Fantasia, "Fast Food in France," *Theory and Society* 24, no. 2 (1995): 201–243.

165 *Some of our friends worried:* The term was apparently originally coined by American sociologist George Ritzer in his book *The McDonaldization of Society* (Newbury Park, Calif.: Pine Forge Press, 1993), but is also used in France. See Claude Fischler, "The McDonaldization of Culture," in *Food: A Culinary History from Antiquity to the Present,* edited by Jean Louis Flandrin, Massimo Montanari, Albert Sonnerfeld, et al. (New York: Columbia University Press, 2008), 530–547; A. Hubert, "Evolution of Food Consumption and Lifestyles in France in the Past 50 Years," *Rivista di Antopologia* supplement 76 (1998): 229–235; Jacqueline Scali, Aurélia Richard, and Mariette Gerber, "Diet Profiles in a Population Sample from Mediterranean Southern France," *Public Health Nutrition* 4, no. 2 (2001): 173–182; Pierre Combris and Jean-Luc Volatier, "L'évolution des comportements alimentaires des Français et de leurs attitudes nutritionnelles," *La lettre scientifique de l'institut français pour la nutrition* 56 (1998): 9–10; J. P. Poulain, "The Contemporary Diet in France: 'De-Structuration' or from Commensalism to Vagabond Feeding," *Appetite* 39, no. 1 (2002) 43–55.

165–66 *Bruno Rebelle, head of Greenpeace France:* Florence Williams, "The Roquefort Files," *Outside,* June 1, 2001.

171 *"Cooking can be an act":* J. Luhrs, *The Simple Living Guide* (NY: Broadway Books), p. 244.

171 *But now it brought to mind:* Rigal, *La naissance du goût.*

Tips and Tricks, Rules and Routines for Healthy, Happy Eaters

212   *For example, kids who have authoritative parents:* Karen Weber Cullen, Tom Baranowski, Latroy Rittenberry, et al., "Social-Environmental Influences on Children's Diets: Results from Focus Groups with African-, Euro- and Mexican-American Children and Their Parents," *Health Education Research* 15, no. 5 (2000): 581–590; Sara Gable and Susan Lutz, "Household, Parent, and Child Contributions to Childhood Obesity," *Family Relationships* 49, no. 3 (2000): 293–300; Heather Patrick, Theresa A. Nicklas, Sheryl O. Hughes, et al., "The Benefits of Authoritative Feeding Style: Caregiver Feeding Styles and Children's Food Consumption Patterns," *Appetite* 44, no. 2 (2005): 243–249. Kyung E. Rhee, Julie C. Lumeng, Danielle P. Appugliese, et al., "Parenting Styles and Overweight Status in First Grade," *Pediatrics* 117, no. 6 (2006): 2047–2054; Kristen M. Hurley, Matthew B. Cross, and Sheryl O. Hughes, "A Systematic Review of Responsive Feeding and Child Obesity in High-Income Countries," *Journal of Nutrition* 141 (2011): 495–501.

212   *In contrast, children whose parents:* J. L. Carper et al., "Young Girls' Emerging Dietary Restraint and Disinhibition"; Jennifer O. Fisher and Leann Lipps Birch, "Restricting Access to Foods and Children's Eating," *Appetite* 32, no. 3 (1999): 405–419; Hurley et al., "A Systematic Review of Responsive Feeding."

216   *This is especially true for lunch:* Mathé, *La gastronomie s'inscrit dans la continuité du modèle alimentaire français;* SHRM, *Pressure to Work: Employee Perspective* (Alexandria, Virginia: Society for Human Resources Management, 2009).

217   *And some scientific research does show:* L. L. Birch and M. Deysher, "Conditioned and Unconditioned Caloric Compensation: Evidence for Self-Regulation of Food Intake in Young Children," *Learning and Motivation* 16, no. 3 (1985): 341–355; de Castro et al., "Culture and Meal Patterns."

225 *Basically, science doesn't provide:* P. K. Newby, "Are Dietary Intakes and Eating Behaviors Related to Childhood Obesity? A Comprehensive Review of the Evidence," *Journal of Law, Medicine & Ethics* 35, no. 1 (2007): 35–60.

227 *This is basic psychology for the French:* Brian Wansink, *Mindless Eating: Why We Eat More than We Think* (New York: Bantam, 2006)

228 *The result, as nutritionists warn:* Piernas and Popkin, "Trends in Snacking."

231 *And strictly serving only healthy:* Susan L. Johnson and Leann L. Birch, "Parents' and Children's Adiposity and Eating Style," *Pediatrics* 94, no. 5 (1994): 653–661; L. L. Birch and J. O. Fisher, "Development of Eating Behaviors Among Children and Adolescents," *Pediatrics* 101, no. 3, pt. 2 (1998): 539–549; Leann L. Birch, Linda McPhee, B. C. Shoba, et al., " 'Clean up Your Plate': Effects of Child Feeding Practices on the Conditioning of Meal Size," *Learning and Motivation* 18, no. 3 (1987): 301–317; Jennifer S. Savage, Jennifer Orlet Fisher, and Leann L. Birch, "Parental Influence on Eating Behavior: Conception to Adolescence," *Journal of Law, Medicine & Ethics* 35, no. 1 (2007): 22–34.

231 *Studies of adolescent girls, in particular:* Leann L. Birch, Jennifer Orlet Fisher, Kirsten Krahnstoever Davison, "Learning to Overeat: Maternal Use of Restrictive Feeding Practices Promotes Girls' Eating in the Absence of Hunger," *American Journal of Clinical Nutrition* 78, no. 2 (2003): 215–220; Carper et al., "Young Girls' Emerging Dietary Restraint and Disinhibition"; Fisher and Birch, "Restricting Access to Foods"; Fisher et al., "Parental Influences"; Amy T. Galloway, Laura Fiorito, Yoonna Lee, et al., "Parental Pressure, Dietary Patterns, and Weight Status Among Girls Who Are 'Picky Eaters,' " *Journal of the American Dietetic Association* 105, no. 4 (2005): 541–548; Yoona Lee, Diane C. Mitchell, Helen Smiciklas-Wright, et al., "Diet Quality, Nutrient Intake, Weight Status, and Feeding En-

vironments of Girls Meeting or Exceeding Recommendations for Total Dietary Fat of the American Academy of Pediatrics," *Pediatrics* 107, no. 6 (2001): E95.

French Recipes for Kids: Fast, Simple, Healthy, and Tasty

234   *According to the Harvard Center for Health:* chge.med.harvard. edu/programs/food/nutrition.html. Accessed 1 November 2011.

Index